ALASDAIR MIL...
Director-Gener...

MICHAEL CH...
Depu...
Director-G...

Engineering   Personnel   Finance
                                    BBC   BBC
                                    Enterprises Publications

External
Broadcasting
(World Service)

Public Affairs
Regions

ALAN PROTHEROE
Assistant
Director-General

Dramatis Personae (picture supplied by BBC)

THE LAST DAYS OF THE BEEB

The LAST DAYS OF THE BEEB

MICHAEL LEAPMAN

ALLEN & UNWIN

London   Sydney

First published in Great Britain by Allen & Unwin 1986
This book is copyright under the Berne Convention. No reproduction
without permission. All rights reserved.
Copyright © Michael Leapman 1986

Allen & Unwin (Publishers) Ltd
40 Museum Street, London WC1A 1LU, UK

Allen & Unwin (Publishers) Ltd
Park Lane, Hemel Hempstead, Herts HP2 4TE, UK

Allen & Unwin Australia Pty Ltd,
8 Napier Street, North Sydney NSW 2060, Australia

Allen & Unwin with the Port Nicholson Press
P.O. Box 11−838 Wellington, New Zealand

ISBN: 0 04 791043 7

CONTENTS

ACKNOWLEDGEMENTS

I AM grateful to Alasdair Milne and his staff at the BBC for the considerable assistance given in my research for this book, without which it could not have been written. In the Introduction I mention a very few occasions on which such assistance was refused. I do this not out of pique but because it is important for readers to know exactly how far the BBC have felt able to co-operate with me.

My chief day-to-day link with the corporation was John Cain of the history of broadcasting unit. Kind, helpful and a fount of information and experience, he was keen to provide all the material I wanted, locating it with remarkable speed and precision. The book owes a great deal to him — but I alone am responsible for errors and for the opinions expressed.

Access to the central reference library at the Langham and the radio news information unit at Portland Place were invaluable facilities. I am most appreciative of the help given me by David Evans and his colleagues in the library and Kenneth Gunderson and his colleagues in the information unit. Staff at the information division in Cavendish Place looked out tapes of old programmes and helped me in other respects, in a period when they had many other calls on their attention.

I want to thank those I interviewed, inside and outside the BBC, for being so generous with their time and insights. Scarcely anyone declined to see me. Most were happy to speak openly but a few sought anonymity. I have therefore thought it fairest not to name any of my sources.

For more practical assistance I am most indebted to my wife Olga, whose editorial judgment made for a more coherent text. She also gave me the word processor that makes it unnecessary to thank anyone for typing the manuscript. My agent Felicity Bryan provided valuable early encouragement, while Adam Sisman, senior editor at George Allen & Unwin, has nursed the project with unflagging enthusiasm.

1

INTRODUCTION

I BEGAN work on this book well before the controversial 1985 licence fee settlement and the appointment of Professor Peacock's committee to examine the future financing of the BBC. In August of that year came the Real Lives furore, provoked by the governors when they initially complied with a request from the Home Secretary to forbid the screening of a documentary on Northern Ireland. By then the book was nearly finished. Because the dispute illuminated two of the principal issues I discuss – the relationships between the governors and management and between the BBC and politicians – I took extra time and have included a detailed chapter on the Real Lives saga, including much previously unpublished material.

Yet although the balance of the book changed during the writing, its theme and purpose have remained the same. I have charted the decline of the BBC from its strong, self-confident position in the mid-1960s, when Hugh Greene was director-general. Today, enfeebled by what seems a chronic lack of purpose, the Beeb can find no effective defence against the sniping of a government ideologically opposed to the concept of a large publicly funded corporation embracing a liberal philosophy.

Inevitably, then, this is a portrait of an institution in disarray, very different from the seemingly invulnerable yet benign bastion of the cultural middle ground created by Lord Reith, the first director-general. That was certainly the BBC I first came into contact with in 1958. A raw 20-year-old, fresh from National Service, I had written out of the blue to the producer of the morning breakfast programme Today with the suggestion that I should read over the air daily extracts from James Thurber's *Fables for our Time.* It was a long shot and, even at that optimistic age, I was surprised to receive a reply inviting me to Broadcasting House for an audition.

The place overawed me – the high ceiling of the entrance hall, the snooty receptionist, the multiplicity of uniformed attendants; then the long trek through silent swing doors along endless corridors lined with eerily blinking lights, to the thickly carpeted studio where the audition was to be held. I remember vividly the dominance of the colour brown – a greyish, metallic shade. It was in the carpets, the microphones, the walls and the furniture: everywhere. It was a comfortable, autumnal hue, sobering in its lack of garishness, implying that nothing unseemly or over-exciting was going to take place. After the audition, the producer was much too polite to tell me just how dreadful my reading had been. A considerate woman, almost the personification of Auntie BBC herself, she observed that people generally read their own words best. She suggested that if I had any interesting or funny personal experiences that could be made into radio talks, why not send her some scripts?

The first one I tried was about that visit to the Beeb. She rejected it but over the next couple of years she did accept four or five talks, mostly about my time in the Navy; and my intermittent broadcasting career was launched. Nearly thirty years later it would be virtually impossible to duplicate the experiment, but I doubt whether a direct approach of that kind, unsupported by any personal acquaintance, would stand a chance of being entertained today. The concept of the gifted amateur, on which so much broadcasting in those times was based, has gone out of style.

It has been replaced – and a good thing too – by a high degree of professionalism in programme-making. The trouble is that the administration of the BBC has not evolved with it. The only gifted amateurs left in the corporation are the people who have the ultimate responsibility for running it: the governors. That has been the traceable cause of much that has gone wrong in the last twenty years. In particular, the governors' insistence on imposing their choice of controller for BBC1 in 1981, against the advice of professional management, contributed to the ratings crisis three years later when an outsider, Michael Grade, had to be called in to restore the position.

The period covered by this book coincides broadly with the career of the present director-general, Alasdair Milne. He has been close to the centre of power at the BBC for much of his time there and he plays a role in many of the events I describe. My technique has been to select dramatic and significant incidents from the corporation's recent past, often disputes or enforced resignations, and to report them in detail, using interviews with the participants as my prime source. Examination of how people behave at critical times, and why, provides insights into them and the institutions to which they belong. The narrative style of journalism is better suited to that purpose than the more generalised and analytical approach of the historian. In the final chapter, I sum up my conclusions in question-and-answer form. I recognise that by concentrating on the bad news I invite the charge of ignoring the many things that have gone right for the BBC during this period; but this is not meant to be a comprehensive history. I leave that to Asa Briggs, in the monumental volumes I list in the bibliography.

Chronologically, the first of the melodramas I describe is the resignation in 1965 of Donald Baverstock, chief of BBC1. It makes a suitable starting point because it was the first occasion on which a major BBC row was acted out on the front pages of the newspapers. The days of the discreet arm round the shoulder and the bland, face-saving public announcements were over. It was also significant because Baverstock was without much doubt one of the most talented people in television. That the BBC could not contain his talents and employ them properly was a sign that something was going wrong. The safe men were taking over. As a result, many of the Beeb's highest flyers, less safe but more creative, flew right away from the nest in the ensuing years.

The greater part of this book is about the television service, because it has the highest profile of the BBC's three main components and it is where most of the significant boardroom dramas of the last twenty years have been played out. Radio no longer occupies its former central position in the national culture;

but it has adapted skilfully to its new subordinate role and provides an indispensable service to many millions of listeners.

I have written little about the external services. While they are technically part of the same organisation, controlled by the same boards of management and governors, they do not share the licence revenue. Instead, they receive a direct grant from the Foreign Office. This is a crucial difference. Despite their successful insistence on a measure of editorial independence, the external services are in the final analysis a part of the Government's overseas information effort. That is what the Foreign Office pays for and what, with only occasional exceptions, it gets. Broadcasting under these circumstances raises fundamentally separate issues from those relating to the home services, which are financed by a levy on their audiences. Two of my main themes – the Beeb's relations with governments and the discussion of its future funding – have no relevance to the external services, whose *modus operandi* in both those areas is unique.

The BBC has traditionally set great store by its universality and cohesion, summed up in the slogan 'One BBC'. But it is a spiritual cohesion only. Physically, there is little interaction between its three main sections except at the very highest management level. One television executive put it eloquently to me:

> One of the snags about BBC television is that it's self-contained. It's a club, a regiment, a school, a university all rolled into one. It is all-embracing in many ways. You can arrive there in the morning and you don't have to leave the White City/Shepherd's Bush area until late at night. The comradeship and the friendships mean you don't need anywhere else. It's a major expedition to have lunch in town – three hours out of the day, if not more. So you're apt to stay behind and lunch at your desk, in the club, the canteen or the senior dining room. I spent most of Monday to Friday there. That's bad. The BBC envelops you and doesn't want to let go. Everything is there.

One result of this claustrophobic atmosphere is that in arguing the case for the preservation of the BBC in its present form, its senior personnel make assumptions that, although taken for granted inside their closed circle, are not automatically accepted by outsiders. To put it at its simplest, they argue that because the BBC makes the best television programmes in the world, and because any change in its financing might jeopardise that achievement, there should be no such change. That is a seductive argument until you question its premises. The word 'best' is so subjective and unspecific as to be valueless in the context. Moreover, were I to rate myself the 'best' writer in the world, I would expect people to pay for my books voluntarily, rather than be forced to subscribe to them in order to be allowed a licence to read any books at all. The BBC's case also ignores the implications, in terms of compromising its editorial independence, of having the licence fee set by the government – implications highlighted by the Real Lives affair.

I found it difficult to breach these preconceptions when discussing the issues with BBC executives. It was like questioning the existence of God with militant Christians: if you do not share the faith there is little hope for you; if you are not with us you are a heretic and therefore against us. This came out most clearly in the intriguing squabble between the BBC and *The Times*. When that newspaper ran a series of editorials advocating the fragmentation and privatisation of the BBC, Milne made a speech suggesting that it was motivated by the desire of its proprietor, Rupert Murdoch, to buy the most lucrative parts. The suspicion of such a motive warrants examining the newspaper's arguments closely but it does not, as Milne appeared to assume, of itself invalidate them. (*The Times* though, did nothing to strengthen its case by mounting an absurd investigation by its 'independent' national directors into Milne's charge, clearing itself of any wrongdoing.)

The BBC's ambivalence towards outside examination, and its sensitivity to criticism – actual or potential – became apparent as I was writing this book. From the start, senior management seemed to be in two minds. Before I started work on it I wrote to Alasdair Milne, the director-general, asking whether I could expect the corporation's help. I received a cordial reply from Michael Bunce, who enjoys the Orwellian title of controller of information services. He said he and his colleagues would give me all the help they could.

This imprecise formula turned out to mean almost unlimited

access to senior people at the Beeb and some valuable research facilities. Documents, though, were often difficult to obtain; and a short time after I began the work I thought I detected a new, wary attitude from BBC people. One incident stood out. When I went to interview Brian Wenham, director of television programmes, he suggested I should attend the programme review meeting that he takes on Wednesdays in the basement of Television Centre. It would never have occurred me to ask but he persuaded me that it would be valuable. He said I should make arrangements with Bunce's office. I conveyed his message and for weeks nothing happened. Neither Bunce nor his deputy returned my calls. Eventually Bunce told me that 'it had been decided' (by whom he did not specify) to turn down my request on the grounds that no outsider had ever before been admitted to programme review meetings and my presence would inhibit people from talking frankly. I pointed out that I had not made any request but had been invited by the man whose meeting it was; to no avail.

Then I received a letter from Bunce's deputy asking me to promise not to pass on any information from my interviews to gossip columns – a ludicrous proposition since every Fleet Street column has numerous direct sources inside the Beeb and would certainly learn any worthwhile gossip before I did. I satisfied the commissars on that and continued to get good access to senior people, though documents became ever harder to prise out of them.

Two refusals seemed especially irrational. In September 1985 the Glasgow University Media Group made a programme for the BBC's Open Space slot in which they planned to quote from the minutes of meetings in the current affairs department concerning coverage of the Falklands War. The minutes had already been leaked and published in the Glasgow group's book *War and Peace News*. Alan Protheroe, the assistant director-general, refused to allow them to be quoted on the screen, even though the purpose of Open Space is to permit free expression of controversial views. In a letter to the *Sunday Times*, Protheroe said that he had imposed the ban not because the minutes were confidential ('they were declassified many years ago') but because the group planned to use them out of context. I therefore asked him whether, since they were not confidential, I might see them in full and thus appreciate the context. He refused. Protheroe has made impassioned speeches on freedom of information but on this occasion did not feel able to apply the principle to these 'declassified' documents. My quotations from them in Chapter 7 are perforce based on the extracts published in *War and Peace News* (see bibliography).

The second denial of access was to a letter that Sir Jack Johnston, who retired as a governor last August, used to send to new governors, explaining what was expected of them. I wanted to see this in the wake of Real Lives, where the role of the governors was called into question. I was not allowed to, presumably because it referred to the convention that governors do not view programmes in advance – the convention breached in the Real Lives affair, with such dire results. I imagine the letter has now been revised or withdrawn.

The documents I did get permission to see dated mainly from the first part of the period covered by the book – the 1960s and early 1970s. Most of my text is based on around 100 interviews with employees and former employees of the BBC, governors, ex-governors, politicians (including two Cabinet ministers), trade unionists, academics and independent authorities on broadcasting. Because the Real Lives incident occurred late in the research, I had a second interview with major participants in it. An exception was Michael Checkland, deputy director-general, who cancelled two appointments where I would have asked him to explain his key decision not to advise Alasdair Milne to return to London for the meeting at which the governors banned the programme. References to Checkland in Chapter 9 must therefore be read with that in mind.

It is possible that, having absorbed my conclusions in Chapter 10, BBC management will regret having co-operated at all. All I can do is assure them that I have no malign motive. I am, however, convinced that what is best in British broadcasting will not be preserved by keeping the existing set-up inviolate; and that attempts to do so are in the long term self-defeating.

Chapter 1

DYNASTY

SIERRA ALTA WAY is one of the pretty lanes that twist up the foothills of the Santa Monica Mountains from Sunset Boulevard. Driving west from downtown Los Angeles, you pass through the tawdry Hollywood motel section, then the phoney dazzle of the Sunset strip, to make a sharp right turn just before the Boulevard penetrates the lush, ordered avenues of Beverly Hills, where tourists in air-conditioned coaches gloat at the mansions of film stars.

The people who live in Sierra Alta Way and its surrounding streets are a rank or two below the big-money household names that are the targets of the sightseers. For sure, many are in the entertainment industry, and they would not be able to afford the six-figure house prices if they were not reasonably successful at it. They are the vital back-room personnel – producers, managers, publicity staff and the like – along with the kind of actor who stays busy without ever reaching the very top.

Most of the houses and bungalows are in the Spanish style, painted white with patios and swimming pools. Some have Spanish names engraved on wooden signboards at the end of the drive: Hacienda, Casa Mia. . . Baskets of flowers in wrought-iron holders hang near the front doors. The pocket-sized gardens contain palm trees and colourful semi-tropical blooms; some giving off their strongest scent after dark, making the night-time fragrance heady.

All the same, and despite the normally balmy weather, Americans do not often venture outdoors at night on foot in residential areas, preferring the comfort and protection of the motor car. So anybody who saw a good-looking couple walking slowly with their dog along Sierra Alta Way, towards midnight on 23 May 1984, might have taken a shrewd guess that they were English.

Their accents would have confirmed it, for they were engaged in an earnest and emotional discussion of a matter that affected them both profoundly.

Michael and Sarah Grade lived at number 1300, on the corner of Cordell Drive, set back from both streets behind flowering shrubs and trees. They had been in California since their marriage at the Guards Chapel in London nearly two years earlier. Michael had lived in Hollywood on his own for nine months before that. A nephew of the colourful show-business tycoon Lew (now Lord) Grade, he was an energetic, affable, outspoken and occasionally indiscreet man with a fresh, classically handsome face dominated by eyes that stared and sparkled a little too brightly, giving him an oddly manic aspect. At 41, he had enjoyed a varied, mostly successful and always surprising career in television on both sides of the Atlantic. After a false start as a sports columnist on the *Daily Mirror* he had become a talent agent and then, at 30, head of entertainment at London Weekend Television, one of the five leading commercial companies. Three years later he was appointed its director of programmes.

People in the business were taken aback when, in 1982, Grade was offered the job of president of Embassy Television. This is an independent Hollywood production company founded by Norman Lear, a producer who made his name with the series All in the Family based on the British hit Till Death us do Part, and then Sanford and Son, derived from Steptoe and Son. Grade had been recommended for the job by Jerry Perenchio, an acquaintance from his days as an agent.

Such positions command high salaries and involve commensurately high risks. In Grade's first year, many of the series that Embassy sold to the big three American networks were cancelled after one season. Working in Hollywood may be glamorous – the

Embassy office is on the showpiece Universal Studio lot – but it involves having to adapt to the quickfire (in many senses) Hollywood way of doing business.

From the start he had received conflicting signals of what was expected of him. The all-powerful money men in the organisation were constantly looking over his shoulder. One of the series he had initiated was taken off with the press printing rumours of drug abuse on the set. Grade found it all too frenetic, too much like a caricature of Hollywood tycoonery, very different from the comparative cosiness of British commercial television. After eighteen months he gave up his senior position to become an executive producer on the Embassy payroll.

Almost simultaneously, he began to receive unexpected signals from the BBC in London to the effect that if he were ever to think of returning to Britain they would like to talk to him about taking a key job with them. The hints were unexpected because the BBC does not generally operate in that fashion. Senior posts on the programme side, of the kind he was qualified to hold, are customarily filled from inside the corporation, after interviews of three or four leading contenders. It would be unprecedented for a senior job in television to go to a man whose only previous contact with the Beeb had been as a competitor; so resourceful and committed a competitor that those BBC executives he had crossed thought of him as downright unscrupulous.

He did not have the *gravitas* or the comfortable complacency of the BBC stereotype of popular mythology. He had been an iconoclast since childhood, leaving the select Stowe public school after a year at his own insistence, because of what he judged to be snobbishness and anti-Semitism. Not having been to a university was not in itself a disability. Several of the current team of senior corporation executives had equally not enjoyed the advantages of higher education. But they had all spent most of their careers with the BBC and had acquired the corporate mind-set, the wristy self-confidence, the subtle skills of composing incisive memoranda, the bland conviction of their superiority. That these people would now consider hiring a figure so unconventional – at least in their terms – was an indication of how desperate the BBC management felt their present plight to be.

Grade's only close friend there was Bill Cotton, former controller of BBC1 and now on the corporation's board of management. (Grade's father Leslie had been an agent representing Cotton's father, the radio band leader Billy Cotton.) Cotton had been dropping Grade's name into discussions with his colleagues for more than a year, until he had eventually secured agreement to sound him out. Grade's talks with Cotton and other senior BBC people had been proceeding off and on for seven months: now, on 23 May 1984, a decision could be postponed no longer.

The first significant approach to Grade had come in September 1983 – not from Cotton but from Brian Wenham, the urbane and thoughtful director of programmes for BBC television. Every two years the Royal Television Society organises a major conference for the industry in Cambridge and Grade had flown from Los Angeles to attend it. Talking with Wenham in the bar, he had the unmistakable impression that the BBC perceived itself to be deep in a trough of despair and failure – and could see no easy way out of it short of an infusion of new ideas and people, with a consequent removal of some of the old ones.

A critical factor in this collapse of confidence at Television Centre was the arrival of Channel 4, the second ITV channel, towards the end of 1982. After a poor start, the new channel was now contributing usefully to ITV's share of viewers. Before its launch, the BBC, with two channels to ITV's one, could without too much effort command the half share of the total audience that it then believed it needed to sustain its claim on licence fee revenue. Now, with Channel 4 and BBC2 competing for the highbrow audience, the BBC's share of audiences on the four channels combined had dropped to around 40 per cent. Unhappily, the coming of Channel 4 coincided with an apparent lack of inspiration on BBC1. It had been some time since any new series of programmes on the flagship channel had really caught the imagination of both viewers and critics. Where were the new Steptoe and Son and Z-Cars? There were weeks when ITV commanded eight or nine places in the ten most watched TV programmes, with the BBC offerings (often Esther Rantzen's That's Life or the Nine O'Clock News) slipping in apologetically somewhere near the bottom. Occasionally no BBC programme made the list at all. They could not even console themselves with the thought that, although failing in ratings terms, they were producing serious, enterprising and influential programmes on current affairs. In 1977 the Annan Committee on Broadcasting had remarked on the inefficacy of BBC television journalism in the seventies as compared with the sixties, and things had not noticeably improved since. Many of the most innovative current affairs people had set themselves up as independent producers to service Channel 4. Annan had detected in BBC current affairs output a fear of offending people in authority – and with the licence fee up for consideration by Parliament again in 1985, that factor would not diminish.

The corporation had also been criticised for wasting money by competing with the new ITV breakfast television programme. Although the BBC's Breakfast Time had been a comparative success in ratings terms (partly because of the initial chaos at ITV's TV-am) there were many who wondered why it needed to be done at all. It was seen as part of a driven obsession with getting the corporate finger into every broadcasting pie, regardless of cost or reason. Wenham had nagging worries, too, about the new successor to Nationwide, the current affairs programme that followed the 5.40 news on weekday evenings. Because of the resistance of the BBC's regional centres to the radically altered programme originally proposed, Wenham feared – rightly, as it turned out – that the new 60 Minutes would go off at half cock. There were still viewers who kept their sets tuned to the same channel for hours on end, a phenomenon known as the inertia factor. So capture of the early evening was important in the contest for ratings.

While Wenham was running through this litany of misfortune in the Cambridge bar, Grade began to suspect that he was not bemoaning his fate merely to get it all off his chest, but that there was an ulterior purpose. He was casting a bait to see if there was any chance at all that Grade would nibble at it.

Grade at first reacted in two conflicting ways – emotionally and pragmatically. From a purely financial viewpoint it would be madness to leave Hollywood. He would not want to join the BBC at a salary disproportionately higher than anyone else's there, even if it were possible to envisage such an offer being made.

14

The best the BBC could pay him would amount to only a fraction of his six-figure stipend at Embassy. In terms of the actual job, though, Wenham's hint had been seductive. At this stage no specific post had been mentioned; but to be among the top half-dozen television executives in Britain's largest entertainment conglomerate was an appealing prospect. While Hollywood had provided a formative experience that he would not have missed for anything, London was where Grade felt most comfortable, and always would.

Then there was a third factor, perhaps the most important and certainly the most difficult. Sarah had fallen on her feet in Hollywood, happily and effectively running the West Coast office of Don Taffner, an agent connected with Thames Television in London. She is Grade's second wife. He was still feeling guilt over the failure of his first marriage – brought about, he was certain, at least partly by his absorption in his career and consequent neglect of the family. He was determined not to let his new marriage go the same way. That meant that if Sarah insisted on their staying in Hollywood, stay there they would. His response to Wenham's tantalising half-suggestions reflected these contradictory emotions. But it was sufficiently positive to persuade the BBC man, with his nose for nuance, that Grade would welcome a chance of re-entry into British television at a high level. They agreed to keep in touch. In the weeks before Christmas letters were exchanged, but no concrete proposals emerged from either side. Like cautious boxers in the first round of a title fight, they were taking each other's measure, weaving and dodging, neither of them prepared to open up his own defences or seriously probe his opponent's.

In January Wenham flew out to Los Angeles. Senior TV people enjoy their trips to California. Until the most recent round of economies, they usually happened twice a year, in January and May, when the Hollywood production houses hold screenings of their new series and invite offers from both British networks. The BBC men have their favourite hotel, the Bel-Air, which they like to describe modestly as 'a small watering hole'. It is in fact one of the most exclusive hostelries in the area, secluded in woods well off Sunset Boulevard, midway between Hollywood and the Pacific Ocean, a good half hour's drive from anywhere they are likely to want to go. It resembles a colonial hotel in the tropics, with the accommodation in bungalows, accessible by a network of outdoor paths from the central bar, restaurant and reception section. You walk in from the car park (valet parking only) across a hump-back bridge over a picturesque moat, where swans drift serenely. The bar is an established haunt of the rich and powerful: on any evening you are likely to come across high-priced lawyers fixing deals for astronomical sums on the counter telephone, and show-business divorcees drinking away their alimony.

On this trip Wenham arranged to drag himself away from the swans and screening rooms for a day and drove to Grade's house in Sierra Alta Way. It was a fine day, typical of what passes for winter in southern California. With temperatures hovering around 70 degrees, it was warm enough to sit by Grade's outdoor pool but not to venture into the water. In any case it was an improvement on the raw London January that Wenham had left behind. The talk was long enough – he arrived in the morning and did not leave until evening – but inconclusive. In the BBC Wenham is known as a man who plays his cards close to his chest, keeps his options open, sees no point in committing himself to a course of action until the last moment necessary for a decision.

This feline characteristic has stood him in good stead at the BBC, where he has risen remorselessly from producer of Panorama to a point at which he could challenge for the post of director-general next time it becomes vacant. On this occasion, though, he overdid the inscrutability. The two men spoke in general terms of the BBC's problems, of the scene in Hollywood and of Grade's position there. Much good gossip was exchanged, as it always is when media people come together. At the close of the day a frustrated Grade could sense that there had been a hidden agenda to their conversation, but it was so well hidden that for all practical purposes it might never have existed. He could not see any way of advancing the discussions further.

In the light of that, after Wenham left he and Sarah had a long discussion about the future. Their long-term aim was to work together as producers. They planned to stay in America for at least five years, then perhaps to return to Britain when they had accumulated a great deal of money. Grade would still be in his mid-forties, not a bad age to get back into British television if he had acquired a successful track record in California.

When Wenham returned to London, he found the BBC in the midst of one of the periodic bouts of disfavour and abuse to which the British press and public from time to time subject it, only more severe than usual. The BBC and its audience are like a long-established married couple. They lose patience and make dire threats of ending it all, but find in the end that they cannot live without each other.

The particular programme seized on for criticism in January 1984 was The Thorn Birds, a melodramatic mini-series based on the best-selling novel by Colleen McCullogh. It was typical Hollywood schmaltz and drew predictably high ratings; but it was unlucky enough to coincide with Granada Television's much-praised production of The Jewel in the Crown, drawn from Paul Scott's Indian novels. That is the kind of series the BBC has traditionally done well. The odious comparison between the Jewel's home-grown quality and the BBC's imported pap was provoked by Douglas Hurd, a junior minister at the Home Office, who briefed lobby correspondents to the effect that the BBC could not expect an increase in the £46 licence fee if it produced such trash. Others wondered why Panorama had been bumped from the schedule on the Monday to make room for it.

The press took up the theme eagerly, notably Max Hastings in the *Standard* (who had not seen the mini-series). The embarrassment was compounded by the fact that the BBC's major documentary series that season, a genre they used also to do well, was a pedestrian and expensive history of the theatre. Moreover the early evening current affairs programme 60 Minutes had been duly launched in the autumn and had confirmed Wenham's worst fears. The critics were predicting that it would not last long. Morale throughout BBC Television was lower than ever.

In February Grade visited London, had dinner with Alasdair Milne, the BBC's director-general, and a drink with Aubrey Singer, whose imminent removal from the post of managing director, television, was known only to a few senior colleagues. Grade was surprised when the two men raised anew the possibility of his joining the BBC – an issue that, after the abortive meeting with Wenham, he had regarded as dormant. It was now clear that it had been discussed seriously by the board of management.

Singer's 'early retirement', to borrow the BBC's diplomatic phraseology, was announced a few days later. He was replaced by Grade's old friend Bill Cotton, who had been languishing for over a year as director in charge of developments in direct broadcasting by satellite, with no control over programmes. Mulling over the parlous state of the television service he had inherited, Cotton came to the conclusion many senior executives reach when faced with intractable operating problems – the organisational structure was to blame. He hatched a novel scheme to change it, involving the abolition of separate controllers for BBC1 and BBC2, and their replacement with a single programme controller in charge of four 'super chiefs' of output departments – news and current affairs, entertainment and drama, arts and features, and sport. Cotton thought there might be a place for Grade in the new set-up, so he telephoned him to outline the plan and ask whether he would be interested in heading the entertainment and drama division. Grade replied that the proposed structure was too difficult to grasp over the phone: he needed it described in detail. Cotton said he would be in Los Angeles in March and they could meet then.

At a long meeting on 9 March, Cotton fleshed out his scheme. For Grade, it had some attractions. He said he would think about it and talk to Sarah. They arranged to meet again on 13 March, just before Cotton was due to fly back to London. At that second meeting Grade said that what he really missed from his former job at London Weekend was the business of creating schedules. The thought of outsmarting the opposition by some clever shuffling of programmes appealed to his competitive nature. So he was not inclined to accept the post that Cotton proposed. If the BBC could see its way to offering him the top controller's job, which under the new plan would involve creating the schedules of both channels, he would be sorely tempted. Alternatively, if they decided not to go ahead with Cotton's reform, he would like to be considered as controller of BBC1 under the existing arrangements.

The barrier to the first of those proposals was Brian Wenham. As director of programmes he would be the natural choice for the new joint controllership. The only way to get round that would be to move him out of the reckoning. The BBC works in machiavellian ways and it was about this time that hints began appearing in the press that Wenham was a candidate for managing director of radio at Broadcasting House, or of the external services at Bush House.

Douglas Muggeridge, then managing director of the external services, was seriously ill. (He died in 1985.) One scenario was that Wenham would replace him, another that Richard Francis, the managing director of radio, would go to Bush House, leaving the radio job for Wenham. But Wenham is a past master at resisting job switches if he thinks they would harm his long-term prospects. In 1980, when he had been controller of BBC2 for two years, he discouraged suggestions that he should move to BBC1. Now, when he had been director of programmes in television for little more than a year, he thought it untimely to go to radio, although it would have meant a technical promotion to managing director.

So Cotton could not bring Grade in by that route. After mulling it over for some weeks with Alasdair Milne, they decided to stick with the existing structure and proposed to the board of governors that Grade should be offered the job of controller of BBC1, replacing the luckless Alan Hart, who had held the position for three and a half years. By virtue of the peculiar institutional procedures that often hamper the BBC's efficiency, the governors have to approve appointments at this level, and normally insist on going through the traditional formality of advertising vacancies and interviewing a short list of candidates. This time, recognising as well as anyone that emergency action was required to stem the loss of confidence in the television service, they agreed that, if Grade accepted the position, the usual formalities could be dispensed with.

For anyone with a true professional commitment to television, there is no more fulfilling role than to control a national channel. It is where the real power lies. The controller allocates the channel's budget, having the absolute power to approve or to kill projects put up to him by the heads of programme-making departments. He thus decides what programmes to make and when they shall be shown. Even people notionally superior to him in the hierarchy – such as the director of programmes and even the managing director, television – have less actual influence on what appears on our screens.

Cotton telephoned Grade and put the firm offer to him. Grade flew to London and spent all of Thursday, 17 May, going over the ground with Cotton in a private hotel room: there had already been guarded suggestions in the press about the appointment and they did not want to fuel further speculation by meeting at Television Centre, where Grade would certainly be recognised. Cotton explained in detail how the BBC worked, with its peculiarly baffling layers of diffused responsibility. He gave Grade the assurances he sought on his freedom of action if he were to accept the appointment. He would have complete control of the BBC1 budget and would not be plagued by interference or recrimination from the top – a practice that Americans call 'second-guessing' and one that Grade had come to detest in Hollywood. The matter of his salary was disposed of quickly: he settled for the BBC rate for the job. At around £50,000 a year, that was less than a third of what he was earning in Hollywood.

He did not accept there and then. There was still the all-important matter of Sarah and her career to consider. He would need to go back and talk to her about it again. He warned Cotton that his agreement was not definite, but promised an answer soon after he returned home. That evening he and Cotton had dinner with Alasdair Milne. The director-general is in some respects a quixotic figure and Grade was surprised that he wanted to talk less about what Grade might do to rescue BBC1 from its present plight than about the last time the two men had been in professional contact. They had been on opposite sides of a spectacular squabble between the BBC and ITV that revealed volumes about the BBC's arrogant and blinkered attitude towards its opposition. That, at least, was how Grade then saw it. The fuss was about football coverage, and Grade had provoked it.

When he became director of programmes at London Weekend in 1977, he already knew what was the most formidable obstacle facing him. His station was on the air only on Friday evenings,

Saturdays and Sundays, and for years the BBC had poured a disproportionate amount of money and effort into its weekend programming – especially on Saturday, when it had built a nearly impregnable position. The evening began with Basil Brush and Dr Who, continued with Bruce Forsyth's Generation Game, The Duchess of Duke Street, The Two Ronnies, Starsky and Hutch, the News and then Match of the Day – taped highlights of a couple of the most interesting soccer matches played that afternoon.

The Football League, fearful of the effect of television on its anyway dwindling attendance figures, had never allowed live coverage of its matches. Under a cosy arrangement that had been in force for ten years, the BBC and ITV between them paid £500,000 a year for the right to tape matches for screening after the event. The BBC had always insisted that they must do it on the Saturday of the match itself, while ITV had to make do with Sunday lunchtime. Grade is not a person who believes that because something has always been done in a certain manner, it cannot be tried any other way. In November 1978 the three-year agreement between the Football League and the two networks was due for renewal. There had been the usual bargaining over the price, with the League seeking a 30 per cent increase in the fee and the TV people saying they could not afford it. Yet while BBC and ITV negotiators were hammering out their joint proposals, Grade was masterminding a simultaneous unilateral approach to the League that would give ITV exclusive rights to soccer for three years, at the greatly increased price of £5m.

He worked in the utmost secrecy. Although the heads of the major ITV companies knew what he was doing, he thought it prudent not to inform Gerry Loftus, the ITV negotiator on the joint team with the BBC. His attempted coup began in the House of Commons bar, where he discussed it with Jack Dunnett, Labour MP for Nottingham East, chairman of Notts County football club and a member of the League's management committee. Dunnett relayed the ITV offer to other committee members and found a generally favourable reaction. The following week Grade hammered out the details with soccer's ruling figures in a series of meetings in London flats and hotel rooms. On Thursday, 16 November, the League clubs accepted the deal by 50 votes to 1 – the single dissenting vote coming from Coventry City, whose chairman Jimmy Hill was Match of the Day anchor man.

The press covered the story on a massive scale. SNATCH OF THE DAY was one of the clever banner headlines. Grade was portrayed as a buccaneering fixer who had taken the fuddy-duddy Beeb men for a ride. As for the fuddy-duddy Beeb men themselves, they were furious, lashing out in all directions with pained statements, and setting their lawyers the task of challenging the agreements.

'It looks like war,' said Cliff Morgan, head of outside broadcasts. Alasdair Milne, then managing director, television, invited himself on to Nationwide to describe the ITV pirates as 'Mafia with cheque books very much in evidence'. His implication was that the unsullied and unworldly men of the Beeb had been done down by vicious and greedy agents of commerce. Ian Trethowan, the director-general, spoke of 'damaged trust' between the BBC and ITV, declaring that it would be hard to engage in joint discussions with them on any subject in the near future. In a letter to Sir Brian Young, director-general of the Independent Broadcasting Authority, he complained about the casting aside of the 'concordat' – a fine BBC word borrowed from the arcane reaches of nineteenth-century diplomacy to describe the agreement between the two channels on carving up the soccer coverage.

There were cooler heads at the BBC, but they did not prevail over the rage, motivated by corporate chauvinism and wounded pride. The veteran administrator Stephen Hearst, then controller of the Future Policy Group, told Milne he was making too much fuss. He was convinced that soccer was a declining interest and that the BBC would not be irredeemably weakened without it. In the long term he would be proved right, but Milne and Trethowan were in no mood to be mollified.

Bill Cotton, who had recently taken over as controller of BBC1, agreed with Hearst's analysis. He phoned his old friend Grade asking what he was playing at. He believed that whatever the moral rights and wrongs, ITV was paying more than the football was worth. As part of the BBC's strong Saturday schedule, Match of the Day averaged some 14 million viewers. Take it out of that schedule, said Cotton, and you may get no more than 8 million.

'You're off your head,' he advised Grade genially.

'I had to try to break you,' replied the tyro, between puffs of a large cigar – a habit he had picked up from his Uncle Lew and now a family trade mark.

The lawyers did not take long to act. By the following week Gordon Borrie, the government's Director-General of Fair Trading, had been persuaded to look into Grade's coup to see if it infringed the Restrictive Trade Practices Act. A few days later the BBC issued a writ seeking an injunction against the deal and damages for ITV's alleged breach of their joint agreement. Even the European Commission in Brussels announced that they were examining whether the contracting parties had flouted the rules on competition embodied in the Treaty of Rome.

The dispute smouldered over the following months. In January Borrie ruled that the agreement between ITV and the League was invalid on the technicality that insufficient notice had been given to the Office of Fair Trading. This, plus the continuing threat of the BBC court action, persuaded ITV and the League to renegotiate, this time including the BBC. The result was a four-year deal whereby the two channels would alternate Saturday night soccer coverage from year to year, with the other one doing it on Sundays. It was back to the *menage a trois* although under the new arrangement ITV's conjugal rights would be equal to those of the BBC, not subordinate to them. Grade was later to claim that this was all he had sought in the first place, but the cost was high. Under the new agreement the Football League would receive £10m for the four-year package – compared with a mere £500,000 for the three-year deal that was just ending. In the final analysis Grade had done more for football than for broadcasting.

Milne, dining with Grade and Cotton on that May evening five years later, could not fail to appreciate the irony of the position. Here was a man whom he had characterised – he thought with justification – as a corrosive blend of Machiavelli and Al Capone. Yet today he was asking him to play another role, that of Sir Lancelot, mounted on a white stallion to rescue the BBC from its deep distress. Milne rationalised this singular reversal by telling himself and Grade that his form of competitiveness was just what the BBC needed and had until now lacked. And there was an extra irony: the man Grade would replace as controller of BBC1, Alan Hart, had been the BBC representative on the joint team negotiating with the Football League. While Grade was dealing behind his back, Hart had been much too gentlemanly to suspect anything. Grade maintained the position that his final acceptance of the BBC's job offer would have to wait until he had discussed it with Sarah. He stressed to Milne and Cotton that this was no mere formality: if his wife had insuperable objections to the move her view would prevail. He had no intention of jeopardising his second marriage for the sake of the BBC. He returned to Los Angeles and for the next five days he and Sarah talked of little else. Sometimes they stayed up much of the night, rehearsing the arguments for and against a return to London, hoping that, if they went through it all again for the umpteenth time, they would come across the elusive clue, the clinching argument that would make the decision self-evident. But there was no clue. It was an intractable dilemma.

Sarah was not so much concerned with her own career prospects as with Michael's. Although she could see that in professional terms the BBC job would be satisfying, she admired the way he had adapted to Hollywood and overcome his difficulties at Embassy, not allowing them to shatter his confidence. Their plan to stay for five years and to work together was not, she felt, simply a self-indulgent ruse to spend more time with each other, but could well result in a powerful and successful professional partnership. And other factors were involved, aside from their careers. Grade supports and pays for the education of the two teenage children from his first marriage: he did not want their life style to be affected by a decision to take such a steep drop in salary. Why should he sacrifice their interests on what some might see as a whim?

Although he is far from indecisive by nature, the more Grade thought about the impending decision the tougher it appeared. He thought back to his days as a journalist and recalled that nothing concentrated the mind so effectively as a deadline. He needed to know the last possible moment when he could reach his decision. He telephoned Bill Cotton to find out.

'There's a governors' meeting on Thursday,' Cotton told him. 'I'll need to know by then so I can tell them my fallback plan if you don't accept. So call me first thing Thursday morning.'

Eight o'clock on Thursday morning in London is midnight on Wednesday in Los Angeles. Grade had his deadline.

On Wednesday, 23 May, he and Sarah went to dinner with friends and returned home shortly before 11 o'clock. With an hour to go, they still had not decided what to do. Maybe the night air would help. They walked up the slope of Sierra Alta Way, away from Sunset Boulevard, until the lane ended in a semicircle of three houses surrounding a tight turning space for cars. They turned and walked back again.

A decision was finally taking shape. Grade felt that if the process of making up his mind was so painful, he could not truly want the job. He would turn it down. But now Sarah had reached a decision, too: the precise opposite.

'I can see it's what you want to do,' she told him. 'So take it.'

It was a few minutes to midnight when they got back to the house. On the hour Grade picked up the phone and began dialling.

'What are you going to say?' Sarah asked.

'I'm going to tell him I'm not going to take it.'

There followed a scene that could easily have come from one of the soap operas he was in charge of at Embassy. Sarah grabbed the phone and banged it down before the connection had been made.

'You're going to take it,' she said sternly.

Grade shrugged. The deadline had squeezed a joint decision from them, although he was far from certain it was the right one.

'Okay, I'm going to take it.' He made the call.

'I knew', said Bill Cotton at the other end of the line, 'that it was an offer you couldn't refuse.'

* * * *

Before taking over as controller of BBC1 that September, Grade sought the advice of a man who had held the job longer than anyone – Paul Fox, now managing director of Yorkshire

Television and among the most respected and powerful figures in British television. Fox, thick-set and greying, is regarded at the Beeb as the Man Who Might Have Been, a talented professional who would certainly have been in the running for director-general had he stayed on and resisted the financial lure to go north. Indeed before Ian Trethowan was appointed in 1977 Fox, by then four years at Yorkshire, was invited by the BBC chairman, Sir Michael Swann, to be interviewed as a candidate for the top job. Fox replied that he would agree to an interview if they were making him a firm offer, but saw no reason to risk being rejected for a post he had not sought. Exactly who, he wondered, did they think they were?

In his time at the BBC he had gained a reputation for bluntness, but in middle age he had become avuncular, an elder statesman of the industry. When Grade sought his advice, he gladly offered it.

'The important thing', he declared, 'is not to worry about what buttons to press; but you must make sure there are certain buttons you *don't* press. There are things you must leave well alone. There are some pompous, boring men in the BBC. Steer well away from them.

'There's a way of getting on in the BBC. Work with colleagues you know and keep away from those who try to interfere. Being a network controller is a lonely job. The only staff you have is your secretary. But you have the two most important things that matter – budgets and programme slots. You're a very powerful person.'

Pondering the advice, Grade reflected that his two-year exposure to Hollywood lunacy might stand him in good stead after all.

Chapter 2

TO THE MANOR BORN

SINCE IT began in 1976, the Edinburgh International Television Festival has been well supported and greatly enjoyed by the most articulate people in an industry that by its nature appreciates the sound of its own voice. Occupying three or four August days in the middle of the Edinburgh Festival proper, it gives delegates a chance to sample a variety of cultural treats – some suitable to be snapped up for the small screen – between bouts of contemplating their professional navels.

Michael Grade had been a keen participant in early festivals but in August 1984 was too busy moving from Los Angeles to London to afford the time. Instead, he contributed a merry article to the festival brochure, called 'Thoughts on Re-entry'. It was in essence an attack on the way the American networks run prime-time TV, where nothing matters except ratings.

'America has taught me that more channels can equal *less* choice and that the regulated structure of British broadcasting may seem anachronistic to some in this day and age. . . I'm glad I went. I'm glad to be coming home.'

It was a shame that Grade could not be there in person because the final debate went to the very heart of the BBC's problem that Wenham had outlined to him during their talk at Cambridge a year earlier. The session was called 'Public Service Television – the Thorn in the Crown', a title that reflected the passionate debate over BBC standards that had taken place the previous

27

January, when Granada's Jewel in the Crown on ITV had been countered by the mini-series The Thorn Birds. Even the BBC felt obliged to admit of The Thorn Birds in its 1985 annual report: 'The series was much criticised for wooden stereotyping of many characters, for thin writing and implausible melodrama and for its placing in the schedules. . . But the series had a narrative drive that proved compulsive. It drew enormous audiences.' Later Alasdair Milne was to confess that the BBC had once considered making Jewel in the Crown itself, but passed it up so that it could afford a number of other series, including a well-received set of nature programmes called The Living Planet, and the less successful history of the theatre.

Douglas Hurd's lobby briefing, linking the apparent drop in BBC standards with its forthcoming claim for an increase in the licence fee, provided Fleet Street with the opportunity it had apparently been waiting for to savage the Beeb. Almost in unison, editorials expressed sympathy with his view. In some cases the newspapers' reservations about the direction the corporation was taking went much farther than the minister's. The *Telegraph* said the purchase of the series marked a low point in the corporation's decline. The *Economist* wondered: 'What is the BBC for?' But none was as vitriolic as Max Hastings in the *Standard,* who knew he had been invited to Edinburgh as a sacrificial offering.

'In a few short broadcasting evenings', he thundered, 'The Thorn Birds has accomplished what the problems of current affairs, the controversy over local radio and the satellite fiasco never achieved. The programme has called into question in the minds of a growing number of politicians and members of the public the function of the BBC.' The failure to compete with ITV had been a fact of life for many months. 'Now, incomparably more serious, comes the avowed collapse of its commitment to quality and excellence.' On two Monday evenings, the flagship current affairs programme Panorama had been dropped for 'one of the most paltry, tawdry, imported soap operas that any TV channel has ever had the contempt to inflict on the viewing public.'

Hastings warmed to his theme: 'Never has the leadership of the BBC seemed more pitifully inadequate, bankrupt of ideas, lost for a course. . . The BBC has become like a great fat man incapable of seeing over his own bulk to his toenails. . . Remorseless mediocrity usually prevails in the struggle for promotion.' He referred to the rumours, soon to be fulfilled, that Alan Hart would be made a scapegoat for the low ratings on BBC1, leaving the 'hapless' Milne and the 'abrupt and graceless' Wenham unscathed.

Opening the festival debate in the high-ceilinged Victorian auditorium in Queen Street that is now the BBC's Edinburgh studio, Hastings took up where his article had left off. The future of the BBC was the most important current issue in television, he maintained.

> Even five years ago it would have been unthinkable that thoughtful, moderate people in the broadcasting industry should be asking questions about the very rationale of the corporation's existence. The successes of ITV and Channel 4 make people ask why, if commercial broadcasting is performing so many of the traditional functions of the BBC so well, the British public should continue to be called upon for a licence fee. As technology expands, why should the BBC's appetite for an ever widening range of activities be indulged?

The BBC's civil service structure meant that producers were not allowed to risk experiment and there was too much dead wood at the top, Hastings maintained. And he introduced a more topical instance of the apparent drift to trivialisation: during the week of the TUC conference the following month, Panorama was again being rested to make way for an American mini-series, this one called Master of the Game.

The luckless Brian Wenham had been deputed by the BBC to speak for the defence. Sir Robin Day, chairman of the session, called on him to reply to the tirade straight away. Wenham can be a smooth and persuasive talker, but on this occasion he seemed determined to conform to Hastings' characterisation of him as graceless. Red-faced, and with an air of gruff ill temper, he poured scorn on the criticisms levelled at the BBC and answered them by reciting an inordinately lengthy list of high-quality programmes that had emanated from BBC television in the previous year. Attacks on the corporation, he asserted, were aimed at turning it into a second-class service, like the national channels in Australia and Canada.

When Day pinned him down on the question of dropping Panorama in TUC week, Wenham could only assert that it was taking its annual holiday. He listed the other programmes that would be covering the conference – including the new-format Six O'Clock News that was then replacing the unsuccessful magazine 60 Minutes. Overall, looked at objectively, Wenham's arguments were convincing, and senior BBC people were quick to hail him as having routed the Hastings faction. But the corporation labours under an image of smug self-satisfaction that it has proved impossible to eradicate. The effect is that any defence of itself, however soundly reasoned, is interpreted as evidence that its senior officials regard themselves as virtually infallible, not open to criticism; while if they do not mount any defence they are seen as having conceded the point. This classic no-win position derives from the public's reaction to those years during and after the Second World War when the BBC was seen as a national asset beyond reproach. Its executives failed to recognise early enough that the mood of the 1980s was opposed to the large, benevolent, liberal institution of which the BBC is the most significant surviving example.

The other two speakers on the platform were both, like Wenham, former editors of Panorama. Jeremy Isaacs, head of the minority Channel 4, was already being mentioned by the more speculative journalists as a possible successor to Milne should he forfeit the favour of the governors. He was noncommittal on Hastings' main theme. He saw some merit in the criticism that the BBC was too big but, like all ITV chiefs, resisted any suggestion that the corporation should sell advertising time. It would be wrong for the two main TV services to be competing for the same source of revenue, leading inevitably to lower programme standards.

Paul Fox said the BBC wanted to have things both ways: it wanted respectability and ratings. Some of its game shows (he singled out Blankety Blank) were more moronic than those on ITV. But it did have an obligation to appeal to a mass audience: if it catered only to minorities it would become a third-rate outfit, irrelevant to the nation's life. As a senior ITV figure and a former

BBC executive, it was he who appeared guilty of having it both ways. This central question of whether the BBC could combine high standards with mass appeal was one taken up by speakers from the floor. The ousting of Panorama by a soap opera proved an irresistible symbol.

The two men most responsible for working out a solution to the dilemma sat in on much of the debate but did not contribute to it. Alasdair Milne, the director-general, and Bill Cotton, his new managing director of television, tried to make themselves unobtrusive in the gallery of the Queen Street studio. Milne would explain later that since Wenham had been deputed to present the BBC's case it would unfairly have cramped his style to have his boss share the limelight – although from Wenham's uncomfortable demeanour throughout it could be guessed that he would have welcomed any such relief.

Milne and Cotton grew angry as the discussion proceeded. They were especially annoyed when two members of the BBC staff were openly critical of their superiors. Peter Ibbotson, the editor of Panorama, spoke of the threats of erosion and marginalisation of current affairs. Over the years the current affairs output on BBC1 in prime time – broadly between 7 and 10 in the evenings – had shrunk to Panorama and Robin Day's discussion programme Question Time, both occurring once a week. That must, said Ibbotson, be the irreducible minimum. He complained that the current affairs department was starved of resources and that there had been an erosion of programme leadership. That was what the argument over The Thorn Birds had been about. A commitment to current affairs meant that the programme had to be there when people expected it.

A few minutes later Roger Bolton, a former Panorama editor and now head of the network production centre at Manchester, spoke in Ibbotson's support. He said the question of prime time was crucial. Minorities were being catered for, but not in the most popular viewing periods. 'You must put before people in prime time a range of programmes that they may not have thought of watching before.'

Wenham was able to reply that there were twenty-five minutes of prime-time news on BBC1 every weeknight. News and current affairs are separate departments in the BBC, the first based at Television Centre and the second at Lime Grove. Although they have moved towards a measure of co-operation in recent years, there still exists a powerful rivalry between them. And he pointed to the regular Newsnight on BBC2 as evidence of the BBC's continuing commitment to current affairs – an irony because when he was controller of the second channel he had stoutly resisted its introduction.

Milne saw the interventions of Bolton and Ibbotson as a direct criticism of his and Cotton's leadership. Returning to his office in London, he composed tart notes to the two men, saying it was disloyal to make such comments in a public forum. Someone leaked the letters to the press and a small row ensued. Milne was accused of trying to stifle free expression.

The matter soon blew over. But Milne was engaged in a more important long-term struggle for authority, not with the always volatile creative people beneath him but with those who notionally run the BBC, the appointed and non-professional part-time governors. Previous directors-general had clashed with the governors but it seemed to many of Milne's colleagues that the particular board he had to work with contained the potential for serious trouble. A few years earlier, they had intervened disastrously in a key appointment, with consequences that had contributed to the corporation's present loss of confidence and the need to seek a saviour in Michael Grade. Since then, new governors appointed by Mrs Thatcher's government had given the board a more hostile and opinionated composition. Sensing trouble, Milne sought to discourage division within the ranks of his management and senior producers that would give away any unnecessary tactical advantage. Sure enough, within the next twelve months, the struggle for authority between governors and management was to become public in a dramatic and contentious manner.

* * * *

Press reports of Grade's appointment naturally stressed his family links with Bill Cotton. It was suggested that the deal had been fixed between the two old friends, with Milne playing only a marginal role, in effect being presented with a *fait accompli*.

Certainly Cotton was a prime mover, but that interpretation suggests a distant relationship between the director-general and his managing director of television. That is not the case. As over the years they scaled opposite slopes of the executive pyramid at Television Centre – Cotton came from light entertainment, Milne from current affairs – they forged an unlikely liaison. Each saw in the other qualities they felt lacking in themselves. The sharp, restless Milne, with the impatient Winchester-bred intellect that was hard to distinguish from arrogance, was aware he lacked the common touch Cotton had inherited from his music-hall family background. Cotton, podgy and down-to-earth, knew that, however high he rose in the BBC, he could never compensate for all he had missed through not enjoying Milne's formal classical education. A master of the one-line gag, Cotton once said of himself: 'The great thing about being mediocre is that I'm always at my best' – a joking response to the disdainful attitude that some of his sharper, flashier colleagues displayed towards him. Between them, the two men felt they embodied all the important qualities needed to lead an eclectic television service combining popular appeal with a sense of high purpose. But each depended on the other.

They are an odd couple. Joining the BBC in the mid-1950s, when independent television began, they found themselves in rival camps in the battle for the corporation's soul. Cotton was a fervent admirer of his father, the band leader Billy Cotton, whose rumbustious Sunday lunchtime radio show, later translated to television, had become an integral part of many people's weekend. For easily understood reasons, when the young Bill joined BBC television as a producer he made it a condition that he should not be asked to work on the band show. But his father persuaded him to change his mind and they had only one serious argument in the years they worked together. Father and son shared the same philosophy about television: it was about having a good time. The next best thing to having a knees-up was watching someone else do it. When Cotton ran light entertainment, and later when he became controller of BBC1, he was known for his belief in the star system, in the drawing power of such as Morecambe and Wise, Ken Dodd, Vera Lynn, Des O'Connor. It was back to the music hall tradition, where success depended on how many famous names you could pack on to your posters. When adventurous, experimental comedy reached the screen, his colleagues felt that it was in spite of Cotton rather than because of him.

Milne and the temperamental Welshman Donald Baverstock ran the Tonight show, created in 1957 to fill the previously empty air time between 6 and 7 in the evening. They were consciously trying to develop a new style of reporting current affairs, informal but riveting, a distance from the inflexible and pompous techniques then applied in news bulletins and political programmes.

Until the end of the 1950s, BBC news had been a solemn ritual, containing little except official statements, and nothing that had not been confirmed by at least one source apart from the corporation's own reporters. The last head of news who insisted on these rigorous and restricting standards was the New Zealander Tahu Hole, eased out of the job for that very reason in 1958 by Hugh Greene when he was director of news and current affairs. The same year Greene asked Baverstock and Michael Peacock, editor of Panorama, to prepare a report on how television news coverage could be improved. They wrote a devastating account of the existing operation, criticising excessive caution and dullness in both the choice of items and the language of the bulletins.

> We were disturbed by the 'BBC-ish' flavour. . . We noted the emphasis placed on the arrival and departure of Cabinet ministers; the inclusion of quotations from nondescript official or semi-official figures; the way in which the platitudes and cliches uttered by an accepted public figure are so often presented to the viewers as a significant statement; the tendency to concentrate on 'official' pronouncements and attitudes and to ignore, at least for a long time, the existence of 'unofficial' views.

They were, in effect, writing the obituary of 'Auntie' BBC and of the days when the news, carefully pruned of anything offensive and untoward, had taken on the nature of a religious observance. Many subsequent improvements in BBC news coverage derive from that report. It started the process of loosening artificial restraints and bringing standards into line with public taste as reflected in Independent Television News and the contemporary press. Yet it was a slow process. As late as 1967, the BBC News Guide was warning editors against using squalid crime stories as 'audience bait', explaining: 'This would be to pander to the public and so offend against our tradition of responsibility.' And the guide still contained this relic of the Reithian Beeb, a warning against over-adulatory obituaries of celebrities:

> The fact that a person has attracted in his lifetime a large personal following does not necessarily mean that his achievement is worthy of uncritical acclaim. You may feel obliged to note the death of an entertainer of meagre talent whose gramophone records – thanks to the activities of financially interested parties – have sold in vast quantities and who has been the recipient of such doubtful accolades as a place in the so-called 'Top Twenty'. We do not have to speak of him in terms more appropriate to a Menuhin or a Klemperer or a Fischer–Dieskau.

Baverstock and Milne were not in the business of lionising pop stars, either, but they did develop a more relaxed, less stern approach to current affairs. Much of what is taken for granted in television journalism today derives from their pioneering work on Tonight. The interviews in particular – by Cliff Michelmore, Derek Hart and Kenneth Alsop – were probing and intrusive, with none of the deference that had become customary. The filmed reports by Fyfe Robertson, Alan Whicker and Macdonald Hastings (Max's father) were high-spirited, quirkish and often very funny. The production people took themselves and the programme enormously seriously. Inspired by the loquacious Baverstock, they would engage in long analyses of their procedures and motivations from both an ethical and a technical viewpoint. A part of his talent was to convince his staff that whatever they were working on was 'important' – one of his favourite words, rolled lovingly round his Welsh tongue. The corollary was that other people's endeavours were less so.

The contempt of the off-screen Tonight team for much of the existing BBC output spilled over into their personal relations with the people responsible for it. They soon won a deserved reputation for arrogance and cliquishness. Some thought them quite off their heads. They trod on the toes of people in other departments deliberately and with apparent relish, usually emerging victorious in the frequent battles over resources and priorities. On Mondays they would sneak a look at the schedule for Panorama and try to implant an item into Tonight that would pre-empt the more prestigious show. On one well-remembered occasion, when a notable scientist died, Milne, on behalf of the Tonight programme, purloined a piece of film from an as yet unscreened interview with him done by Aubrey Singer's science features department. Singer was furious but Milne unrepentant. He was a firm believer in loyalty and *esprit de corps* and inculcated it into his staff: but it was a loyalty primarily to Tonight rather than to the BBC or the television service as a whole.

Alasdair Milne joined the BBC as a general trainee in 1954, after coming down from Oxford and being rejected for management training posts by four business concerns. Born in India to Scottish parents in 1930, he was brought up in Edinburgh by his grandparents for the first six years of his life before his father, a doctor, returned to England and settled in Kent. At Winchester, the public school for the very cleverest boys, he rose to be prefect of hall, a position that counts as head boy in the school's complex hierarchical system. From that point, being head of things came naturally to him. And although he denies having his eyes on the job of director-general in his early days at the BBC, it was said that Grace Wyndham Goldie, the formidable assistant head of talks who took Milne and several other potential high-flyers under her protective wing, had singled him out as a natural contender for the post after he had been working in her department for only two years. Her view was shared by Hugh Greene, who became director-general in 1960.

As a general trainee Milne was assigned tasks as varied as producing talks on the external services and writing handouts in the press office. He arrived at Lime Grove just as Donald Baverstock had launched Highlight, the twenty-minute interview programme that was the precursor of Tonight. The two men took an immediate liking to one another and found they could work well together. It was a different relationship from the one that Milne was later to forge with Cotton. Baverstock, like

Milne, was an Oxford graduate although he had not been to a public school. He was articulate and sparkling in a way the reserved Milne could never emulate. Six years older than Milne, Baverstock inspired in his lieutenant a regard that came close to hero-worship. Because the obsessive Baverstock was prepared to put in immensely long hours on the programme, so was Milne – so long that his wife Sheila, whom he had met at Oxford, once rang Baverstock to complain how little she saw of her husband. Baverstock, later a close family friend, sympathised but was not prepared to compromise over his working techniques or on the level of commitment he required from his right-hand man. Milne even borrowed from his mentor the Welsh habit of addressing nearly everyone, regardless of status and sometimes of gender, as 'boy' – an affectation both men have retained to this day.

The pair shared an office and would bombard each other with ideas for Tonight items. Ex-colleagues remember them as both looking rather seedy, stained at the lapels, Baverstock in a grey Burton suit and Milne in one the colour of putty, a shade he still favours. Both could drink without losing their faculties – an important skill in the days of mainly live television, when catering in the hospitality suite was more lavish than it is today. Baverstock believed in leadership by irritation, in making a nuisance of himself as a way of bringing out the best in his subordinates, in changing things at the last minute to keep people on their toes. He called it *elan*. Others called it cussedness. Whatever it was, it worked on Tonight, even if it proved counter-productive later.

In the legends about the programme that have grown in the two decades since it expired, Baverstock is cast as the original ideas man, throwing half-formed schemes to talented producers such as Tony Jay, Gordon Watkins, Derrick Amoore and Ned Sherrin. They would interpret them as best they could and it was left to Milne, with his flair for direction and practical organisation, to shape the elements into an actual programme. While most of the Tonight survivors endorse that account of how things worked, Milne does not remember it like that. He can be offended at being cast in the essentially non-creative role of an aide-de-camp and insists that he had as many usable ideas as Baverstock. It was simply that when it came to discussing them with colleagues, the terse, self-contained Scot was overwhelmed by the garrulous Welshman.

The Tonight crew had little to do with the light entertainment department although they were not shy in expressing their opinions when something they saw on the screen seemed excessively dim – witted. One occasion was the much-vaunted debut on British television, in July 1961, of the American satirist, Mort Sahl. The traditionalists in the BBC had expressed strong doubts as to the wisdom of putting such a man in front of a family audience. He had a reputation for iconoclasm. He had made jokes critical of American foreign policy and occasionally referred to sex. As it happened, the programme did have a long-term effect on British television, but for perverse reasons.

Bill Cotton was assigned to produce the show and, no doubt by design, did it in a way that drew many of Sahl's teeth. The audience was packed with celebrities waiting expectantly to be shocked. The camera picked them out – Peter Sellers, Spike Milligan, Sidney James, Lord Boothby, Dr Bronowski, Tony Benn, and the cast of the satirical review 'Beyond the Fringe'. Before the star appeared there was a coy introduction by Frank Muir and Denis Norden, the script-writing team even then approaching the status of BBC veterans. They explained how, as BBC consultants on comedy, they had recommended booking Sahl. 'And they did it,' declared Muir, on a rising inflection. 'Auntie BBC went and booked Mort Sahl. This is the most controversial figure in the world of entertainment. . . But old auntie, she took a great deep breath and her stays twanged like telegraph wires and she said: "Have him brought over." '

If that build-up was not enough to sink the bewildered American, Cotton had a still more lethal torpedo in reserve. Half way through Sahl's monologue he brought on the dancing girls. It was back to the music-hall again. If the comedian had been a bit too outrageous, the sight of naked legs flashing across the stage, keeping time with a hummable tune, assured the audience that it was all a bit of cosy fun, not to be taken seriously. Sahl made a lame joke about the Queen and several obscure ones about President Kennedy. After the show, it was widely agreed that he had been a disappointment. The young Turks of Tonight sneered at Cotton's lack of sophistication, but the show offended another, more significant critic. The director-general, Hugh Greene, fumed at the asinine staging and especially the Muir-Norden introduction. He told Kenneth Adam, his director of television, that if the BBC was to launch a satire show – as was being discussed in the wake of the stage hit 'Beyond the Fringe' – it should not be done by the light entertainment division.

Saturday night satire, in That Was The Week That Was (TW3) and its successor programmes, is the innovation for which Greene's long term as director-general is best known. (When he criticised the BBC for bowing to government pressure in the 1985 dispute over the IRA interview in Real Lives, the *Sun* wrote of him: 'He unleashed the plague of satirists who sneered at cherished beliefs. More than any other individual he was responsible for the decline of the BBC's standards.') The original idea for TW3 was not his, but it is legitimate for him to take the credit – or blame – for creating an atmosphere in which the experiment could be tried, and for being willing to resist the inevitable pressures from authority to have the programme abolished or modified. It is inconceivable that it could have happened under his predecessor, Sir Ian Jacob, a former soldier who ran the BBC in military fashion, holding regular cocktail parties to which he invited only those of his colleagues who had held commissions in the services. In the early years of Tonight, Jacob had insisted that Baverstock and Milne should cancel the weekly appearances by the young satirist Jonathan Miller, after he performed a sketch that made fun of Lord Nelson.

Following Greene's instruction, Kenneth Adam assigned the Tonight team to begin working on a new satire programme. By now, Baverstock had been promoted to assistant controller of television programmes, while Milne was soon to become head of Tonight Productions, a self-contained unit within Lime Grove formed to give the distinctive flavour of Tonight to other enterprises. Ned Sherrin, a Tonight producer, was put in charge of the satire project, reporting to Milne, and with Baverstock taking a paternal interest. The barons of light entertainment were not pleased.

That Was The Week That Was, launched in the autumn of 1962, was an immediate success and provoked rather fewer rows than most people expected. This was partly because Sherrin and Milne were skilled at determining just how much freedom they could give David Frost, the compere, and the young team of writers and performers. Sherrin was a realist and invariably gave way when Milne – and occasionally Grace Wyndham Goldie – thought he had gone too far. Greene deliberately distanced himself from day-to-day supervision of the programme but let it be known that he was sympathetic to its aims and that complaints to him were unlikely to produce results. Most important, his relationship with the board of governors was such that nobody thought of complaining to them. On programme matters he was completely in charge – or at least that was how it appeared to outsiders. He knew how to anticipate trouble and head it off. That was why he abruptly announced at the end of 1963 that TW3 would be withdrawn because 1964 was to be an election year. Nobody on high had openly pressed him into the decision, although his authorised biographer Michael Tracey says he feared that at least one governor would resign if the iconoclasts remained uncurbed. Just as important was his belief that the programme was losing some of its freshness and compensating by trying to stretch the bounds of the permissible that little bit too far. Better to curtail it when there was no overt pressure to do so than to be seen to give way to gubernatorial or political influence later. Milne, like all those connected with the programme, was angry. They saw Greene's action as the first significant retreat from his avowed purpose of guiding the Beeb to mature adulthood. With the advantage of twenty-three years hindsight, that seems a reasonable judgement: for although satire returned to the screens it could never quite avoid, as TW3 had done, the sense that it might be over-stepping the mark.

In 1963 Milne saw the issue from the point of view of the dog being fitted with a muzzle. By 1985, when he had become chief dog-handler, it looked different. Having to cope with a torrid censorship issue for himself, and to do it in public, he was able to appreciate and to envy Greene's pre-emptive finesse. But by then the whole relationship between the governors and the management, always an ambiguous one, had changed – in his view for the worse.

* * * *

When broadcasting began in 1922, it was run by the British Broadcasting Company, owned jointly by a number of radio manufacturers. The prickly, self-important John Reith was the general manager. It quickly became apparent that the new medium was an immensely powerful instrument for communication and influencing opinion. Two government inquiries concluded that it was potentially too important to be left in private hands. In 1927 the company was transformed into a public corporation, with Reith as director-general and a board of governors (originally five, now twelve) to protect the public interest by ensuring that the air waves were not exploited for profit or propaganda.

The governors are political appointments, made by the Queen on the advice of the Prime Minister. There have been numerous attempts to define their exact responsibilities. For many years the textual authority was a paper called the Whitley document, drawn up in 1932 by Reith and J. H. Whitley, chairman from 1930 to 1935. Copies of it were given to all new governors. It said in part:

> The governors of the BBC act primarily as trustees to safeguard the broadcasting service in the national interest. Their functions are not executive. Their responsibilities are general and not particular. They are not divided up for purposes of departmental supervision. . . With the director-general they discuss and then decide on major matters of policy and finance, but they leave the execution of that policy and the general administration of the service in all its branches to the director-general and his competent officers. The governors should be able to judge of the general effect of the service upon the public, and subject as before mentioned, are finally responsible for it.

Even that seemingly clear statement left many areas of dispute. In practice the powers the governors take upon themselves depend mainly on the character and inclination of the chairman and the director-general, and on the quality of the relationship between them.

The governors have two distinct roles, not always compatible. One is as the final authority in the administration of the BBC, to 'discuss and then decide on major matters of policy and finance'. The director-general is thus answerable to them in all areas. 'The governors *are* the BBC,' is how that function is often explained. Lord Beveridge, chairman of a post-war committee on broadcasting, described them more vividly as 'completely masters in their own house'.

Yet they are also expected to act as watchdogs to prevent the BBC doing anything untoward, 'to judge of the general effect of the service on the public'. It is a futile watchdog that barks at its own shadow, but the governors by their terms of reference are obliged to do something very like that. While leading and supporting the broadcasters they are simultaneously the last line of defence against their (in other words against their own) excesses. Many of the most spectacular rows about programmes and people, including the Real Lives fiasco of 1985, have either stemmed from that contradiction or been fuelled by it.

The professional broadcasters in the BBC's senior management have always tried to limit the extent to which the governors exercise their powers. Lord Hill, who became chairman in 1967, wrote in his diary: 'How the senior staff resent the governors showing the slightest signs of governing.' And the report of the Annan Committee on Broadcasting in 1977 noted:

> Both Lord Hill and Sir Michael Swann (who succeeded him in 1973) have told us how hard it is to get BBC top management to accept proposals put to them by the governors. Months of defensive action ensue, and all too often efforts are made to blind these interfering amateurs with the science of the profession. . . It would do worlds for the reputation of the BBC with the public if the governors were seen to govern. . . The BBC does itself untold harm by its excessive sensitivity. At the first breath of criticism the corporation adopts a posture of a hedgehog at bay. That is not the best way to disarm one's critics.

In the 1970s at Television Centre it was the fashion to refer to the board tersely as the 'sodding governors' – a concise indicator of how they and their function were regarded. Michael Swann used to compare the management's attitude with that of senior civil servants to their ministers, trying to find harmless ways of occupying the governors' interfering minds and keeping them out of mischief. The conduit for these efforts was the discreetly manipulative Colin Shaw, who as BBC secretary was the formal link betwen the governors and management. Swann teasingly referred to him as the 'thought police'. But in the harsher and less conciliatory political climate of the 1980s, the governors became ever harder to mollify. They made more and more mischief as they discovered what fun it could be.

People who discuss BBC politics customarily grade chairmen and governors on a scale of 'interventionism', measuring the degree to which they exercise authority over the director-general and his board of management. Lord Normanbrook, chairman from 1964 until his death in 1967, did not like the word. How, he wondered, could governors be said to intervene in what were ultimately their own responsibilities? The conventional view has it that Normanbrook was the last of the non-interventionist chairmen and Sir Hugh Greene, director-general throughout his chairmanship, the last chief executive to dominate the BBC as comprehensively as Reith.

When Normanbrook died, Harold Wilson, the Prime Minister, appointed Lord Hill, once the BBC's cosy and authoritative radio doctor, then a Conservative minister, but more recently the combative, high-profile chairman of the Independent Television Authority. This was interpreted as a move to curb Greene, although both Hill and Wilson denied that this was ever explicitly discussed between them. Calculated or not, that was the effect of the appointment. Greene was persuaded to resign as director-general eighteen months after Hill's arrival. They were too assertive to co-exist. Both enjoyed the limelight and did not relish sharing it. What persuaded Greene to go quietly was the unique honour of being appointed a governor after being D-G. But he found it an anti-climax and left the board in less than two years.

A politician by instinct, Hill was stronger on gestures than on substantive action. His first move on arriving at Broadcasting House was to have his office shifted from the third floor, where the director-general sits, to the fifth. Only in an organisation as introspective and conspiratorial as the BBC would this change in the housekeeping arrangements be examined closely for an ulterior meaning. Hill's explanation that he needed more space was dismissed derisively: it was apparent to the *cognoscenti* that he was snubbing Greene by moving away from his floor.

If it was a deliberate gesture, Hill would have been justified in making it, given the arrogantly ungracious welcome he received in his new job from Greene and other senior BBC men. They were mortified at being saddled with the former leader of the despised enemy. It was a cruel blow to their team spirit and their self-regard. 'It was the end of the BBC as I knew it,' wrote Sir Robert Lusty, the vice-chairman. Greene told his biographer Michael Tracey that his first reaction was: 'How can I work with a man for whom I have the utmost contempt?' And David Attenborough, controller of BBC2, told Hill to his face that it was as if Rommel had just been appointed leader of Montgomery's Eighth Army: 'We know you're a good general but we don't know if you're on our side.'

The Annan Committee had no doubt about the significance of the Hill appointment. 'Lord Hill', they wrote, 'was determined that, although the general management of the BBC must rest with the director-general and his staff, on some major issues the governors should not only discuss but decide matters of general policy, even if their decisions ran counter to the advice of the director-general.' The report noted Hill's determination to be a less shadowy figure than his predecessors.

Yet the notion of a passive Normanbrook being succeeded by an interfering Hill is only partly true. In the history of institutions as of nations, changes are seldom as clear-cut as that. Normanbrook did in fact exert his authority over Greene quite often. When Ian Smith, the Rhodesian leader, visited London in 1965, just before making his unilateral declaration of independence, Normanbrook, under pressure from Harold Wilson, would not allow the BBC to interview him. (Independent television ignored the government's appeal and went ahead with an interview.) On another occasion Normanbrook and his fellow governors forbade an interview with Baldur von Schirach, the former Nazi Youth leader. And he refused to allow the broadcast of 'The War Game', a powerful and deliberately horrifying film about the effects of nuclear war which was not shown on home screens until 1985, twenty years after it was made. (The eventual screening made less public impact than was expected because it came in the middle of the 'censorship' row over Real Lives.)

Greene made no overt fuss at the time about interference by the governors, because he was anxious to maintain his reputation as an enlightened director-general who had shaken the dust off the corporation and dragged it into the sixties, high-kicking and occasionally screaming. Greene enjoyed taking credit for giving his programme makers a free hand, keeping the timid governors at bay. His liberal reputation – to a large extent deserved – would have been compromised if it were known that he felt obliged from time to time to bend before the authority of the governing board.

In the 1960s it was still possible to conduct such business the old-fashioned way, through discreet and confidential exchanges over lunch at the club, avoiding the embarrassing glare of publicity. Relations with the government generally followed the same pattern. Representations from Whitehall about programmes and policy would, with few exceptions, be made privately, as often to the director-general as to the governors. There was not then the assumption that was to grow in the 1980s that the governors were watchdogs placed by the government to keep an eye on the unreliable professional broadcasters. Essentially, they were still on the professionals' side – even Hill, as he was to show in the furore over the programme Yesterday's Men in 1971 (see Chapter 8).

But the days of governance by nod and wink were ending, both in the wider world and in the BBC itself. It was appropriate – or perhaps poetic justice – that the first major dispute at the top of BBC television to receive sensational press coverage should involve Baverstock and Milne, those apostles of the public's right to be treated as responsible citizens, unprotected by those who thought they knew best.

* * * *

The introduction of the second BBC channel in 1964 meant a huge influx of new staff to service a programme output increased overnight by more than 50 per cent. It also meant strengthening senior television personnel. Greene looked to the two authors of the 1958 forward-looking report on news. Baverstock was appointed chief of programmes for BBC1 and Peacock for BBC2. Both reported to Stuart Hood, controller of programmes, a thoughtful but indecisive Scot. Above him was Kenneth Adam, director of television.

Peacock did not make a success of BBC2. He had an original – but in the event unworkable – idea known as the 'seven faces of the week'. Each night on the new channel was to be devoted to a separate subject: entertainment, education, music, etc. The idea was to pin down audiences with specific interests to the channel for the whole evening, but in programming terms it imposed an inflexibility that proved impossible to handle. Viewing figures were small. Worse, BBC1 languished too, suffering from sharper competition from ITV and from the upheavals caused in the whole television service by the introduction of BBC2. Baverstock's arrogance and impatience, qualities that had proved a positive advantage when he was editor of Tonight, were a liability when it came to motivating heads of programme departments and co-ordinating their efforts into the output of a single channel. When in the summer of 1964 Stuart Hood suddenly quit at a moment's notice, Greene saw the chance to make a fresh start at running the two complementary channels.

He left Hood's post vacant for eight months while he pondered his options. Eventually, the man he chose as his instrument was Huw Wheldon, head of documentary and music programmes and a popular presenter of documentaries on arts and historical subjects. A soft-voiced Welshman, Wheldon was a tougher corporate in-fighter than appeared on the surface. When Greene asked him to take over the television service, he said he doubted whether he could do the job effectively if that other Welshman Baverstock remained in charge of the flagship channel. Like his fellow departmental heads, Wheldon had found the mercurial Baverstock difficult to deal with. They were not like the old Tonight team, young and highly motivated, sharing their editor's views on the essential nature of television, willing to be loudly abused for the sake of the cause and equally ready to shout back. Those methods had worked within Tonight's restricted framework but it was unrealistic to suppose that they could be adapted effectively to deal with the BBC's entrenched bureaucracy. In the attempt, it was inevitable that Baverstock should make a good many enemies, most importantly Kenneth Adam.

Greene and Adam wanted to switch Peacock, a more adept organisation man, to BBC1, making Baverstock chief of BBC2. When Greene put the plan to him in February 1965, Baverstock refused the move, seeing it as a demeaning demotion, a vote of no confidence. Oddly for an iconoclast, he had a powerful sense of status. It rankled with him that he was called chief of BBC1 rather than controller (a title given to his successors). Greene was adamant that he must leave BBC1 and put to him three alternatives: he could replace Wheldon as head of documentaries; go out to take charge of the Paris office (although he spoke no French); or spend a year travelling the world – an expensive payoff that proved how much Greene was prepared to spend to get him out.

Baverstock discussed the position with Milne, who advised him not to accept the BBC2 post or any of the alternatives but to leave, adding that he, Milne, would probably quit with him. Both felt that the guardians of the old and in their view deplorable BBC ethic, the enemies of enlightenment, were regaining control. Their double resignation could be the blow needed to reverse the process.

The dispute became public on Thursday, 25 February. The lead story in the *Daily Mail* bore the dramatic headline: TOP BBC MAN OUT. Its author was Bernard Levin, a friend of Baverstock through his script-writing contributions to Tonight and his screen appearances in TW3. Levin made no secret of his sympathies from the outset. The report began:

'A sensational palace revolution at the BBC has resulted in the ousting of Donald Baverstock, the most dynamic and talented man the Corporation has thrown up since the end of the war.'

The 41-year-old Baverstock had been tipped as a future head of the BBC, Levin reported. Now he had been replaced by Peacock, responsible for the 'disastrous' launch of BBC2. Levin revealed that shortly before his dismissal, Baverstock had put to Greene 'a far-reaching and exciting plan for re-organising and re–grouping the BBC's structure'.

But Greene had ignored it. Baverstock 'could not be expected to accept demotion to BBC2,' Levin declared, adding that some of the governors had been waging a campaign against him as 'a threat to the safe, tidy Establishment image of the BBC'. Anticipating that the official line would stress Baverstock's difficulty in forging good relations with his colleagues, Levin insisted that the dispute was 'not a clash of temperament but the result of much manoeuvring for position of the kind that is constantly going on in organisations like the BBC'.

Levin followed up his scoop the following day with another front page splash beneath the ludicrous headline: BAVERSTOCK SPEAKS. The other newspapers, following up the *Mail* story of the previous day, had failed to track down Baverstock, who was taking a short holiday in the south of France. Levin knew where he was and flew from dull, chilly London to Nice, where the temperatures were not exactly tropical but were at any rate an improvement.

Levin had no experience in news reporting for the popular press but he had read plenty of it and thought he knew what was required. His discovery of his friend's holiday retreat was given a build-up on a scale more appropriate to Stanley's tracking down Livingstone.

'As the storm at the BBC raged tonight,' the story began, 'I found Mr. Donald Baverstock, the man in the middle of it all, in the south of France. I joined him and Dame Peggy Ashcroft for dinner.'

Unluckily, so far as the story was concerned, Baverstock was unwilling to say anything concrete, even to his old friend, on the subject of his dismissal. He had 'no harsh words for his enemies'. Apart from declaring that he was 'not interested in power and I never have been', his talk was of a general, philosophical nature.

'Though the lines of worry have bitten shockingly deep, these last days and weeks, into his face, his eyes lit up with the familiar gleam of enthusiasm as he talked of his first and last professional love.'

The trouble was that for *Mail* readers, involved in television only on the receiving end, the talk was scarcely riveting. Baverstock bubbled on about the organisational structure of the BBC, about there being too many bureaucrats inserted between producers and their viewers. After a few paragraphs of this, 'tired and pained – pained at being let down by men he trusted – Mr. Baverstock, despite his legendary inexhaustibility, began to flag.'

Inside the paper on the same day was a column by the television critic Peter Black that offered a more balanced and thoughtful perspective on Baverstock's departure. 'The pre-eminence of the journalist is over,' he wrote. 'When the news of his eclipse broke yesterday a lot of voices inside the BBC greeted it with relief and thanksgiving. What had gone wrong?' As part of the answer, he quoted a view that Baverstock would refuse to give consideration to creative ideas with which he was out of sympathy, and mentioned his difficult relationship with Sydney Newman, the influential head of drama. Black concluded: 'The BBC badly needs its Baverstocks. His resignation will convert a setback into a disaster.'

And what of Alasdair Milne, whose BBC career was closely bound with Baverstock's and who still regarded the Welshman as his mentor, even though the roles had been reversed when Baverstock was seeking advice on his resignation? Levin questioned him about his future. 'You can say', Milne replied carefully, 'that if the BBC can't contain Donald Baverstock it is unlikely to contain me.'

Indeed it did not. As he had predicted to Baverstock, Milne resigned from the BBC soon afterwards. Although part of the reason was certainly his disgust at the way Baverstock had been treated, there was a second contributory factor. A little over two years earlier, wishing to broaden his experience with a view to the future, Milne had sought a transfer to Scotland, which while not his birthplace was the land he most identified with. The post of director of programmes in Glasgow had fallen vacant and he applied for it. At the appointment board, he received his first tangible indication that the Tonight people, their programme philosophy and their arrogant cliquishness, were far from everyone's cup of tea. As it happened, Scotland was at that time among the strongholds of BBC traditionalism. Although Scottish viewers liked Tonight as much as anyone else, the administrators disapproved of it deeply, and would later be even less enamoured of TW3.

The controller for Scotland, Andrew Stewart, was clearly opposed to Milne's application. At the board, his first question was aimed at proving that Milne was not a real Scot. 'Which is your favourite among the ballads?' Stewart asked. He was referring to the Gaelic ballads. Milne did not yet speak Gaelic and rather unwisely tried to hedge. 'Which part of the corpus are you talking about?' he countered. While it could not sensibly be maintained that a detailed knowledge of the ballads was a requirement for the job, he certainly needed Stewart's good opinion, which he had forfeited. Not a man who accepts failure with equanimity, Milne was upset at being rejected and resolved to learn Gaelic before he tried for a job in Scotland again.

By 1965 he had largely come to terms with that disappointment, but it still made it a mite easier for him to decide to leave the BBC with Baverstock. It was appropriate that the Tonight productions unit should be disbanded as soon as they left, and the programme itself was taken off the air the following June. Late-night satire, which had continued in several guises since the demise of TW3, expired soon afterwards.

Free from the constraints of the Beeb, Milne and Baverstock teamed up with Tony Jay, the former Tonight producer who had left the BBC and gone independent some months earlier. Jay had discovered a market for professionally made films for industry, and with the other two formed a company called Jay, Baverstock, Milne. It was never a huge success, although later Jay would transform it into the highly profitable firm of Video Arts. Milne and Baverstock did some freelance assignments for ITV companies and Milne was involved in a consortium that bid unsuccessfully for the Scottish commercial TV franchise. It seemed likely that both would take the opportunity, were it offered, of reverting to full-time television executives.

Greene would have liked to lure them both back. Other senior BBC figures were more enthusiastic about Milne than Baverstock. While recognising the Welshman's indisputable talent, they could not forget how difficult he had been to deal with. Even if Levin was right in believing that he had been the most talented man produced by the BBC for twenty years, they seemed to have survived well enough without him. With Peacock and then Paul Fox heading BBC1, and the personable David

Attenborough in charge of BBC2, things were going from strength to strength. Why invite the bull back into the china shop? In 1967 Wheldon asked Milne, the more acceptable face of the old Tonight philosophy, to return as head of current affairs. Milne felt it too much like the job he had quit as head of Tonight Productions, and in any case he was by now determined to get a Scottish job if he could. It happened that the posts of controller Scotland and controller Wales became vacant at about the same time, due to retirement. Greene had a master plan for Milne to fill the first and Baverstock, despite the residual antagonism toward him, the second. Although Greene's sense of mischief had been dulled by years of making compromises with governors and governments, it was still sufficiently alert to recognise that letting a bull into a china shop, provided it was a bull with discrimination, could prove effective in getting rid of some of the damaged and less pleasing old crocks. The difficult part, as he was to discover, was coaxing the bull back in.

When Greene asked Baverstock whether he would like the Welsh job, Baverstock assumed he was being made a firm offer. Greene said he would have to meet some of the governors first, but still Baverstock assumed that this was a formality, a chance to get to know each other. He was surprised and horrified to discover that he was attending a full-blown selection board and, worse, that he had to wait outside while three other candidates were going through their paces. Later he insisted that if he had known he was going to be 'boarded' he would never have allowed his name to go forward. His ill-temper showed when he was finally ushered in to see Greene and the group of governors. When the Welsh governor, Professor Glanmor Williams, began putting questions Baverstock regarded as banal, he flared with irritation. The board found no difficulty in preferring an alternative candidate. As it turned out, Baverstock had lost his last chance of returning to the Beeb.

Milne suffered no such debacle. Although curt with colleagues, he has a smooth, practised way with selection boards. Remembering Stewart's trick question five years earlier, he had already begun taking Gaelic lessons from William Carrocher, a Foreign Office diplomat (later to join the BBC and become Milne's trusted confidant).

Milne's appointment as controller Scotland, succeeding Stewart, was quickly confirmed.

Controlling a BBC region is a deft balancing act. The aim is to contribute as much as possible to the national network, for the sake of prestige and morale, while gaining maximum autonomy from headquarters in London. Milne did it well. He knew just how far he could go on his own without provoking London to make an issue of it. The difference between the national regions – Wales, Northern Ireland and Scotland – and the others is that they have their own governors, so any important dispute involving them becomes a matter for the board of governors as well as the board of management. The professionals hate inviting the governors to adjudicate in a dispute between them. The tactics developed over the years have been to present the governors with a united management position rather than a range of options – just as civil servants like to give their political masters one recommendation for action, not a choice. Milne exploited his understanding of that to gain for BBC Scotland more independence than his predecessors had achieved. He was fortunate that the external political climate was in his favour, with much talk of devolution.

His view of Scotland was a romantic one. For him, it was the land of the pipes and the ballads, the kilt and the Highlands and the heather. Among the most notable programmes to be made there during his stewardship was a series of plays based on the works of Lewis Grassic Gibbon, period pieces set in Angus. They were sensitively done and marvellous to look at. But his critics thought this folk vision of Scotland was misleading. They believed he had too little understanding of the real, gritty Scotland, the central industrial belt with its poverty and unemployment. He stayed in Glasgow for five years, until in 1973 he became director of programmes at TV Centre in London. He replaced David Attenborough, who had grown tired of administration: he had held the post for five years and wanted to return to making his nature programmes. Wheldon believed that if Attenborough stayed on he would be a contender for director-general when Charles Curran retired, but he was not to be persuaded.

With Attenborough's withdrawal from the fray, Milne, still

Alastair Milne's BBC career 1954–1986

Leaves Oxford and joins BBC as trainee

Starts *Highlight* with Donald Baverstock

Deputy Editor of *Tonight*

Editor of *Tonight*

Head of *Tonight* Productions

Leaves BBC to become independent producer

Rejoins BBC

Controller, BBC Scotland

Director of Programmes, Television

Managing Director, Television

Deputy Director-General

Director-General

1954 55 56 57 58 59 60 61 62 63 64 65 66 67 68 69 70 71 72 73 74 75 76 77 78 79 80 81 82 83 84 85 86

only 43, must by now have seen himself as very much in the running for the top job. His position was strengthened when, the same year, Paul Fox left the corporation after six years as controller of BBC1, to become director of programmes with Yorkshire Television (replacing Donald Baverstock, who had been in the job since 1967). Michael Peacock, his other outstanding contemporary, had quit several years earlier. It was in one sense upsetting that the BBC was losing so many talented people, but it did clear the log-jam for promotion at Milne's level. He had been a regional controller and was now controller of all television output. The next step ought to be managing director of one of the three output services. Wheldon, managing director since 1968, was expected to retire by the end of 1976. If Milne were chosen to replace him he would be well poised for his challenge for Curran's job before reaching 50.

As it turned out, that scenario did not fit the plans of Sir Michael Swann, who had replaced Lord Hill as chairman in 1973. Swann recognised that Milne had better professional qualifications than anyone else in the top stratum of administration, but doubted whether they were really what was needed to be an effective director-general. He thought perhaps not. Many of the most important aspects of the job involved dealing with the governors, Whitehall and other powerful pressure groups. Experience in programme-making was not much of a qualification for that. Swann's gaze fell instead on Ian Trethowan, managing director of radio. He was a former lobby correspondent and on-screen presenter for both BBC and ITV, who had been singled out by Lord Hill for the radio post, with an eye on the possibility that he might rise further. Both Hill and Swann believed that his polished tact and experience in dealing with politicians would serve him well in his relations with outsiders. Milne, on the other hand, had a reputation for abruptness. He was impatient, easily bored, apt to switch off after a few minutes if a discussion did not interest him. He had that irritating habit of recognising within moments the direction an argument was taking, and trying to cut it short. He did not suffer fools gladly; and as director-general he would have many fools to suffer.

Trethowan's weakness was that, though he had appeared on television many times, he had no experience in its administration. In 1975 Swann and Curran remedied that by persuading Wheldon to step down as managing director at the end of the year – several months earlier than he would normally have expected – to make way for Trethowan. This would give him nearly two years experience on the sixth floor at TV Centre before Curran's retirement, pencilled in for 1977.

Milne was furious when he was told about it. As director of programmes he regarded himself as Wheldon's heir apparent. For days he was sulky and dangerous to approach. He recognised the appointment as part of Trethowan's work experience training for his forthcoming promotion to director-general; and that meant that his own ambition of becoming DG would be deferred. When his anger cooled he was able to appreciate something else: that he was going to have to learn to work closely with Trethowan for the next few years. To engage in any vendetta would simply spoil his own prospects for the succession.

Trethowan, for his part, was never comfortable with Milne. His friends believed he could not avoid an irrational sense of guilt over having leapfrogged the younger but more experienced man. He was overawed by Milne's brisk and decisive manner, and even more by his Winchester and Oxford education. Trethowan had been to public school – Christ's Hospital – but did not apply himself sufficiently to gain a place at university. (His own explanation is that he had 'a low threshold of boredom'.) Whenever he was in Milne's presence he was reminded of that and could not help feeling a bit of a sham. Sometimes, relaxing with colleagues and their wives after dinner, he would confess that if only he had Milne's intellectual prowess he would make a better DG.

Partly to purge that feeling, he determined to do all he could to see that Milne would be his successor. Some of their colleagues thought they detected an implicit understanding between the two, an unwritten non-aggression treaty under whose terms neither would do anything to thwart the ambition of the other. Whatever the truth of that, when Trethowan retired in 1982, the governors chose Milne to replace him. Nearly forty years after Winchester, the boy most likely was head of school again.

* * * *

On 18 February 1982 several dozen television veterans, most of them well into middle age and some frankly old, gathered in the executive hospitality suite on the sixth floor of Television Centre. They were the survivors of the talented young team that created Tonight, and were there to celebrate the twenty-fifth anniversary of the start of the series. Programmes come and go on television, usually without being marked by such reunions. That the Tonight team had come together every five years, starting with the tenth anniversary in 1967, was partly an indication of the sense of *esprit de corps* they still enjoyed, but more importantly because of the commitment of Alasdair Milne, who took the 1982 reunion so seriously that he found time to organise it even while preparing to assume the office of director-general.

Milne is one of the few Tonight people who have stayed with the BBC. Others fulfilled their promise in different ways and some never did anything as worthwhile again. Milne regards his time on Tonight as among the most important and fulfilling stages of his career. Sceptical colleagues see the reunions as an attempt to re-live those comparatively carefree years. Milne and the others were still proud enough to believe that it had been not only the prime of their lives but a golden age of British television, never equalled since – a view shared today by many who were not directly involved in the programme.

Milne had not only organised the party but was the originator of the anniversary programme, consisting of clips from old editions of Tonight and interviews with its personalities. It was to be broadcast that same night on BBC1 after the news. The plan was for guests at the reunion party to watch the programme as it was being transmitted. They gathered early in the evening in the sixth floor hospitality suite where Cliff Michelmore gave an elegant speech of welcome. The star guest was Grace Wyndham Goldie who, although nearing 80, was still boisterous enough to roar 'Boring' – an old Tonight catchphrase – when Michelmore launched into a tribute to her. The most important absentee was Baverstock himself, kept at home in Yorkshire by health and family considerations. Lamenting this, Michelmore praised Baverstock as 'the man who really began this programme and told us that we had to be irreverent, we had to be enterprising, we had to be lively, we had to be relevant, important and funny, the man who drove us on from the very first day'. He went on: 'He was a very, very great influence on the life I think of everyone in this room, and a very, very important man, certainly in my life.'

Nobody recognised that more than Milne. In 1976 he had sought to repay part of his debt to Baverstock for the inspiration of those early years. After quitting Yorkshire Television, Baverstock had nowhere obvious to go. Milne devised the touching scheme of teaming him up again with Ned Sherrin, in a Sunday evening programme called Terra Firma. It was a quirkish magazine-style show, an attempt to revive the informal, spontaneous qualities of Tonight, but it did not succeed. Some of the difficulties were caused by the logistics. As part of the BBC's scheme to farm productions out to the regions, it was decreed that this one should emanate from Manchester. It meant that Baverstock had to drive across the Pennines every week from his home at Ilkley, and most of the cast had to come up from London – hardly conducive to the mood of relaxation the programme tried to convey. It was a flop. Milne had tried, but there was nothing more he could do for his old mentor.

Michelmore ended his speech by wishing Milne well in his new job as director-general. 'We hope Tonight gave you a good enough grounding to look after all those terrible people you'll have to look after when you get into one of the most important positions in public life in this country. We all raise our glasses and wish you well.'

Milne had no time to reflect just how terrible those people might be, for it was his turn to make a little speech. True to his reputation as an impeccable organiser, his remarks were almost entirely about the practical arrangements for the evening: 'We should have not too many more drams, but eat. I thought we should move out of this room about 9 p.m. but not too much later and we should go down the stairs. . . We shall watch the programme in solemn silence and there shall be no ribald interruptions. And we'll come back afterwards for a proper discussion of the nature of the programme (laughter) and then we'll have twa or three drams and go home. . . And Cliff, thank you boy, very much, for a marvellous speech.'

So a little after 9 the party trooped down seven flights of stairs to the basement auditorium where the weekly programme review meetings are held. They fell into silence as, on TV sets dotted round the room, they watched Michelmore introduce the programme. Baverstock had been well enough to take part in the film and tears welled to many eyes as they heard him, looking puffy and out of condition, state the Tonight philosophy: 'We were not servants of the state. We were not servants of the establishment. We were not educators, we were not preachers. . . We were people questioning what was going on in the world, lifting our eyebrow at it, celebrating it sometimes.' The tears in the room were not entirely nostalgic. They reflected sadness for Baverstock, whose career, despite Milne's 1976 bid to revive it, never truly recovered from his being eased out of the BBC in 1965. Milne had been bold enough to resign with him but canny enough to clamber back on to the corporate roundabout a few years later. The qualities of stubbornness and clear thinking that had made Baverstock the consummate producer of his time were inconsistent with the tact and diplomacy needed for corporate advancement. Milne, the ADC, the competent organiser of that emotional evening, was always the one destined for the top.

Chapter 3

GRANDSTAND

THE JOB Alasdair Milne had laboured so patiently to secure was beginning to turn sour several months before he began it. Two important decisions by the governors on appointments – made against his wishes and, in one case, against the unanimous advice of management – meant that he would begin his term of office with the wrong men, in his view, in strategic positions in the television service.

The key to controlling an organisation lies in the power to appoint its senior management. The governors of the BBC have that power and the extent to which they use it is a measure of the board's strength. Exactly how many management appointments should be made by the governors has never been precisely defined. In 1974 the chairman, Sir Michael Swann, told a lecture audience: 'Far more important than anything else in a body like the BBC is the making of senior apppointments. The board itself makes the top 30 or 40 of them, down to the level of controller, and it takes the job very seriously indeed. For in the long run, it is the choice of these men and women that determines what sort of body the BBC is.' Three years later the Annan Committee wrote: 'At present the governors are responsible for some 35 of the top appointments. We think this is too many. We recommend the governors should appoint only the top tiers of management.' Since then the number of appointments claimed by the governors has gone up, not down. Nobody is prepared to give a precise figure, but estimates fluctuate between forty and sixty. From the top down, these comprise the twelve-man board of management plus the secretary; the twenty-six people with the word 'controller' in their title, and the managing director of BBC Enterprises. This makes forty-one. Below those are appointments where the governors like to be consulted but which they do not always insist on making themselves. A joint sub-committee of governors and management does most of the detailed work on appointments, including the interviewing. Their decision then has to be ratified by the full board.

As part of his strategy to increase the power of the governors, Lord Hill insisted that they should become more involved in making appointments. Under his predecessors, the board was generally content to take the advice of the director-general, on the grounds that he and his management colleagues had intimate knowledge of the capabilities of the rival candidates and of the professional qualities the job demanded. If Hugh Greene told the board that there was one obvious choice and they should look no further, they would take his advice. Hill, bent on controlling the character of the institution, was not prepared to see that critical power forfeited so casually. Charles Curran, who succeeded Greene as director-general under Hill, wrote in his book *A Seamless Robe:*

> Under Lord Hill, the practice of bringing candidates before the whole board became more common – in fact, almost usual. Even when it seemed to me, as director-general, that there was an obvious and outstanding candidate, I was sometimes required to bring others before the board so that this view could be checked. . It sometimes meant that people who had little chance of being appointed were drawn through the somewhat harrassing process of being seen by a board of as many as 12 people. . . The process of interview by the full board of wider lists of candidates than can have realistic hopes of appointment is demoralizing for those not selected and insidiously undermines the authority of the director-general.

The practice did not end with Hill's departure. Power is like any other addiction – it is easier to acquire than give up. Even under the benign Michael Swann, the governors insisted on their right to make a wide range of appointments and see a diverse list of candidates. When Curran retired in 1977 it was apparent that his successor would be Ian Trethowan, who had been carefully groomed to take over. Yet the governors advertised the post and even invited selected people to apply. Paul Fox, head of Yorkshire Television, declined to take part in such a charade, but the governors did interview Harold Evans, editor of the *Sunday Times;* Claus Moser, the statistician and chairman of Covent Garden opera; and Robin Day, the BBC's own political interviewer. None had the slightest chance of getting the job: if by some mischance the governors had taken against Trethowan they would have appointed Gerald Mansell, managing director of the external services, the safe in-house choice. The uncharitable but unavoidable conclusion is that the chief purpose of putting such a galaxy of famous names through their paces was to make the board feel mightily important.

Swann's successor, George Howard, was as determined as Hill not to allow interference from below stairs in the governors' divine right to govern. And it was during his period as chairman that the inevitable happened: someone put up by management as a makeweight candidate for a senior post, to give the governors a field to choose from, was awarded the job.

Mansell's retirement as deputy director-general at the end of 1980 allowed scope for a limited redeployment of senior people. Alasdair Milne, already earmarked to succeed Trethowan in a couple of years, was made his deputy, while keeping his position as managing director of television. But because he would now have to spend part of his time dealing with non-television matters, Milne himself needed a high-powered deputy at Television Centre. Bill Cotton was given the job, leaving vacant the key strategic post of controller, BBC1, which he had filled in a competent but unspectacular fashion for three years.

The most obvious candidate was Brian Wenham, who had brought stability to the current affairs group as John Grist's successor. He had been controller of BBC2 since 1978. But a simple switch of channels would have been a mistake in terms of Wenham's career prospects. Although BBC1 was the senior, he would still merely be exchanging one controllership for another. More important, there would obviously have to be a significant reshuffling of senior jobs when Trethowan stepped down in 1982.

By then, if Wenham took the BBC1 position, he would have been in it for little more than a year – probably too short a time to be moved. So he would not be considered for any of the more senior television posts that his colleagues assumed he coveted.

With few exceptions (Bill Cotton is one), people at the highest level of management of BBC Television have come from the areas of current affairs or documentaries. Milne and Trethowan shared that background, although Trethowan had been a presenter rather than a producer. So when the two men learned of Wenham's reluctance to be considered, it was scarcely surprising that they should look in Lime Grove for the new controller of BBC1. They lighted upon John Gau, who had taken over the current affairs department from Wenham in 1978. Professionally and intellectually, Gau towered above any of his potential rivals in a thin field. There was one snag. Not many months before, in the view of a powerful faction on the board of governors, he had seriously blemished his record. For under his tutelage the current affairs department had become involved in the saga of Carrickmore – an incident that not only brought Gau's BBC career to a premature end, but also set the stage for the even more contentious Real Lives debate six years later.

* * * *

As the most intractable domestic issue over the last twenty years, it is scarcely surprising that the Irish question should from time to time have been the source of friction between the government and the broadcasting authorities. In December 1971 the Home Secretary, Reginald Maudling, urged the BBC not to go ahead with a programme planned for the following month, a live discussion called The Question of Ulster, set up as a mock tribunal. The government in London and in Belfast thought it would provide a platform for critical and uninformed attacks on its policies, while people were being killed in the province. They objected to what they termed trial by television. The government and most Unionist politicians boycotted the programme. In a lecture three years later Desmond Taylor, then editor of news and current affairs, said it amounted to 'the most sustained attempt to keep it off the air that any of us have ever experienced'. All the same, Hill and the governors refused to ban it. Ever since Lord Reith declined to give Winston Churchill the run of the airwaves during the 1926 General Strike, the BBC has felt it necessary to assert its independence of the government, except during all-out war. Responsible views critical of government policy are sought and broadcast, despite the near-certainty of official protest. It happened during the Suez crisis of 1956 and, more recently, the Falklands war of 1982. When The Question of Ulster was broadcast on 5 January 1972, the consensus was that the three-hour debate had not been subversive, merely tedious.

Five years later came the notorious 'Battle of Culloden'. The board of governors is a peripatetic body. When in London it meets at Broadcasting House or Television Centre, and more rarely at Bush House in the Aldwych, home of the external services. From time to time it feels obliged to venture into the provinces, and in November 1976 it was the turn of Northern Ireland. Until that year it had been the custom for the BBC team to stay at one of the hotels in the middle of Belfast, and to have the official dinner there on the evening of the meeting. But because some of those hotels had been subject to bomb attacks it was thought safer to move the headquarters to the Culloden Hotel near Holywood, some six miles north-east of the capital.

The dinner was attended by many of the powerful people of the province, chief among them Roy Mason, Secretary of State for Northern Ireland in the Labour Cabinet. At the end of governors' dinners the chairman customarily asks the main guest to start a discussion. Unconscious of any danger, Sir Michael Swann invited Mason to do so. The minister had been sitting next to Roy Fuller, the poet governor, and the pair had been desultorily swapping reminiscences of growing up in the north of England. But as soon as Mason got to his feet he ripped off his mask of cordiality and launched into a ferocious attack on BBC reporting of Ulster affairs, accusing the corporation of giving encouragement to terrorists, murderers and enemies of the state. A specific point of contention was an interview with a wounded Republican supporter, who had said she wanted all British troops to go home in coffins. Mason declared that unless the BBC mended its ways, the government would not be favourably disposed to any claim for an increase in the licence fee – a threat always present by implication but rarely made openly by ministers.

His fury was shared by most of the local people at the dinner. The BBC representatives were unprepared for the onslaught and one or two made feeble attempts at a defence, provoking still greater hostility from the majority. The atmosphere was beginning to approach that of a lynch mob until the emollient Richard Francis, controller in Northern Ireland, smoothed things over with a speech of great diplomatic skill, expressing some sympathy with the complaints while making no concessions on the principle that the BBC must report and reflect all views, both for and against the government. The governors were impressed with – and grateful for – Francis's performance. It stood him in good stead when promotion time came round again: he was made director of news and current affairs, a newly created post.

The BBC Handbook for 1978 describes the event coyly as a 'long and frank talk' with Mason. It says it provoked the BBC into re-examining its editorial policy for the province. 'Once again, in no spirit of self-satisfaction or complacency, we came to the conclusion that the only justifiable policy was one of open reporting within the law and the constitution.' Not long after the Culloden meeting, as if to test this restated resolve, the governors had to decide whether to broadcast allegations of brutality made by Republican prisoners against the Royal Ulster Constabulary. They let the programme go ahead and another small row ensued.

Shortly before the general election of 1979 Airey Neave, a leading Conservative politician and close friend of the party leader Margaret Thatcher, was murdered by a car bomb while driving out of the House of Commons garage. A group called the Irish National Liberation Army (INLA) claimed responsibility. A few weeks later a spokesman for INLA was interviewed on BBC1, disguised to prevent identification. The broadcast angered many people including Mrs Thatcher, the newly elected Prime Minister, who denounced it roundly in the House of Commons. Ian Trethowan, the director-general, had given his personal permission for the interview to be shown, and in his memoirs *Split Screen* he declares that he was probably wrong to do so, despite its indisputable news value. When Lord Mountbatten was assassinated a few weeks later, Trethowan gave an assurance to the government that no more such interviews would be conducted for the foreseeable future. 'From now on,' he told his management colleagues, 'as far as Northern Ireland is concerned we're in a new ball game.'

It was against this background that the producers of Panorama, the weekly current affairs programme, decided to devote an edition to examining the Provisional IRA (Irish Republican Army). A film crew with David Darlow as director and Jeremy Paxman as reporter went to Dublin and made contact with representatives of Provisional Sinn Fein, the IRA's political wing, explaining the purpose of the programme. On the afternoon of 17 October they received a telephone call in their hotel room advising them to repair right away to Carrickmore, a village of 400 people in County Tyrone, Northern Ireland, 17 miles from the border with the Republic.

Without telling anybody, they gathered their gear and drove to the village, to find it had been taken over by masked Provisional gunmen. To judge from their film of the incident it was a low-key, even comic affair. The masked men set up roadblocks and waved their rifles at car drivers who reacted with weary good humour, patently having seen it all before. In less than half an hour, when the camera crew had all the film they wanted, the masked men slipped away. The point of this demonstration of gun law was that a few days earlier the army had issued an optimistic statement that they were now in effective control of the border area. The Provisionals were determined to show that this was not the case. It was a valid news point and Paxman made it in his commentary – never in the event broadcast.

Being invited to report illegal acts (even if, as in this case, there was no specific mention of illegality in the invitation) is a thorny problem for TV journalists to handle. They will be accused of encouraging the offence by their presence, of sustaining the law-breakers by giving them, in a telling phrase Margaret Thatcher was to use about a comparable event six years later, 'the oxygen of publicity'. If the demonstration in Carrickmore was carried out only for their benefit, then the Panorama team were helping create the news rather than reporting it. There were bound to be suspicions that they had gone further and actually colluded with the gunmen in planning the incident. In fact there was no such collusion and Roger Bolton, editor of Panorama, was able to collect damages from the *Daily Telegraph* for suggesting that there was.

There is a complex body of procedural regulations in the BBC covering such difficult areas of news judgement as interviews and contact with terrorists and other undesirable groups. They are constantly being updated and issued either as memoranda or in plump booklets. These written statutes are occasionally reinforced or modified verbally at meetings of news and current affairs producers. Some of the procedures involve not just reference up, to an immediate superior, but also reference across, to other departments of the BBC. When decisions about news coverage have to be made quickly it is virtually impossible to go through all the designated procedures, although even that eventuality is covered in the 1975 *ABC for BBC editors,* which rules that 'lack of time for reference or inability to get a quick answer is a reason for not conducting an interview, not a reason for getting it while it is still available'.

Connoisseurs of bureaucratic practice will appreciate that the effect – and possibly the intention – of such convoluted reference rules has been not to prevent unauthorised activity by news teams but to establish that any subsequent blame lies at the point at which the correct reference was omitted. That makes it easy to identify a scapegoat, and provides a means for people higher in the chain of command to dodge blame. It also leaves scope for argument about degrees of consultation. Broad approval of an intention to make a programme may not necessarily cover the specific steps necessary to complete it. As the row over the Carrickmore filming began to develop, the question crystallised not into 'Who did what?' but 'Who knew?'

James Hawthorne had been appointed controller in Northern Ireland in 1978, after seven years running the broadcasting service of Hong Kong. A tall, bearded individualist, fond of caravanning, he had joined the BBC almost by accident in 1960 when, as a schoolteacher, he was seconded to educational programmes. Because his career had not followed a conventional corporation pattern the governors went to unusual lengths to check his fitness for the sensitive Belfast post, even telephoning Sir Murray Maclehose, the Governor of Hong Kong, for his view.

Sir Murray was warm in his praise and Hawthorne, a native Ulsterman, proved a popular appointment in the province (where he succeeded Richard Francis, the hero of Culloden).

In a corporate sense, though, his weakness was that he had been away from the BBC for seven years and knew few of its senior people. He did attend management meetings in London about once a fortnight but the colleagues he met there were unsure quite what to make of him. Heads of programme departments and producers, because they hardly knew Hawthorne, would not automatically think of telephoning him to discuss what they were planning to do in his territory. Instead, they would often prefer to raise it with his predecessor Francis, whom they did know and who was conveniently to hand in London.

On Thursday, 25 October 1979, more than a week after the Carrickmore incident, Hawthorne hosted a dinner party in Lockets, a Westminster restaurant popular with politicians and civil servants. Humphrey Atkins, Secretary of State for Northern Ireland, had been invited but was forced to cancel at the last minute. In his absence the chief guest was Jim Hannigan, a senior civil servant and Deputy Secretary of State. The purpose – ironic as it turned out – was to improve relations in the province between the BBC and the government. In the course of the discussion Hannigan casually raised the matter of Panorama 'staging that IRA thing'. Hawthorne had not the slightest idea what he was talking about and said so, adding that he doubted whether it had happened. He pointed out that under the 'reference up' procedures he was entitled to be told what visiting crews from London were doing in Northern Ireland. It was apparent – and scarcely surprising – that Hannigan did not believe his protestation of innocence, for it transpired that David Gilliland of the Northern Ireland Office had taken part in a long discussion of the incident with John Gau, head of the television current affairs group, at a party at Hawthorne's own house a full week earlier.

The NIO had been informed by the army, who had learned of it through their intelligence sources in Carrickmore only hours after it happened. Early in the morning following the visit, Darlow and Paxman, by then in Belfast, had received a call from a security official enquiring about it. Immediately after receiving that call Darlow had phoned Roger Bolton, the editor of Panorama, at his London home at breakfast time. But Bolton had not had the chance to confide in Gau, his immediate chief, who coincidentally was on a visit to Northern Ireland.

Hawthorne's party was held the evening following the incident at Carrickmore. A team from the current affairs programme Nationwide happened also to be filming in Northern Ireland, although less surreptitiously. Hawthorne had taken the opportunity of inviting some senior current affairs executives to his house to meet local people. Gau was taken aback when Gilliland, after exchanging conventional pleasantries with him, asked: 'What the hell are your people up to?' After hearing Gilliland's account Gau went to join his deputy, Christopher Capron, at the other side of the room. 'Christ,' he whispered to him. 'There's trouble.' Neither thought of mentioning it to Hawthorne.

The chubby, bespectacled Gau had been running the current affairs department at Lime Grove for less than two years. It is a notoriously exposed position and Gau's tenure of it had been marked by a greater than average incidence of high-level rows. Apart from the Irish dilemmas, he had twice quarrelled seriously with Ian Trethowan, the director-general, first over programmes examining the security services and then about allegations that doctors were authorising organ transplants from people not clinically dead. Current affairs programmes are the ones politicians and BBC governors watch. The head of the department has to absorb pressure from those pillars of the establishment who believe programme makers are by instinct dangerous radicals bent on undermining the state, and should be severely curbed. At the same time he is constantly being urged by those very programme-makers to extend the bounds of what is permissible and to resist what they see as pernicious pressures from vested interests. But Gau is a man of great resource; tough, realistic and thoughtful. Trethowan, despite their disagreements, had already marked him out as possessing 'bottom', an elusive quality he sought in people earmarked for advancement in the BBC. It suggests a clear view of what has to be done, combined with the strength of character to see it through. The director-general was not alone in thinking Gau would go far – as he surely would have done, had it not been for the events now unfolding.

Returning to London after Hawthorne's party, Gau confirmed the facts about Carrickmore with Bolton and went to see Bill Cotton, controller of BBC 1. 'It might blow up in our faces,' he warned. In case that did happen, the two men drafted a statement setting out what the Panorama team had done and the journalistic and ethical justification for it. They agreed that Cotton should release the document at the first sign of the affair being made public. But when that did happen two weeks later, the fire spread too fast to be doused by a statement – or at least by that statement – and it was never issued.

Even Cotton did not think of raising the matter with Hawthorne, who was thus caught entirely off his guard by Jim Hannigan at Lockets. Returning to Belfast the day following the dinner, Hawthorne found Jeremy Paxman there and was briefed by him. Paxman said that, as far as he knew, there had been full consultation in advance. While Hawthorne was puzzled that this had not included him, his immediate deputies were not available that day for questioning and he might have settled for a brisk internal investigation the following week. But late on Sunday evening he received a telephone call from Lady Faulkner, the BBC's national governor for Northern Ireland.

Lucy Faulkner is a steely, determined woman, the widow of the province's former Unionist Prime Minister, Brian Faulkner. She had been telephoned earlier that day by Gilliland at the personal request of Humphrey Atkins, who had been told about Hawthorne's unsatisfactory responses to Hannigan's questions the previous Thursday and was suspicious. Officials were angry not just about the IRA takeover as such but because Paxman and the crew had not reported it to the police or military as soon as they left the village.

Hawthorne was at least now able to confirm to Lady Faulkner that there had been a Carrickmore incident, although he was still uncertain about its exact significance. So far he had been able to speak to none of his senior colleagues about it. He promised her that he would make more enquiries on Monday. On doing so he discovered that his Belfast news editor, Robin Walsh, had known about the affair, and had given Paxman and Darlow a sombre but unspecific warning to 'establish the proper channels of consultation' upwards. There had certainly been no advance discussion at the senior level demanded by the news guidelines, which say that any programme proposal concerning Northern Ireland must be cleared by the controller personally.

Hawthorne then acted in an instinctive BBC fashion: he composed a long memorandum and sent it by telex to Francis, director of news and current affairs, with a copy to John Gau. This document, laced with a streak of fierce indignation, was to become important in determining the corporation's defence strategy when the affair eventually became public knowledge.

'It would appear', wrote Hawthorne, 'that the NIO no longer sees much value in discussing matters of this kind with BBC management executives – considering my defence to Jim Hannigan, can you blame them? Lady Faulkner's dismay and embarrassment are at least as great as mine – i.e. extremely acute. And that is putting it mildly.' The memorandum was guarded about pinning responsibility for the foul-up but it criticised Roger Bolton, who had in September given Hawthorne's staff a broad indication of his intention to make a programme about the IRA, but had not fleshed it out. Hawthorne recalled that Bolton had been the producer of the programme containing the INLA interview earlier that year. 'It is inconceivable that Roger Bolton – the man who brought you the INLA affair – should not be aware of the paramount need for close and detailed consultation with the Northern Ireland management before embarking on a major Irish project.'

The memo ended on a didactic note: 'I now require a full report on everything that has happened so far in this matter and everything that is proposed, including a view of all the film shot at Carrickmore. Regardless of Panorama's deadlines or commitments I shall want to see every item of the proposed programme before transmission and in sufficient time to allow for amendment or abandonment as appropriate. May I please have your support.'

Francis thought it was time to refer the matter further upwards. Ian Trethowan, the director – general, was in hospital following a mild heart attack and his functions were being undertaken by Gerry Mansell, the good-natured BBC stalwart who had spent most of his career in the external services.

When Trethowan had been appointed DG two years earlier, Mansell had been the only serious alternative. Now only a year away from retirement, he had been propelled by accident into the top job, if only for a few weeks, and was enjoying immensely this autumnal taste of supreme power. Hearing of the Carrickmore incident, he summoned Francis and Bill Cotton to see him. They agreed to keep a close watch on the proposed IRA programme and to make sure they were fully informed before it went on the air.

So far the matter had been kept concealed from the public and all except a handful of politicians, although with the Northern Ireland Office in the know it would have required an unusual amount of luck to keep it quiet permanently. Nothing happened for more than a week following Mansell's meeting. Then a reporter from *Hibernia,* an Irish journal, went to Carrickmore and was given an account of the incident and the BBC's involvement in it. The *Financial Times* in London picked up the story in its editions of Thursday, 8 November, and other Fleet Street papers cobbled together versions of it later. Although the *Hibernia* story stated specifically that the Panorama crew had no advance knowledge of what they would see in the village, the tabloid press was not slow in asserting that the BBC had helped stage the incident.

The Cabinet were meeting that morning. Mrs Thatcher, still indignant about the INLA interview, was furious when she read the *Financial Times* report. She sent William Whitelaw, the Home Secretary, out of the Cabinet room to phone Sir Michael Swann, the chairman of the governors, who were by chance also in the midst of their fortnightly meeting. Whitelaw gave Swann a vivid description of the Prime Minister's anger and told him that some public act of contrition would have to be made to pacify the Cabinet. 'It looks ugly,' he confided.

Swann immediately reported the substance of Whitelaw's call to the other governors and asked Mansell what he knew. Mansell assured Swann that he had not been told about the incident until after it had taken place. Since it was not strictly speaking an IRA interview he was not required to give advance authority – but there were procedures laid down for this kind of thing and he was not sure they had been properly complied with. He would certainly look into it.

Two members of the board were especially insistent that something had to be done. One, for obvious reasons, was Lady Faulkner. Fellow governors had the impression that she might well resign unless decisive action were taken. The other was George Howard, the plump, flamboyant country gentleman, owner of Castle Howard in Yorkshire, soon to take over from Swann as chairman. They had been angry about the INLA interview a few weeks earlier, but since this had been approved in advance by Trethowan there was nothing they could do without implying a lack of confidence in their director-general. But Trethowan had assured them then that he would have control procedures tightened up. Now, only weeks later, this had happened. Howard and Faulkner were determined that the management should not be able to get away with bland assurances this time.

Before question time in the House of Commons that afternoon, further kindling had been piled on to the fire in the shape of a report in the London *Evening Standard* that gave a greatly exaggerated account of what had happened at Carrickmore. It put the number of IRA men in the village at 140 – about ten times the real figure. It said they were armed with a rocket-propelled grenade launcher, which was ludicrous. And it added that the incident had been set up solely as 'a stunt for Panorama'. Mrs Thatcher, asked in the Commons about the reports, gave a fine display of indignation. 'The Home Secretary and I think it is time the BBC put its own house in order,' she stormed, adding that it seemed to be a matter for the police and the Director of Public Prosecutions. Mr James Molyneaux, leader of the Ulster Unionists, said: 'It seems to me to be at least a treasonable activity.'

Swann told Mansell to institute an inquiry. To placate the governors and politicians, it seemed that at least one sacrificial head would have to be offered them. Mansell set about the task with a will. Although butchery was far from his peaceable nature, he did find, rather to his surprise, that to be pitched into the central role in so contentious an affair made his adrenalin flow –

especially since it had happened quite by chance and so late in his career. He spent the next week busily interviewing all the participants. His conclusion was that of a bureaucrat, concentrating on the breach of formal consultation procedures rather than on the harder, central issue of the rights and wrongs of the Carrickmore venture itself. The critics in Parliament did not care about procedure. Their complaint had been that by filming illegality the BBC was encouraging it. The corporation, typically, diverted the main argument into the more easily codified and investigated question of whether the right people had been consulted.

Mansell found that the single definable offence had been the failure to inform Hawthorne of the visit in advance. He saw this not so much as an oversight but as an example of the conscious resistance of journalists and producers to political control. The two men he blamed were Roger Bolton, Panorama's editor, who should have seen to it that Hawthorne was told, and John Gau, who, Mansell believed, ran the current affairs department on too loose a rein. He also hinted mischievously at a criticism of Ian Trethowan. It was, as Mansell saw it, the job of the director-general to create an atmosphere in which people told each other what they were doing. The mood in Trethowan's BBC did not encourage that.

He presented his conclusions to a special meeting of the governors on Thursday, 15 November. They issued a statement the following day accepting Mansell's report, exonerating the Panorama crew from the charge of collusion with the IRA, but criticising the breach of internal consultation rules. 'We are in total agreement with the acting director-general's diagnosis', the governors wrote, 'and we endorse his decision, amongst other things, to take whatever disciplinary action may be appropriate.'

That action was under way by the time the statement was released. First Gau and then Bolton were summoned to a hearing conducted by Mansell and Mike Bett, the director of personnel.

* * * *

Lime Grove is a scruffy street of cramped terraced houses, running between Uxbridge Road and Goldhawk Road, just west of Shepherd's Bush Green. On the east side, roughly half way along, is the ugly grey lump of the old film studio that the BBC bought in 1950 as the temporary headquarters of the television service. When the purpose-built Television Centre – about half a mile north on Wood Lane – opened in 1960, the current affairs department stayed at Lime Grove. It has been their headquarters since. Over the years the BBC has bought much of the surrounding property and converted it piecemeal to its own use. That makes it a confusing warren of a place, its offices and studios linked by haphazardly sited corridors. At the end of one of them is room S7, a hospitality suite used for relaxing important guests before interviews and restoring their shattered nerves afterwards.

Every Friday at lunchtime, current affairs editors meet in S7 for a buffet and a few drinks, to keep each other up to date with what they are doing and, more interestingly, to exchange gossip. The lunch on 16 November 1979 was imbued with tension. Vincent Hanna, a current affairs reporter and a national official of the National Union of Journalists, had been telephoned at home in the morning by Mansell. 'You should know', he had been told, 'that I'm calling Roger Bolton in and disciplining him.' Although strictly not senior enough to attend the editors' lunch, Hanna repaired to S7 to await the outcome.

John Gau was the first to return from his ordeal. A silence fell as he pushed open the door. He staggered in clutching his bottom, acting the role of a schoolboy returning from a sound magisterial beating. 'Cor,' was his only comment. It took the company a few seconds to size up what was happening, then, mightily relieved, they hooted with laughter. When that subsided, Gau told them he had received an official reprimand – serious enough because it would go on his BBC file, but apart from that it has no deleterious consequences. He gave an hilarious account of the meeting, impersonating Mansell incisively. He was treating it as a joke. The others gratefully took their cue from him.

The mood, therefore, was jovial by the time Bolton returned half an hour later. Loosened by modest doses of BBC house wine, voices were being raised just that fraction too high, compensating for the strain of the earlier part of the lunch. As Bolton entered an ironic cheer went up, and a few catcalls. The editors looked forward to a repeat of Gau's bravura performance. Then they saw that Bolton did not look at all perky, but pale and crestfallen, as if about to be sick. For the second time in less than an hour, they had misread the position. There was a sudden silence. Bolton filled it with a strangled whisper: 'I've been sacked.'

It was a slight exaggeration. He had not been fired from the BBC but Mansell and Bett had decided to remove him from the contentious world of current affairs programmes into an administrative position in the secretariat. Mansell reasoned that it would give him a less blinkered perspective on the corporation, show him that chains of command were important and journalistic values not necessarily paramount. Bolton did not see it that way. He interpreted the proposed move as professional assassination by stealth. Current affairs was his field and his career plan was to climb as high in that area as he could before moving up to perhaps even greater things. A switch to the administration department, within the most obscure recesses of Broadcasting House, would take him off that track, and he knew how hard it would be to get back on it.

At the disciplinary hearing, Bolton had made two points in response to the charge of inadequate consultation. Although he agreed he had not told Hawthorne of the Carrickmore visit, the crew had consulted Robin Walsh, the Belfast news editor, and had a right to assume he would mention it to the controller. The other issue was how much Richard Francis knew. Francis never denied being told about the programme in outline, but Bolton maintained he gave him fairly full details of his plans at a Blackpool oyster bar during that year's party conferences. Bolton had taken Helen Jenkins, leader of the NUJ Lime Grove chapel, to the hearing with him. She argued to Mansell that they had not been given time to prepare a proper defence and that the proceedings should be adjourned. Mansell, with his powerful sense of what was proper, agreed. But he told Bolton there was no chance of his sentence being modified.

On hearing Bolton's account Vincent Hanna picked up the telephone in the hospitality room and got through to Mansell and Bett. He said it was unfair to prejudge the result of next week's resumed hearing by determining the sentence in advance. He warned of the possibility of industrial action by journalists. Mansell agreed to reinstate Bolton pending the outcome of the new hearing. In S7 the current affairs editors, horrified and indignant, agreed that something should be done at the highest possible level to save Bolton. Gau's own involvement made it inappropriate for him to initiate any action but his deputy (and eventual successor) Christopher Capron volunteered. He would draw up a petition for Bolton's reinstatement and have it signed by as many senior people in news and current affairs as would agree. He called a meeting in his office late that afternoon of people whose names might add authority to the petition. Peter Woon, the editor of radio news and current affairs, attended and so did two men from the features department at nearby Kensington House, Desmond Wilcox and Paul Bonner. They agreed that Bolton was being made a scapegoat and should be defended. Capron would compose a document and they would sign it over the weekend, with a view to presenting it to Mansell before the hearing resumed on Tuesday.

Capron worked on the draft on Saturday, having found a secretary willing to spend part of her weekend typing it out. He was aiming for a form of words that would make clear the belief of the signatories that Bolton was being victimised, without being so extreme as to deter senior people from signing. On Sunday he took it round to as many potential supporters as he could trace. His first port of call was a conference centre near Abingdon, where many of the leaders of the news and current affairs departments were taking part in a weekend meeting that had, coincidentally, a bearing on what had happened at Carrickmore. Its subject was how the press and broadcasting organisations should respond to acts of terrorism and revolution, and how far they should co-operate with the authorities in modifying their reporting to thwart the aims of the terrorists.

It was a high-level conference, organised by Richard Francis, with participants from Europe and America. The Lords Goodman and Scarman were there, as well as senior police officers, editors, lawyers and civil servants. Fictional scenarios were played out, with many of the delegates acting the part of themselves: 'You're an editor and you get a news flash of a siege. Who do you contact first?' Discussion was frank and not always as earnest as the subject might suggest. (Hearing a description of Britain's Official Secrets Act and the curbs it imposed on reporters, a Texas police chief drawled: 'Sure wish we had something like that at home. I'd put journalists so deep into the jail you'd have to pump in daylight.')

Outside the conference sessions the talk among the BBC participants was all of Carrickmore and the threat to Bolton, which had been reported in Saturday's newspapers. Francis seemed irked that an obsession with this piece of internal BBC gossip should detract from the vital global concerns of his conference. He was even angrier when Capron arrived with the petition during the tea interval. The BBC people broke away from the knots forming around Francis's high-powered guests, the biggest names in British security, and grouped instead round the boyish, pink-faced Capron, who was not a big name in anything at all. Everyone Capron approached agreed to sign. He had not been quite sure of Alan Protheroe, the fiery, unpredictable Welsh editor of TV news (later to become deputy director-general). Relations between the news and current affairs departments were traditionally sticky. Protheroe was always energetic in fighting for old-fashioned hard news values against what he regarded as the gimmicky, showbiz practices of Lime Grove. But his view of Carrickmore was that journalists had reacted professionally to a news tip-off and he had no hesitation in signing. Capron did not solicit Francis's signature. Quite apart from the question of how much he may have known in advance, there was a feeling at Lime Grove that as director of news and current affairs he had stayed notably silent when he might have been expected to rally in defence of his juniors. After picking up a half dozen good signatures at Abingdon, Capron headed back down the M4 and went to the homes of the others he wanted to sign. Luckily most senior BBC people live in riparian south-west London – Barnes, Putney and Richmond – and by the end of the evening he had collected fifteen names. On Monday, the day before the resumed hearing, he sent the petition to Mansell. Gau, meantime, had penned an angry letter to Swann, with copies to a dozen senior management people, saying that the Carrickmore incident was justified journalistically and the governors should resist official pressures to victimise anybody on account of it.

By themselves, the Capron petition and the Gau letter would probably not have persuaded the acting director-general to alter Bolton's sentence. He would have been able to dismiss them as the natural – indeed quite creditable – reaction of colleagues to the distress of a man they admired and liked. Mansell's primary concern had to be to satisfy the governors that decisive action had been taken. But against that, he now had to consider the more formidable opposition of Vincent Hanna and the National Union of Journalists. Hanna had the power to stop programmes and cause trouble. If he did that the issue would drag on, rather than die away as Mansell now so profoundly desired: for his initial surge of adrenalin had by now run dry.

At the hearing Hanna presented a long memorandum arguing that the procedural guidelines for reference up were not as clear as had been maintained. Bolton was justified in thinking that by telling Robin Walsh of the Carrickmore plan he had done his duty by the Belfast office. As for how much he had told Francis, that had to remain an uncertain question. Mansell thought the arguments had merit. Although he did not relish having to explain his climbdown to Swann and the governors, he reduced Bolton's punishment to the same as Gau's, an official reprimand. The reprieved man remained, for the time being, editor of Panorama. Seven months later he was switched to the early evening programme Nationwide, before becoming deputy head of current affairs and, in 1983, head of the network production centre in Manchester. So far his career has stayed on course.

Mansell was right to fear the governors' reaction when, lifting the cover on the silver platter he presented to them, they found he was offering not the severed head they expected, freshly dripping with blood, but yet another lame explanation that severed heads were out of season, along with an unconvincing promise that they would surely be luckier next time. The fiercest critics of the Carrickmore visit – notably George Howard – saw Mansell's climbdown as another deplorable example of the weakness of a management more interested in defending its own people than in taking the necessary tough action. That view was shared by Mrs Thatcher and most of her Cabinet, who had precipitated the furore by their initial outraged reaction to news of the incident. A few weeks later the Attorney-General, Sir Michael Havers, wrote to Sir Michael Swann saying that although he believed an offence had been committed by the Panorama team, he would not go ahead with a prosecution. The letter ended with a fresh polemic about the BBC's record in such matters. Trethowan, when Swann showed it to him, thought it a disgrace. He believed it blurred the distinction between Havers the politician and Havers the law officer of the Crown. A similar contradiction was to be displayed in a more famous letter to a BBC chairman nearly six years later, this time from the Home Secretary.

As for the frustrated governors, there was nothing they could do just then about the management's refusal to sacrifice Bolton or Gau as a scapegoat. But a few months later, when the time came to appoint a new controller of BBC1, their latent resentment was to rise to the surface, with incalculable long-term consequences.

* * * *

Gau was far from confident that he would be offered the controllership of BBC1, not only on account of Carrickmore, but because of the other differences of opinion with Trethowan during his tenure at Lime Grove. He was sure – and he was right – that Trethowan regarded him as a troublemaker. Their worst row was over the two projected Panorama programmes about the security services. From the moment the journalists began their enquiries, Trethowan came under pressure from Whitehall to ban the project. He summoned Gau, who persuaded him to let them at least complete the programmes: decisions about possible changes could be taken then. When Trethowan saw the completed films he objected.

'John. I don't think this programme should go out,' he had told him. 'Why don't you pull it?' Gau replied that he thought it should go out and if Trethowan disagreed, why did *he* not pull it.

'If I did, it would cause such an enormous kerfuffle,' Trethowan sighed. Instead, he suggested sixteen alterations, some of them in Gau's view absurd. Someone told the press, who ran it as a 'BBC censorship' story. Trethowan was furious and blamed Gau, not for the press leak but for reacting so sourly after he had appeared to accept in advance that changes might have to be made.

(In 1985 a scoop in the *Observer* revealed that MI5 actually had an agent inside the BBC, monitoring sensitive appointments.)

Gau was wrong in assuming that these clashes with Trethowan would automatically rule him out of consideration for controller of BBC1. Trethowan's reputation at the BBC was as a political wheeler-dealer, keen to avoid offence to the establishment and adept at smoothing ruffled feathers when something untoward slipped under his guard. That is a fair analysis of how he performed the function of director-general but it misses a vital part of the truth about him.

Trethowan has a strong belief in people fulfilling their appointed role. Because he saw his function as DG as being to ease relations between the boards of governors and management, he was inevitably viewed as an appeaser. But equally he recognised that the role of the head of current affairs is to fight his corner and try to get provocative and stimulating material on the air. He knew that Gau was under constant pressure from those below him who regarded any restriction on their programme-making as part of a conspiracy against truth. So although Trethowan felt obliged from time to time to stay Gau's hand, that did not mean he thought less of him in professional terms. On the contrary, he respected him for doing his job so conscientiously. He had a curiously detached view of such things. In his book *Split Screen,* there is a revealing passage about absorbing external pressures:

> I felt what was important was not whether someone tried to bring pressure on the BBC, but how we responded. To dismiss all pressure seemed to me as foolish as automatically to give way to it. Sometimes those exerting pressure had a legitimate point. On the other hand there were times when we were palpably being pressed to depart from an honest, truthful policy, and there we had to stand firm.

He believed that, just as it was legitimate for interested parties to put pressure on him, so too could he transfer that pressure to his subordinates – and it was up to them to respond in accordance with their view of the merits of the case.

The second reason why Trethowan was willing to go along with Milne's desire to appoint Gau was the unspoken pact the two had operated since Trethowan was preferred to the younger man for director-general. In his last months in office, he did not want to queer the pitch of his appointed successor by saddling him with executives he did not want, whatever his reservations about Gau.

In the autumn of 1980, Milne and Cotton went to see Gau in his narrow office in the row of Victorian terraced houses that had been incorporated into the Lime Grove studio complex. They told him of Cotton's coming promotion and of the vacancy for controller BBC1. 'We think you're the man,' Milne told him.

'Hang on a bit,' said Gau, ever a realist. 'It's less than a year since I had an official reprimand. Surely I'm not the person you should be putting forward?'

Milne smiled. 'Don't worry,' he advised. 'We think you're the man and we've squared the DG. He sees it's a bit sensitive but he's behind our endorsement.' Gau wondered. His political instinct told him the appointment would be more than 'a bit' sensitive and the governors would have a view on it. Still, he assumed Trethowan had cleared it with the board. The job was one he would dearly like to have. He saw no reason why he should not allow his name to go forward.

It was unlucky for him – and for Milne and Trethowan – that this was the first important appointment to come up since George Howard had taken over as chairman in August. A demonstrative widower, often in the gossip columns because of his fondness for extravagant clothing such as kaftans, Howard had been surprised and pleased to be offered the chairmanship after eight years as a governor. His only experience of administration and public affairs prior to his appointment had been as president of the Country Landowners' Association, a member of the Countryside Commission and a councillor of the Royal College of Art. He was virtually a full-time member of voluntary committees, without commercial or professional involvements; so as a governor of the BBC he was able to absorb himself in the affairs of the corporation in greater detail than most other board members, who had broader outside interests. Because he had no alternative arena in which to deploy his energies and his ebullient personality, he asserted himself at board meetings, making a loud show of his sometimes tendentious opinions, occasionally based on an incomplete understanding of the facts. He believed fervently in a strong board of governors exercising firm control on the broadcasters. That was why he had backed Lucy Faulkner with such conviction in her insistence that something had to be done over Carrickmore.

Howard had not – and he knew it – been the first choice as chairman. A number of people outside the board of governors had been approached, including Michael McCrum, former headmaster of Eton and now master of Corpus Christi college at Cambridge. (He would have been almost a hereditary choice, since he was married to the daughter of Sir Arthur fforde, an earlier chairman: but he declined.) Amongst board members, the most suitable candidate in terms of competence and qualification was Mark Bonham Carter, Swann's vice-chairman and a former chairman of the Race Relations Board. His disqualification was that he came from a distinguished family of liberals. William Whitelaw, the Home Secretary, called him to his office and told him regretfully that he and the Prime Minister, Mrs Thatcher, had decided that Conservative back-benchers would not approve the appointment to so vital a post of a man with his leftish views. In the light of later events, that was a significant benchmark in the history of relations between the governors and the government. Until then, party politics had been kept at a distance from appointments to the board. The clearest example was Lord Hill, made chairman by Harold Wilson although he had been a Conservative minister. Yet by the mid-80s, when relations between Westminster and Portland Place reached a point of crisis, all the governors had been appointed by the Thatcher government and most were sympathetic towards its philosophy. Bonham Carter, although he would have loved to be chairman, had, as early as 1979, enough political sense to understand what was happening. He knew too that Howard was an old friend of Whitelaw's, a fellow member of the Northern gentry.

Partly because he was aware of being a second or third choice,

Howard was determined to make his name as a strong chairman in the Hill tradition. Where Swann had been tough in a discreet way, Howard preferred bombast to subtlety. He wanted to be seen to be in charge. So when Trethowan suggested that the controllership of BBC1 should go to John Gau without a contest, Howard would not hear of it. This was by tradition a governors' appointment and the governors would make it.

Trethowan was surprised by this reaction because he had always been close to Howard: indeed among all the governors it was Howard who had campaigned hardest for Trethowan's appointment as director-general. But he could not accept his reasoning about Gau. After all, when Trethowan had discussed the running of the current affairs department with the board, in the context of Carrickmore and the other controversial issues, he had often expressed the opinion that Gau was too much under the influence of the 'wild men' at Lime Grove who resisted interference from their seniors. Now he was recommending that very man for one of the most influential jobs in television, where potential for harm is that much greater. Although Trethowan had been able to persuade *himself* that there was no inconsistency in this, it was not the same as persuading Howard.

With the governors insisting on a contest, Trethowan and Milne tried to think of other candidates they could nominate plausibly, but who would stand no serious chance of gaining the governors' favour. One was Humphrey Burton, the attractive and energetic head of music and arts. Milne, encouraging him to apply, assured him he had the necessary stature and weight; but that opinion was not widely held. Although a gifted producer and an on-screen presenter with a pleasing manner, Burton had been the victim of several items of gossip in the satirical fortnightly *Private Eye* concerning both his private and professional life. His administration of the department was thought to be extravagant. Some of his colleagues believed that his enthusiasm for appearing on screen and producing his own programmes left him too little time for essential work at his desk. A running joke at Kensington House – the BBC outpost that music and arts share with sport and general features – was that whenever you wanted Burton he was in 'make-up or Munich'. Though realistic enough to recognise that his chance of becoming controller was slender, he agreed to appear before the board.

Another nominee was Graeme McDonald, later to become controller of BBC2. The third was Alan Hart, head of television sport. Tall and fair-haired, amiable and fluent, Hart was lucky in the timing of the BBC1 vacancy. It came up not long after he had made an impressive appearance before the governors arguing the case for limited coverage of the 1980 Moscow Olympics. The Americans were boycotting the games to protest against the dispatch of Soviet troops to Afghanistan but British athletes were not prevented from taking part if they wanted to. The BBC was in something of a dilemma. There was genuine interest by viewers in the performance of the British competitors but, with the government sympathetic to the American boycott, it would be inappropriate for the national broadcasting organisation to give the Games the customary saturation coverage. The governors, many of whom had never met Hart before, asked him to attend a board meeting in Bristol to discuss his plans.

He went before them with a well-prepared proposal, supported by charts and diagrams, for coverage at about 25 per cent of the usual level. He argued that this would reflect the essential elements of the Games without letting them dominate the two channels; and it would allow people to follow the progress of British sportsmen. Hart's presentation was orderly and the argument logical. 'He laid it out before them like a good clerk would in the Middle Ages,' said someone who was present. 'You could see it was the kind of thing the governors liked.'

Nobody denied Hart's clerical attributes. What he lacked, in Milne and Trethowan's view, was that elusive 'bottom'. While the two men were not doubting Hart's strength of character, they saw little evidence of the necessary vision. The range needed by the controller of the BBC's prime channel was very much greater than that of a head of sport. It was true that two former controllers, Paul Fox and Brian Cowgill, had come from the same professional background; but that did not necessarily mean that Hart was up to it.

The candidates attended an appointments board at Broadcasting House a few weeks before Christmas. Trethowan and Milne sat on it, and among the four governors, ominously for

Gau, were George Howard and Lucy Faulkner, the sternest critics of the Carrickmore adventure. They questioned him closely about it and, although other topics were discussed, Gau had the impression that this was to be the decisive issue. He admitted that there may have been errors in procedure but insisted that in journalistic terms it was right of Panorama to make a programme about the IRA. In that context the correct editorial decision had been made. He only regretted that the programme had never been shown. Sensing that this was perilous ground, Trethowan tried to steer the discussion towards other topics, but with only limited success. Milne said nothing.

Had the governors been willing to accept the management's recommendation in the usual way, Gau's appointment could have been announced there and then. But Howard and Lady Faulkner refused to go along with that. While willing to rule out McDonald and Burton, they insisted that Gau and Hart should appear before the full board for a final selection. It was too late to arrange that before Christmas. When Gau received a phone call from Milne to tell him that the decision had been postponed until after the holiday, he knew that his chance of getting the job was slim.

Trethowan, now so openly committed to Gau, felt that his personal prestige was at stake. He used the intervening weeks to put his political skills into play. Knowing the chairman was against him, he made a confidential approach to the vice-chairman, Mark Bonham Carter, asking him to canvass and lobby the other governors to build support for Gau. Bonham Carter reported back that there were too many 'don't knows' for certainty but he thought Gau could win. Four governors were firmly committed to the management candidate: Bonham Carter himself; Philip Chappell, a merchant banker; Sir John Johnston, the former British High Commissioner in Rhodesia; and Stella Clarke, a West Country councillor with particular interests in children's welfare. The chairman and Lucy Faulkner were sure to vote for Hart. That left five undecided (there being a vacancy on the board). Gau needed two of those five to win, and Bonham Carter assured Trethowan that he would do his best to talk them round.

The governors are a random bunch of men and women, selected rather loosely as a cross-section of society. Often they are carelessly described as coming from the ranks of the Great and the Good, but that is not borne out by analysing lists of board members over the years. They are less than great and usually only moderately good; a more apt generalisation is that they represent the Worthy. Although most are chosen from specific categories – the trade union governor, the diplomatic governor, the black governor, the Scots, Welsh and Irish governors – they do not regard themselves as representing only their special interest groups. They vary markedly in terms of the interest and energy they devote to corporation business, and in their ability to understand complex issues of technology and programming. In preparation for their fortnightly meetings they are swamped with masses of documentation, which they do not always have the time or the capacity to digest. When they have not done so they are at the mercy of those who have – notably the chairman, who devotes nearly all his time to the job, as against the few days a month the others are expected to put in. For that reason they are generally too diffident to be organised in a boardroom revolt against the chair. Although Bonham Carter knew this – and appreciated too that they might not want to defy Howard on this first major issue of his chairmanship – he was confident that he could, by forceful reasoning, persuade them to give the management the man they wanted in the job.

The five waverers on the appointment were Dr Roger Young, the Scottish governor, principal of George Watson's College in Edinburgh; the Welsh governor Alwyn Roberts, director of extra-mural studies at the University of North Wales; Lord Allen, former general secretary of the Union of Shop, Distributive and Allied Workers (USDAW), the trade union governor; Baroness Serota of Hampstead, a life peer, expert on the treatment of offenders and former Minister of State in the Department of Health and Social Security; and Professor Christopher Longuet-Higgins, the scientific governor, a research professor at the University of Sussex.

When the governors met in mid-January, one was absent. Howard said he was going to take a vote on the issue – again following the example of Hill. Bonham Carter was confident of a victory for the Gau forces. Milne and Trethowan agreed with him, for they had been taking their own soundings and even hazarded the likely result – seven for Gau, three for Hart. But they underestimated the determination of George Howard and Lucy Faulkner. Lady Faulkner had been cancelling out the effects of Bonham Carter's lobbying by opposing Gau in such a determined manner that some of her colleagues feared she might resign if he were appointed. This time the candidates were interviewed more briefly and Gau was not asked about Carrickmore at all. Howard discouraged a long debate and rushed the vote through. The result was exactly the opposite of what the Gau camp had predicted – seven for Hart and three for Gau.

Howard was pleased with himself. In the first major test of his strength he had asserted his authority over the board of management. He would, he believed, from now on enjoy the reputation of being a tough chairman, jealous of his prerogatives. It was a very different approach from the one his predecessor Swann would have employed. Swann had run the BBC the way he had run Edinburgh University – seeking agreement by persuasion rather than by invoking the power of his office. Had the conflict occurred during his term of office (as it could well have done, because he too would have resisted Gau's appointment) he would have talked it through with Trethowan until one of them had been won over to the other's view. It is the difference between a consensus liberal of the seventies and a conviction Tory of the eighties.

It fell to Milne to make the phone calls congratulating Hart and commiserating with Gau. Later he dropped a note to Gau saying that he had been assured by a governor that Carrickmore was not the reason for his rejection. Gau did not believe it and was equally sceptical about the sentence in the letter that was supposed to comfort him: 'Don't worry, your time will come.' Gau did not think it would, and was fairly sure now that he did not want it to. It was not the fact of rejection that bothered him: after all, he only applied for the post because he was persuaded into it by Milne and Cotton. But he did object to the way it had been handled. In his view, Trethowan and Milne had behaved badly and weakly. It is a feeble management that puts up its own candidate for a senior position and then cannot deliver it to him. As head of current affairs he had felt more than once that he was not getting the support he needed from what he saw as wishy-washy management. He preferred not to work for such a sloppy organisation. Six months later he left to form his own production company, making programmes for Channel 4.

Chapter 4

WORKERS' PLAYTIME

IN 1981 it was a novel experience for the board of management
to be outmanoeuvred by the board of governors, although it was
something they would grow used to over the next five years. Six
years earlier, the case of Alastair Hetherington had provided a
flawless example of the reverse process, of how the board of
management succeeded in taking the sting out of a potentially
threatening initiative by the governors, not by opposing it
directly but by doggedly and stealthily chipping away until the
threat disintegrated.

The appointment of Hetherington as controller in Scotland was
the idea of Michael Swann, the chairman. In 1975 talk of
devolution for Scotland was in the political air. The referendum,
in which the Scots decided that they did not after all want a
separate legislature, was yet to be held. At that time the
assumption was that Scotland would opt for internal self-
government and Swann was worried about the future of the BBC
there. Would not a Scottish assembly want a Scottish
broadcasting service, independent of London? It might. Like any
sovereign, Swann did not view with relish the prospect of his
territory being diminished. He believed the best way of reducing
the risk of secession would be to give BBC Scotland as much
autonomy as possible without destroying the national system. He
had in mind the kind of federal arrangements that the old
Colonial Office used to seek to impose – usually unsuccessfully

– on colonies where there was a demand for tribal or regional separation.

Swann's tactic of appeasing the secessionists was opposed fervently by the board of management, for whom the slogan 'one BBC' represented an article of faith. The traditional corporation standpoint is that the BBC can sustain its legitimacy only by exercising firm control from the centre. How can the red blood of the corporate ethic be pumped to the most distant limbs – the local radio stations, to name the most distant of all – if the heart is not sound, strong and indisputably supreme? When Milne was in Glasgow he had taken as much autonomy as he thought consistent with that tenet. Charles Curran, the director-general, was certain that to give more would damage the corporation's fabric, and that view was shared by most of his management colleagues.

At the end of 1975 the post of controller in Scotland would become vacant. Swann perceived that to secure a measure of internal devolution it was no use appointing someone who came from the 'one BBC' tradition. And because the issue was likely to become political, it required a controller tuned into the politics of the world beyond broadcasting. Hetherington had been the successful editor of the *Guardian* for twenty years and, from conversations when they had met socially, Swann knew that he was looking for a change, preferably a change that would allow him to return to his native Scotland. He invited him for a talk at Broadcasting House. Hetherington had sympathy for the cause of Scottish devolution and found that what Swann said about it made a great deal of sense. Another favourable factor was that Curran appeared to be enthusiastic about his joining the BBC. Hetherington's mistake was in believing that Curran's welcome meant that he shared Swann's views on Scottish autonomy and would put them into practice.

He joined the BBC at the end of 1975. Before moving to Glasgow in January he was submitted to an initiation process by the mischievous Huw Wheldon, managing director of television. Wheldon told Hetherington that since he had come from the intellectual end of Fleet Street he should be introduced to 'the realities of life' – television for the popular taste. So the tall, white-haired, ascetic Scot was made assistant floor manager of

Bruce Forsyth's Generation Game (in which members of the public were encouraged to make fools of themselves); then spent a week on Top of the Pops. While working on the Vera Lynn show he received his first lesson in BBC diplomacy. The singer had finished rehearsing a song when the producer roared down the intercom, audible only to the producer and Hetherington: 'Tell her to look as if she cared and put more life into it.' In fact the language was fruitier than that but the floor manager translated it before relaying it to his star: 'Vera, that was wonderful. I wonder if you could put just a little bit more expression into it?' It was all very different from editing the *Guardian*.

Hetherington made the rounds of the departments at Television Centre and Broadcasting House and went to Scotland with as thorough an indoctrination into the mysteries of the BBC as it was possible to acquire in eight weeks. It would soon transpire, though, that as far as the board of management were concerned it was not thorough enough. Almost as soon as he arrived in Glasgow Hetherington, who has a stubborn streak, began a series of clashes with colleagues in London that were to continue throughout his stormy three years in office.

He had been in Scotland only a few weeks when Swann persuaded him to write a paper for the Annan Committee on Broadcasting, then collecting evidence, on his first impressions. Swann asked him to concentrate on the relationship between the regions and the centre. Hetherington was reluctant to commit his thoughts to paper so soon but the chairman was insistent. It was a personal report, not representing the corporation's view, but as a courtesy Hetherington sent copies to Swann and Curran before submitting it to Annan.

As he read through the paper, Curran's fury mounted. His new controller was openly criticising the degree of centralism in the BBC's administration and in particular London's monopoly over appointments. It irked Hetherington that he could not appoint whom he wanted in Scotland – within his budget, naturally – without getting the approval of the personnel directorate in London. (Later he would learn that part of the reason for this was the custom whereby some senior appointments had to be vetted by MI5.)

On receiving the paper Curran phoned Hetherington to confirm that it represented no more than his personal opinion. The following week he rang again to say that he had let the board of management see the document and they might want to talk to him about it. Hetherington had to go to a meeting in Edinburgh that he regarded as important – his first attendance at the church and nation committee of the Church of Scotland. He had been there some forty-five minutes when a note was handed to him: he must return immediately to Glasgow. He stayed with the church committee for another twenty minutes, then apologised and hurried back. The board of management were meeting in a studio at Broadcasting House in London linked for sound with a studio in Glasgow, where he sat on his own. It was a Star Chamber where the prisoner was seated several hundred miles from the examining body. Curran and his colleagues denounced the Scot's heresy and asked him to retract it, or at least alter it before sending it to Annan. Hetherington was firm that he had been asked by Annan and Swann for a personal view, and this was it. After a meeting lasting nearly two hours, he refused to budge. His new job was off to an appalling start.

One of the proposals in his paper was that the regions should be allowed to appoint all but their top half dozen people without reference to London. A few months later he had to face the refusal of the news and current affairs department in London to confirm Helen Liddell in her post as Scottish economics correspondent, which she had already held on a temporary contract for nine months. Rejected for what Hetherington viewed as frivolous reasons, Miss Liddell went back to politics (she had come from the Scottish TUC) and is now Scottish Secretary of the Labour Party. He was also prevented from engaging Isabel Hilton as a reporter because, as it transpired much later, the functionary in charge of security vetting mistakenly asserted that she had been a member of a society advocating closer links with Communist China. Hetherington refused to fill any more vacancies until London agreed to drop its veto on Scottish appointments. He won his point – but at the same time gained a reputation as a trouble-maker.

Apart from personnel, many other aspects of the regions' activities were controlled from London – finance and engineering were two more. And the people who worked for those departments in the regions felt they owed more loyalty to their directorate in London than to their local controllers. Hetherington reckoned he could have saved £1m a year if he had been allowed real power over all the people working at BBC Scotland. He also found it wasteful, both of his time and the corporation's money, to be required to travel to London for meetings at least once a week and sometimes more often. He was appalled by the bureaucracy of BBC procedures, especially the excess of memos and other paperwork. At the *Guardian* there had been a rule that nothing should be put on paper unless it was likely to form part of the archives. Day-to-day business was done by conversation. There was no chance of converting the Beeb to that philosophy.

Glasgow was not the only outpost to feel constrained by the yoke of the central directorates. In the summer of 1976, faced with persistent complaints from the regions and from people on the programme-making side in London, Curran asked Richard Francis, controller in Northern Ireland, to head a three-man committee looking into whether the centralised services were effective. Francis and his two colleagues performed the task thoroughly, taking three months off from Belfast to travel the land and soak up Hetherington's and the other controllers' complaints. The report was highly critical and naturally offended those people at Broadcasting House and Television Centre whose powerful position was dependent on their authority over the BBC's outposts.

As a committee we have been made increasingly aware that there are two schools of thought within the BBC as to how the corporation should be administered. Whilst corporate functions are not in question, a number of long-standing administrative practices are no longer accepted by the majority of senior output staff as the only way of running things. . . To achieve significant savings in administrative overheads, harsh decisions would have to be faced. It would require intellectual resilience to challenge and, if necessary, to change long-standing structures. . . Our study leads us to the conclusion that, within 'one BBC', there are viable alternatives to the present degree of centralisation in some areas. These require something of a Copernican revolution – a fundamental change of direction in the relationship between output directorates and the centre.

Curran was furious – so furious that Francis confided in his friends that he feared his career at the Beeb might be over. Talk of a revolution, even a Copernican one and even as carefully hedged as this, has always been regarded with the gravest suspicion by BBC management. Francis survived, but even today the BBC is so sensitive about his report that it refuses to show it to researchers. It was not until Trethowan succeeded Curran as director-general the following October that any significant progress was made towards giving the regions more responsibility for financial and personnel matters.

Hetherington also managed to quarrel with one of his predecessors, Alasdair Milne, who became managing director of television when Trethowan was made director-general. It is the aim of all regional controllers to get as many of their own productions on to the network as they can. But they have no inherent right to any network time at all, and are forced to lobby for it in London. Hetherington found he differed with Milne about the kind of programmes he should be offering the network. He wanted more gritty plays about the working class and the industrial heartland – the real Scotland, as he saw it, as against Milne's more romantic perception. But it happened to be Milne who controlled access to the network, and he refused several offerings that had tentatively been accepted, arguing that they were not of the quality he required.

Hetherington's terminal row came with Trethowan in December 1978. The director-general was going to Edinburgh to appear before the Broadcasting Council for Scotland, the body of lay people whose job is to oversee the BBC's Scottish output and make representations about it. Hetherington looked on the council as his ally in the battle for autonomy and decided to send them a briefing paper suggesting the lines on which they might question the director-general. He made sure that a copy of the document reached Trethowan in Newcastle, on his way north, so he would not be taken unawares. Trethowan was furious that his Scottish controller should ally himself, as he saw it, with the local pressure group against the BBC management. It smacked of disloyalty. He also believed he should have been shown Hetherington's paper earlier, to give him time to prepare considered replies to the points. (As it happened, the council members did not in any case pursue them as vigorously as Hetherington would have liked.)

'I'm very distressed at what you've done,' the director-general told Hetherington when he arrived in Edinburgh for the meeting. 'We must have a discussion about it.' They agreed to meet in London the following week. It seemed to Hetherington inevitable that he would be asked to resign. Over the weekend intermediaries telephoned him to see whether a face-saving formula could be worked out. Hetherington produced one himself. William Carrocher, the first head of BBC Highland Radio in Inverness, had been made head of publicity in Glasgow. The Inverness vacancy had still to be filled. Hetherington loved the Highlands and thought that controlling a small radio station would give him the chance to do some real broadcasting without becoming too embroiled in administration. Trethowan, relieved that the problem of this over-zealous Scot had been solved for him, readily agreed to the move.

Hetherington stayed at Inverness for a little over a year before becoming professor of media studies at Stirling University. It had been ludicrously optimistic of him to think that he could single-handedly defeat the entrenched bureaucracy in London. In 1985 he was appointed to the Peacock Committee looking at alternative ways of funding the BBC. If he felt wounded by his treatment at the hands of Milne and the London Mafia, and if he were a vengeful man, here would be a golden chance of settling the score.

* * * *

Recurrent pressure for regional autonomy is a symbol of a fundamental fault in the BBC's organisational structure. It was not confined to Glasgow but broke out almost simultaneously nearer home, in Birmingham, where Hetherington's frustration was duplicated by Phil Sidey, head of the network production centre. Sidey's appointment had been recommended by John

Grist, controller of the English regions and a former colleague of Sidey's at Lime Grove. But as he grew into the job, Sidey began to see Grist's own position as irrelevant, a barrier to his own communication with senior executives. He wanted the three network production centres (Birmingham, Manchester and Bristol) to be headed by someone of controller status, with direct access to the board of management. This resulted in acrimonious arguments between Sidey and Grist – and Grist's successors when he was posted to New York. Sidey lost the battle and left the BBC in 1983. Complaints that the rigid hierarchy of the corporation gets in the way of good programme making have echoed through the years, especially in the television service. As early as 1962 Antony Jay, then editor of Tonight, wrote a paper criticising the division of the BBC into a small number of output departments. As the departments grew bigger, he pointed out, it became ever harder for producers to communicate with department heads – their only conduit to top management. He proposed the establishment of small, integrated production units for individual programmes, outside the departmental structure. He warned that producers were becoming frustrated with the bureaucracy that flowed from the existing system and that some were likely to leave. Nothing came of his idea and he fulfilled his own prophecy two years later by quitting the BBC to establish his own production company.

At the end of the sixties the focus of the revolt against the system switched to the general features department at Kensington House. In 1975, a group of producers and programme staff angered management by presenting a paper to the Annan Committee, making a detailed case for the small, integrated, multi-role production unit – or SIMPU, to use the unfortunate acronym by which it came to be known. Technical staff would be integrated into the units, which would be capable of producing programmes over a wide range, cutting across departmental divisions. They would work directly to channel controllers. The units would not replace the present departmental system but would be established alongside it.

In January 1977 Alasdair Milne, director of programmes for television, set up a study group to look into the feasibility of such a change. Chaired by Paul Bonner, editor of the recently introduced community access programmes, the group made detailed calculations of how SIMPUs would work and how much they would cost. Each unit would consist of around thirty people, including four producers, and would work on a number of projects simultaneously. The relationship between the unit and the channel controller would be that of supplier and customer.

The group's report maintained that the change would not only make for better programmes but would improve job satisfaction by fostering 'a common sense of purpose, shorter lines of communication and the treatment of individuals as people rather than functional operatives'. Summing up the drawbacks of the present system, the report declared: 'Many production staff feel trapped after some years in their departments. Well qualified at their own specialism, they lack the breadth of experience necessary to qualify for a job in another department. . . They would welcome the larger number of opportunities for production work opened up to them by a "mixed economy" of SIMPUs and departments.' The recommendation was that one experimental SIMPU should be established at the beginning of 1978.

The management rejected the idea sharply. Bill Cotton, BBC1 controller, and Shaun Sutton, head of drama, saw it as a threat to the centralised control from which, in their view, the BBC derived its strength and legitimacy. Aubrey Singer pointed out that it would increase the costs of programme-making at a time when stringency was being urged on the corporation. He argued that the Kensington House group simply wanted to set themselves up as quasi-independent producers at no financial risk to themselves, because they were being underwritten by the BBC. Three years later Bonner left the BBC to become channel controller of the new Channel 4, where he established a programme buying system similar to the one recommended in the SIMPU group's report.

* * * *

The unrest the study group had detected among Kensington House producers was real enough. Within a few years it was to manifest itself in one of the most spectacular pieces of blood-letting in the corporation's history. Like the easing-out of Hetherington it involved Milne, and again it illuminated some of the BBC's less appealing characteristics. The victim was Desmond Wilcox, manoeuvred into a noisy exit from his job as head of general features.

Wilcox, once a reporter on the *Daily Mirror*, had joined the BBC in 1965 from the London independent company Rediffusion, where he had made a name in the documentary series This Week. He was hired to appear in and edit Man Alive, a weekly series of factual programmes initiated by Christopher Brasher, which were to concentrate on hard reporting, human interest and revealing interviews. Wilcox was adept at bringing out the emotional angles. His most searing programmes became known at Kensington House as 'Desmond's weepies'. But they were much admired and in 1972 he was made head of features, while continuing his role on Man Alive.

He is a loud, demonstrative man, full of energy and ideas, passion and enthusiasm, alternating disconcertingly between bonhomie and bad temper. One former colleague spoke of his 'James Bond complex'. Another compared him with Al Capone: 'If he had somebody knocked off (he was speaking figuratively) you can be sure the biggest wreath at the funeral would come from him.' Wilcox was one of a group of executives in the 1970s who ran their departments as personal fiefdoms and gained piratical reputations. Their names would appear from time to time in scurrilous stories in *Private Eye*. But they also nurtured some of the BBC's best creative work by giving programme-makers the inspiration and leadership to coax their best qualities from them. 'Golden age' theories can be treacherous: in any institution at almost any time there will be people looking back ten years to what they perceived as a uniquely fertile period. Yet it may not be a coincidence that the end of the seventies, when Wilcox was forced out and when boldness and mischief went out of style, was also the time when the talk began to be heard about malaise and crises of confidence in the television service.

That was a long way from anyone's mind in 1974, when a bright and brash young woman in Wilcox's department, who had presented innovative consumer features and investigative reports on the popular programme Braden's Week, was given her own show. Esther Rantzen had begun in the BBC as a researcher and worked her way to stardom through diligence, drive and an indisputable talent. Her new programme, That's Life, was a genial mixture of thorough investigations into consumer rip-offs, suggestive jokes about bodily functions, street interviews with passers-by, misprints in newspapers, campaigns against injustice and bureaucracy. It relied heavily on letters from viewers, which arrived by the sackful. For many months it was the most popular BBC programme and after its first run Rantzen was voted the television personality of the year. It was not only the viewers who were mightily impressed with her. Wilcox's high regard for her work soon developed into something more personal. They began an affair that would eventually lead to Wilcox leaving his first wife and family to marry her.

To edit That's Life, Wilcox had secured the appointment of Peter Chafer, a former actor who had been producing religious programmes. Rantzen had performed some of her early assignments for him and as an inexperienced reporter she had been grateful for his calming influence. From the start, the new programme achieved the confidence and flow that are the hallmarks of success in television. But off screen tensions were growing, all of them to do with the Rantzen/Wilcox liaison. It irritated Chafer, and others who worked on the programme, that in the event of a disagreement the presenter had privileged access to the head of department and could usually have her way. It distorted normal professional relationships.

The annual report and interview are long-standing elements of the BBC's personnel arrangements. Each year staff members are assessed by their heads of department and interviewed on the basis of that report by the head of their service. The interviews are broad and generally anodyne but they give the chance for each employee to meet someone senior in the hierarchy. At the end of the first season of That's Life, Chafer went to the sixth floor of Television Centre for his interview with Alasdair Milne, director of programmes. Overlooking the desolate urban landscape of Shepherd's Bush, they discussed the impeccable report Wilcox had given him and Milne thanked him for his work on That's Life. Then he asked: 'Any other problems?'

Until that point, Chafer had not decided whether to raise the matter of Rantzen and Wilcox. It was not easy for him, because he and Wilcox were friends – not close friends, but they had been sailing together on a couple of weekends. In professional terms, though, he could not see the problem going away. His head of department and his star presenter were growing ever closer. Sometimes when he went to talk to Wilcox, Rantzen would be in the office alongside him. The danger was that, squeezed between this opinionated and forceful lady and her quixotic swain, his role as editor would be neutered. He would be no more than a cipher.

So when Milne put his question, intended as an exit cue, Chafer replied: 'I'd like your advice on something.'

'Work?'

'Yes.'

'You mean Desmond and Esther.'

'How the hell did you know?'

'Paul Fox marked my card before he left. (Fox had gone to Yorkshire Television in 1973.) What's the problem?'

Chafer told him and asked what he should do.

'As editor of the programme you must put your foot down,' Milne replied sternly. 'If you're right you'll get support from me. If you're wrong you won't.'

Ask a silly question, thought Chafer as he waited for the lift, and you get a silly answer.

Nothing happened for three months. Then a Fleet Street paper got wind of the Rantzen/Wilcox affair. Wilcox had moved out of his marital home into a flat of his own. He told the reporter this was because he was writing a book and needed to be alone, and he threatened legal action if anything damaging was published. He was unsure, though, whether that would prove a deterrent and thought it prudent to alert Milne in case anything did appear.

Milne asked him how other people in the department felt about the affair. Wilcox replied that nobody had raised it.

'One of them has with me,' Milne replied. 'One of the men you go sailing with.'

Wilcox, although surprised and hurt by this revelation, did not receive the impression that Milne took the matter too seriously.

A puritan by instinct, with a secure marriage of his own, Milne nevertheless recognised that in a volatile and high-pressure business like television such messy pairings were bound to occur. He thought that people's private lives should be their own concern. Although there was a BBC rule that a husband and wife should not work together, Milne was not sure it was a good one. His public school grounding had taught him to abhor sneaking above all things, and he thought there was an element of sneaking in what Chafer had told him. His first instinct was to take no action. They were all grown-ups, after all; and this was the 1970s.

Later that week Wilcox sent for Chafer.

'Was it you who told Alasdair?' he asked.

Chafer confessed that it was.

'We loved you and you've betrayed us,' said Wilcox, in his most emotional on-screen tones. 'I think we'd better have Essie in.'

The word 'betrayal' received several more airings before the difficult tripartite meeting was over. Clearly there would be no more sailing weekends for Chafer, but it was not that which principally bothered him. For now *he* felt betrayed, by Milne. Annual interviews are supposed to be confidential occasions. Like a confessor in the Catholic church, an executive receiving a complaint is not supposed to go telling tales to the person complained about. Chafer was so angry that he phoned Milne to protest.

'The fool didn't tell you, did he?' Milne asked, exasperated.

'Of course he told me. What did you expect?'

'God. Do you think I shouldn't have told him?'

'Of course you shouldn't. I really am in the shit.'

'You'd better come up.'

Another taxi to TV Centre. And when he got back to Kensington House, another confrontation with the head of department.

'He's sent for me again,' Wilcox shouted. 'I thought you'd agreed to keep your mouth shut.' Chafer this time replied angrily. He thought he was the one who had the right to feel bruised. But it was typical of the BBC that the central issue – Rantzen's influence over Wilcox – had been lost. They were now essentially arguing about procedures, about who had the right to say what to whom.

Milne could see that it would be hard for Chafer to work again on That's Life. He told Wilcox that he was going to move the programme out of his features empire at Kensington House and make it the responsibility of the current affairs department at Lime Grove. That would pre-empt any further complaints about Wilcox's personal loyalty clashing with his professional judgement.

And so it did, for a while, but Wilcox was unhappy with the new arrangement. He thought That's Life was a marvellous programme and he had relished his association with it. Now it was no longer on the premises, he felt a sense of loss. Talking about it when they both got home was not at all the same thing. Rantzen felt the same. She was now producer of the programme as well as its presenter, but that did not compensate for being shifted from Kensington House. It was not just that she liked being with Wilcox. Of all the BBC's buildings scattered around Portland Place and West London, none provokes such loyalty as this nondescript post-war block, in red brick and cream stucco with lots of glass, standing a few hundred yards south-east of Shepherd's Bush Green. It looks insignificant from the front, but it stretches back nearly 100 yards, forming a slight curve as it does so, to provide space for three departments: general features, music and arts, sport. The reason for its unusual shape is that it was built on the line of the long-abandoned track of the old London and South-West Railway, looping north from Olympia and south again to Hammersmith and points west.

But it is the atmosphere, not the geography, that makes Kensington House an invigorating place to work. People in the features department regard themselves as the most creative in television, in the sense that they are not reacting to news, as the current affairs people do, or fleshing out someone else's work, as in drama. They conceive and make their own programmes and believe thay have a right to be arrogant about it. Because they are separated from TV Centre by a taxi ride, they do not feel any weight of authority bearing on them. Controllers and managing directors do not regularly set foot in the place, partly deterred by its reputation as a hotbed of intellectual ferment, confirmed by such incidents as the Kensington House Revolt. Small wonder that when Rantzen was moved to Lime Grove's less elite surroundings, she suffered withdrawal symptoms. After two years she and That's Life were back at Kensington House. The pretext was a series of programmes called The Big Time that she was producing and presenting to fill the gaps between runs of That's Life. It involved a viewer being allowed to fulfil a lifetime's ambition – becoming a jockey, designing a dress for a couture collection, editing *The Times* Diary. It had nothing at all to do with current affairs, so there was no reason for basing the new programme at Lime Grove. Back to Kensington House it came, and Rantzen with it. Since she was also working on the next run of That's Life, it made logistic sense to bring that programme back under Wilcox's ambit as well. Milne, now managing director, agreed. They were, he repeated, all grown-ups – presumably two years more grown-up than they were when the last row occurred.

Wilcox asked Peter Chafer to go back to That's Life as editor. As his price, Chafer exacted a pledge from his star that in the event of disagreements she would no longer run to Wilcox for his support. Wilcox concurred. Things were a lot better for Chafer the second time around – but now came murmurings from other features producers. In the Kensington House bar, they moaned into their gins that a disproportionate amount of the department's resources were being devoted to That's Life, to the detriment of other programmes. The only other series to get decent funding, they maintained, was Wilcox's thirteen-parter on The Americans – a project that, by its nature, involved a lot of expensive travel. And now he was planning a similar costly epic on the Jews, which would effectively rule out a major series that year for any other of his producers. Maybe, they joked wryly, the department ought to change its name to Wilcox/Rantzen Enterprises. Not only that, but the couple had married in 1977 and had produced issue. The baby and nanny became familiar figures in the office, and the proud mother would retire periodically to breastfeed her child. Other producers began to mention their worries to Milne and his deputy, Robin Scott.

Wilcox and Rantzen dismissed the complaints as professional

jealousy. That's Life was by far the highest-rated show put out by the department and it was only natural for less successful toilers to look on it enviously. But the disgruntled producers admitted to no such motive. They felt trampled on by the overweening pair. They likened the department to the court of Louis XIV, and dubbed Rantzen the Sun Queen. The *Sunday Times* described the couple as 'a mutual admiration society, succumbing to *folie a deux*, feeding each other's illusions of grandeur and pushing the limits of BBC conventions'. The article quoted Wilcox: 'We're a high-profile machismatic couple.' But there was that corporation convention that forbids husband and wife to work together.

By the early summer of 1980 the two senior producers in Wilcox's department, Adam Clapham and Tim Slessor, decided that the matter must be brought to a head. Clapham had worked with Rantzen on Braden's Week and The Big Time, while Slessor now ran Wilcox's old programme, Man Alive. A new series of The Big Time was due to be aired in the autumn. On Monday, 2 June, Wilcox and Rantzen left a cool and showery London for a three-week holiday in the sunshine of Corfu, leaving the series in a less advanced state of preparation than their colleagues had hoped. Clapham happened to be making a film about the BBC career of Sir Hugh Greene and took the opportunity to outline the problem to the former director-general and ask for his advice. Sir Hugh said he should take up the matter with Milne or Scott.

With Milne also on holiday, Clapham and Slessor went to see Scott on 5 June. They told him of their fear that Wilcox, by his consuming preoccupation with his own and his wife's projects, was destroying the morale of the department. They stressed that they were talking in confidence, because if Wilcox ever heard about their approach he would make it impossible for them to work under him again. With that understanding, they felt able to speak without restraint. Scott was the longest-serving inhabitant of the sixth floor of Television Centre, having arrived there as head of BBC2 in 1969. A slight, dapper man, he was a competent administrator and had, over the years, acquired an unrivalled understanding of the workings of the bureaucracy. This had stood him in good stead as he pursued his career just below the top stratum of management, never adopting a high enough profile to be considered for the most senior positions. Milne assigned to his deputy the administrative detail he found so tedious. Among Scott's specific responsibilities was handling the personnel side of the television service, and he supposed Clapham's and Slessor's complaint came under that heading. But because it involved the head of a department – and because he was due to retire in a few months in any event – he felt obliged to refer it to the managing director himself. He made a full note of what the two producers had told him, and left it for Milne to read when he returned the following week.

Next Wednesday, 11 June, Milne called Clapham and Slessor to his office. He could now see that he had been naive to believe that, following Wilcox's marriage, everyone in the features department would settle down and behave like adults. Something in the atmosphere of Kensington House seems to preclude that. Although he does not enjoy personal confrontations and tries hard to avoid them, it was apparent to Milne that action was necessary to head off a major mutiny in the department. He had managed to contain the Chafer insurrection by shifting That's Life to Lime Grove but that was a comparatively localised affair. Clapham and Slessor were more senior people – indeed Clapham was Wilcox's deputy. And they were not talking about just the one programme but about the whole conduct of the department. It would need a more radical cure than another rearrangement of the furniture. Milne pondered for a while, then told the mutineers that as soon as Wilcox returned from holiday he would be offered three choices: to sort things out on his own ('which I think is deeply unlikely,' Milne commented); take his wife and her programme out of his department; or leave the department himself.

On 25 June, the day after his return, Wilcox was summoned by Milne and told:'You've got trouble in the ranks.' Milne showed him Scott's notes of his meeting with the two producers. Wilcox's first reaction was that the two men should have had the courage to put the charges directly to him, instead of waiting until he was away on holiday. Milne, with his ingrained sense of hierarchy and fair play, could only agree.'Did you tell them that?' Wilcox asked. Milne confessed that he had not, but added that their back-door approach, however despicable in personal terms, did not invalidate their central argument. How could Wilcox run a department if he had lost the confidence of its senior people? Wilcox replied that two men did not constitute a full-scale insurrection. He asked for time to think and to see what he could do.

It was a dull June day, cloudy with rain threatening. Shepherd's Bush Green looks dismal even in the best of weather, and as Wilcox drove back from Television Centre to Kensington House he wished fervently that he was back in Corfu. The unwelcome turn of events did help direct his mind to a question that he and Rantzen had been discussing spasmodically of late. He had to sort out his priorities. He had been head of features for eight years. Even without this little unpleasantness it was high time he moved on. He had already been turned down for two higher posts – controller of BBC2 and controller in Northern Ireland. (He had been interviewed by the governors for the Irish job but it was already clear that they were grooming James Hawthorne for it. To avoid splitting up his new family, Wilcox had suggested originating That's Life from Belfast if he won the appointment.)

But now he was not sure that he really wanted to jump through the hoops of higher administration. He was happy making his own programmes and he was happy to be involved in his wife's phenomenal success with That's Life. Maybe he could give up his wider role and create a mini-department responsible only for those two enterprises? But as he negotiated the cars parked tightly in the narrow approach to Kensington House, he recognised that none of this long-term musing helped solve the immediate question of how to deal with his disaffected lieutenants. The first thing he did on returning to his office was have a long talk with Rantzen. They decided, even at this late stage, to see if there was any possibility of peace negotiations.

Tim Slessor was now on holiday but they asked Adam Clapham to go and see them. Clearly wounded at what he saw as treachery, Wilcox told Clapham, as he had reminded Chafer some three years earlier, that he had been his patron and supporter. What kind of reward for past favours was this? He did not understand why the present issue was important enough to over-ride personal loyalties. Clapham maintained that the future of the features department was at stake and that was the paramount issue. Although it quickly became apparent that there was little common ground, every day for the rest of that week the two men met for a long talk. Wilcox was exploring every possibility of compromise, and in doing so baring his personal feelings to Clapham in a way he had never done before. At the last meeting of the series Rantzen was again present to hear her husband produce a suggestion that took Clapham by surprise, as it was supposed to: why did not he take over as editor of That's Life? As number two in the department, he would be strong enough to act as an effective barrier between Wilcox and the programme, answering complaints of excessive interference.

It took scarcely any time for Clapham to reject the suggestion. To begin with, he was surprised that it was acceptable to Rantzen. She replied that she would go along with the plan. But Clapham recognised that there was no way he could stop the couple talking shop together at home where – or so it was widely believed in the department – the mealtime conversations were of little else but That's Life. The move, he could see, would be nothing more than cosmetic. But most important of all, it did not answer Clapham's and Slessor's main point, that the argument was about the Wilcox/Rantzen domination of the whole department, not just that one programme. It was as much about her influence on her husband's job as about his interference on That's Life. Clapham said he would not go along with the notion.

'It's the managing director's instruction,' Wilcox told him.

'If that's so I reject it,' Clapham replied.

Wilcox sagged back in his chair and said quietly: 'We're finished, then.'

* * * *

He was not finished by any means. What he had not told Clapham was that, almost as soon as his previous Wednesday's meeting with Milne was over, he had made a private phone call to Michael Grade, the young director of programmes at London Weekend Television. The two men had often bumped into each other in that social underworld peopled by television executives. They found themselves kindred spirits – bold, highly professional and with an eye to the main chance. Grade had once told Wilcox, if ever he was thinking of switching channels, to be sure of letting him know, for he might be able to fix something up. It is the kind of invitation that media executives toss off with as little thought as an American telephone operator wishing callers a nice day; but it had lingered in Wilcox's mind.

He asked Grade whether he would be interested in running a version of That's Life on London Weekend. Wilcox would be the executive producer and his wife would leave the BBC to present it. Obviously the Beeb would not let them use the name but they could call it something easily recognisable: That's Sunday, perhaps; or That's Esther. Grade pricked up his ears. The success of That's Life was a serious problem for London Weekend, hurting them at prime time on Sundays and having a carry-over effect for the rest of the evening. It would be a major capture. He arranged to meet Wilcox for tea in the lounge of the Grosvenor House in Park Lane.

'You get a good tea there,' he confided. 'My grandmother used to live there so I know.'

The tea was such a success that they decided to meet again for lunch, this time at the Howard Hotel, a discreet establishment by the Thames, near Temple underground station. Here Grade confirmed his serious intent by bringing somebody along to deal with the question of money. At a third meeting, Wilcox took Richard Armitage, the agent he shared with Rantzen. By now the odds were in favour of a deal being struck.

Meanwhile, back at Kensington House, events were moving to a climax. Even if Clapham had wanted to keep his representations secret from his colleagues, there is a hallowed tradition in the BBC that such matters never remain concealed for long. On Monday, 9 July, ten features producers wrote to Milne endorsing Clapham's and Slessor's stand. Milne showed the letter to Wilcox who called two meetings the following day – one of the producers who had signed the letter and another of the whole department.

The people who worked on That's Life now felt that they were about to be the victims of emotional blackmail. Trying to anticipate Wilcox, they believed he was going to use them to put pressure on the gang of twelve (the ten signatories plus Clapham and Slessor). They guessed that he would accuse the mutineers of conspiring to send the That's Life team away from the cosy confines of Kensington House and into the fiercer clutches of current affairs or some other department – light entertainment had even been suggested. In fact they did not need to guess, because Rantzen walked around the production offices making just that point and accusing her critics of being motivated by envy.

Some of the That's Life crew decided it was important to determine a common line in the face of the Wilcox gambit. Peter Bazalgette, a young researcher, called a meeting of the programme staff to precede the one summoned by Wilcox. They agreed that they supported the gang of twelve in their bid to reimpose a conventional chain of command in the department. Bazalgette told Wilcox the result of the meeting when he and a few other researchers were called to his office. They were slightly surprised that he remained impassive at the news.

Thursday, 10 July, was one of the coolest days of the summer. The temperature never climbed above 60 degrees Fahrenheit. At 4 p.m. about fifty members of the features department huddled round a long table in a conference room at Woodstock House, an auxiliary office building alongside Kensington House. Wilcox and Rantzen sat at either end of it. Wilcox did what the That's Life team had expected, appealing to their loyalty to him and the features department and painting a lurid picture of how unpleasant things would be at Lime Grove. 'This is a result of your actions,' he declared, seeking the eyes of Clapham and his supporters. Bazalgette had taken on himself the role of spokesman for the under-class of researchers, cheerleading for the gang of twelve. He told the meeting what the That's Life crew had agreed at their own meeting that morning. Wilcox felt especially betrayed by this youngster because he had been personally responsible for bringing him to the BBC. They had met during Bazalgette's last year at Cambridge, when Wilcox had taken part in a debate at the Union. (As often happens on those occasions, Bazalgette had taken pains to make an impression with Wilcox and ask him about the prospects of a job. As happens less often, he was offered one.) Now, as the self-possessed young man spoke on behalf of his colleagues, Rantzen was heard to say in a stage whisper: 'I'd like to stick his head down the lavatory.'

It was a difficult meeting, lasting just over two hours. Wilcox and Rantzen, still at bay, learned how little support they could count on in the department. But if it had achieved no other purpose, the session had cleared the air, and when it was over the participants were infected with a quite irrational sense of exhilaration. All of them – including Wilcox and Rantzen – trooped to the bar on the ground floor of Kensington House and enjoyed a companionable hour. There was a feeling that the matter was now out of their hands, that things were moving remorselessly towards a conclusion that would depend on decisions taken elsewhere – taken, to be precise, on the sixth floor of Television Centre. Like students after exams, they had done all they could and would now have to wait for whatever transpired. A small binge was the appropriate response.

Only Wilcox and Rantzen knew that the key decision on their own future would be taken not at TV Centre but at the headquarters of London Weekend Television on the south bank of the Thames. Their negotiations with Grade were progressing well enough for them to start thinking about their staffing requirements when they moved the programme to the rival channel. If they were going to have the new show off and running by the autumn, they would need people who had experience of how to do it. The researchers were the key. The exposures of dubious business people that are a feature of That's Life are the result of months of careful research using precise and complex techniques. To train an entire new production team would take too long.

On Friday, 18 July, eight days after the Woodstock House meeting, Wilcox called six members of the That's Life team into his office individually and swore them to secrecy. He offered them jobs at London Weekend at salaries some 50 per cent higher than they were getting from the BBC. His choice of people revealed how, even in the vindictive atmosphere prevailing in his department, he still placed the quality of the programme above personal spite. They were selected on the basis of their ability alone. One of them, for example, was the loquacious Bazalgette. He was offered £12,000 a year to jump ship with Wilcox and

Rantzen, compared with the £8,000 he was receiving. He said he would think about it over the weekend.

Swearing a BBC person to secrecy is like asking a dog politely to give up chasing sheep: it is not within the nature of the beast to comply. Wilcox, through having been the constant butt of gossip stories in *Private Eye* and elsewhere, knew this better than anyone. He would complain that whenever a story was brewing in the department, the numerous 'moles' would rush to reserve their phones to be the first to tell the world. So it was scarcely surprising that, almost as soon as the last of the six interviews was over, those who had been approached knew the identity of the other five and how they had responded. Three had swallowed the bait right away, while Bazalgette and the other two had yet to make up their minds. That night the three waverers met in the bar at Kensington House. They decided that they were not sure it was a genuine prospect. Wilcox seemed confident that Grade would take the programme and its staff but, such was the air of unreality that permeated the place, they wondered whether the deal existed only in his mind. They felt like tourists in Paris when someone was trying to sell them the Eiffel Tower. They decided to turn down the offer and told Wilcox on Monday.

That Monday, 21st July, was a bad day for Wilcox in many respects. Being spurned by the three was not the gravest rejection he was to suffer. A clinching meeting with Grade was scheduled that evening at the Wilcox house in Kew. Grade had brought his money man along, while Wilcox and Rantzen had their agent. As soon as he had poured the first round of wine, Wilcox could sense that something was wrong. Grade was wringing his hands about the cost of the programme, and his financial adviser was nodding sagely in sympathy. They calculated that it would cost London Weekend about three times as much to produce That's Life as it did the BBC. The wage bill would be higher. Wilcox would have received £30,000 a year, comfortably more than the £22,000 he was getting as head of features. Rantzen's salary would have gone up in proportion. Grade was also worried about studio facilities. London Weekend had only one studio large enough for the programme and other output would suffer if the facility had to be tied up for so long at the peak weekend period.

After Grade had finished speaking there was a pause, while the others worked out what he was really trying to convey. Then Wilcox spoke:

'I can see you haven't the heart for it now. Shall I let you off the hook? Shall we call it a day?' Grade, with visible relief, said he thought that would be best. Wilcox refilled the wine glasses.

Next morning, at about 10 o'clock, Peter Bazalgette was strolling towards Kensington House. It was one of the rare nice days of that summer, sunny and warm. As he turned towards the main door the Wilcox Rover drew up alongside Peter Bazalgette. Wilcox, with a silent Rantzen in the seat beside him, leaned out of the window. 'Come and see me in my office,' he called out. Bazalgette did so right away. 'The deal's off,' Wilcox told him.

None of the other five had yet been informed and Bazalgette wondered whether, given his rejection of the offer, he was simply being put off the scent. He met his two allies in the bar at lunchtime and they decided that was the most likely explanation. Bazalgette now felt obliged to do something about it. If Wilcox was really plotting to make off with one of the BBC's most popular programmes, was it not his duty to inform someone at Television Centre? He sought advice from some of his senior colleagues, although this was complicated by the fact that many were on holiday. He phoned Clapham on a caravan site in the south of France and raised Paul Heine, one of the programme's subsidiary presenters, on a boat at an Irish fishing village. The consensus of the advice from them and from people in London was that he should take the matter higher. With Alasdair Milne taking another holiday, he made an appointment to see Robin Scott.

To prepare for the meeting, one of Scott's assistants phoned Bazalgette to find out what it was about. When Bazalgette mentioned Wilcox's negotiations with Grade he was stunned that the assistant, instead of reacting with shocked disbelief, replied casually that yes, they knew about that, and was Bazalgette wanting assurances about keeping his job? Now Bazalgette was angry. Here he was grappling with his conscience, pitting his corporate loyalty against his natural antipathy to telling tales, and it was assumed he was simply trying to protect his back. It took all the nobility from the gesture; so he withdrew the request for an interview. How did the sixth floor know? The theory that evolved at the Kensington House bar was that Grade, known to be an old friend of Bill Cotton, had tipped him the wink that one of his executives was trying to flog a major programme to the opposition. This would have been inconsistent with Grade's highly competitive nature.

Wilcox has a simpler explanation. He says he told Milne in person almost as soon as negotiations began. Milne, however, does not recall this.

The affair now moved towards its climax, delayed only by the fact that Milne did not return from his holiday until 4 August. In his absence Wilcox had been discussing possible face-saving formulae with Scott, but fruitlessly. Scott told him that to make him head of a sub-department responsible only for That's Life and his own work would create more tensions than it cured. Moving the programme out of London would not work either.

'What you're telling me is that none of my proposals is acceptable,' said Wilcox, and when Scott signalled agreement sighed: 'If you tell me that I know it's true.'

But it was not in his nature to go down without a fight to the finish. He wrote memos to the board of management and governors defending his conduct of the department. Unluckily for him, he also had to write a note to Bill Cotton, controller of BBC1, explaining that the new series of That's Life could not begin until the new year, partly because of the strains imposed on its presenter by her motherhood. Cotton, who had wanted the series to start in the autumn, was angry. There was one executive whose support Wilcox could certainly not count on.

On 5 August, the day after his return, Milne received a copy of another letter written not by Desmond but to him, by an anonymous group describing themselves as the Kensington House Silent Majority. This expressed support for Wilcox and Rantzen in such extravagant terms that many harboured the unworthy suspicion that they had written it themselves.

Recent events in general features department have created in all of us first astonishment, then distress and now finally shame. It is intolerable that the effect of Adam Clapham and Tim Slessor's visit to DMD Tel (Scott) has been to sabotage your work, when you have been, without question, the best head of general features department and it is now at its most creative and productive. . . It is inevitable that Esther Rantzen and her programmes will now be transferred from general features. We would like to place it on record that we know you have both, at all times, behaved with the utmost integrity. . . Success has been her downfall. As you must realise, the move has been occasioned entirely by professional jealousy. We are aware how bitter you must feel, at the centre of such disloyalty.

That last-minute declaration of support came too late to affect Milne's decision on what must be done. On Friday, 8 August, Milne called Wilcox into his office and said it was time for him to move.

'Upwards, I hope,' Wilcox said.

'We're looking,' Milne replied evasively. 'How about a senior job in New York?'

'I've a working wife and a family here in London,' Wilcox reminded him.

'We'll give you some air tickets,' said Milne.

Getting difficult people out of the country is a technique of personnel management that has evolved in the BBC over the years. New York is a marvellous posting in terms of personal contacts and comforts but no job there is central to the running of the Beeb and few people rise to the top once they have been exiled there. It was clear to Wilcox that the offer had not been thought through and that Milne would have been surprised and disconcerted had he accepted it. Milne had guessed he would resign but tried to talk him out of it – not just out of politeness but because he genuinely regretted it when talented men left the corporation. The two men went for dinner to the Belvedere in Holland Park, near Milne's home. It would have been pleasant on a fine evening but the weather had reverted to the norm for that dismal summer, cool and cloudy. It suited Wilcox's mood, as the two men drafted his resignation statement on the back of a menu.

At a farewell party for his staff, Wilcox was asked whether he had left of his own accord or whether he had been pushed. He replied:

'When you're falling from the 35th floor and someone sticks his head out of the 10th-floor window and asks something like that, you're in no position to discuss it. You just wish they'd run to the bottom and catch you.'

Because he was no ordinary TV executive but was married to a popular personality, the newspapers gave the story detailed and highly excitable coverage. The *Sun* had a front page picture of the couple wielding glasses of champagne and a page three story (next to the naked lady) headlined: ESTHER LASHES OUT AS HUSBAND QUITS BBC. She was quoted as referring to 'faceless critics' who had launched a 'whispering campaign' against her. 'Perhaps I unwittingly aroused jealousy in people I don't even know,' she surmised. And she threw out a hint to other commercial companies that might feel able to take on the programme: 'What I most want to do is to make a consumer programme which pleases and helps viewers. It is of secondary importance whether it is shown on the BBC or elsewhere.'

By Monday the *Sun* had put a face to the faceless man. Under an 'exclusive' tag, they ran a page five interview with Adam Clapham headlined WHY I SHOPPED ESTHER'S HUSBAND. He was quoted as saying that he had begun the whispering campaign because the couple had broken the BBC rule about husband and wife working together. 'I hated having to do this to Desmond but things had to be changed. Esther was working in the Wilcox kingdom. All the best people and money were going to her show, That's Life, at the expense of programmes like Man Alive. The BBC is a damned good place to work. It's a better one now and I'm filled with relief.'

By the following day the *Sun* had decided that the story was so important that it warranted an editorial comment. They were in no doubt whose side they were on – they backed the popular star of the screen against the bland and treacherous face of bureaucracy:

> It can be argued that Desmond Wilcox should have been forced to resign from the BBC. He and his wife, Esther Rantzen, broke a rule about husband and wife working together. There can, however, be no argument about the behaviour of producer Adam Clapham who boasts that, although he worked with Mr. Wilcox for 15 years, he led a whispering campaign against him.
>
> Mr. Clapham says that the BBC is now a better place to work and he is 'filled with relief'. We hope his happiness continues. That, however, will depend on his having colleagues a little more loyal than he was to Desmond Wilcox.

Rantzen did not carry out her threat to take the programme to a commercial station. She was in fact rather attached to the BBC, in spite of everything, and proved it a few months later. She had been a founder member of TV-am, a group formed by David Frost and Peter Jay to bid for the new breakfast television franchise. Soon after the group was awarded the contract the following December, she quit it, preferring to stay with That's Life and the Beeb.

As for Wilcox, he was commissioned by Milne to produce his thirteen-parter on the Jews, to follow up the series on the Americans, but in an economy drive a few months later it was axed. The work he had already done was turned into a three-part series instead. Then he began making successful network documentaries for BBC Scotland. He was succeeded as head of features by Will Wyatt, a producer and administrator of great competence with a good track record, whose soothing, low-key touch was, Milne believed, what the department needed. If that was what it needed, that was what it got; for were Wyatt to resign it probably would not rate the front page of the *Sun*. He lacks Wilcox's dynamism. The BBC in the 1980s has no room for such large, charismatic figures, difficult to keep under control. They mean trouble. And if their departure means you lose a handful of inspirational programme ideas, it is worth it for the quieter life.

Chapter 5

100 GREAT SPORTING MOMENTS

WHATEVER Wilcox may have thought about it, Milne was deemed by his management colleagues and the governors to have handled the affair of the resignation well. Certainly it did not count against him when the time came for his succession as director-general to be confirmed. But it was not, all the same, to be a smooth assumption of power. For George Howard, having asserted his authority by persuading the governors to make Alan Hart controller of BBC1, was not content to let it rest there. Within a year, he insisted on another appointment that would make the new chief's job harder: Milne was not going to get the man he wanted as managing director of television, either.

Largely at Milne's instigation, Bill Cotton had been appointed his deputy when Robin Scott retired in 1980. The idea was that Cotton, the man Milne thought complemented him so ideally, should get a year or so's experience as his understudy before becoming managing director proper, and a member of the board of management, as soon as Milne vacated the post. Cotton and Milne had continued to pursue divergent courses after the early days at Lime Grove, as both placed their feet on the lower rungs of the ladder of television administration. In 1962 Cotton was made assistant head of light entertainment programmes. The following year Milne was put in charge of Tonight Productions. When, after quitting in 1965, Milne returned three years later as

117

controller in Scotland, Cotton was still doing the equivalent of his old job, but was now called head of variety. He took charge of the light entertainment group in 1970.

Three years later Milne was appointed director of programmes. With little experience of comedy and variety he relied on Cotton's judgement as the two worked closely together for the first time. In 1977, the year Milne became managing director of television, Cotton was made controller of BBC1. Their partnership and their mutual reliance grew. Occasionally, on his way home in the evenings from Television Centre, Cotton would drop round for a drink at Milne's house in Holland Park Avenue.

Milne knew that Cotton would not be the only candidate for managing director when he took over as director-general. A looming presence was Aubrey Singer, the plump, innovative former producer of science programmes who had been a well-regarded controller of BBC2 from 1974 to 1978, when he was made managing director of radio. As a member of the board of management he was senior to Cotton, and since most of his career had been spent in television there was no doubt that he had the necessary experience to take over from Milne.

Singer, both in appearance and by instinct, is a mandarin, enjoying nothing so much as the manipulation of people and budgets to create the programmes he wants to see made. He was a tougher corporate in-fighter than his roly-poly appearance would suggest. How else could he have won his way through to his present eminent position since joining the BBC in 1949, without benefit of a university education? In the looser structure of the television service in the sixties and seventies, he had been one of a group of powerful departmental heads who had an immense amount of autonomy in programme-making – more real power even than the channel controllers, who held the purse strings. His reputation was based on a number of major scientific documentary series for which he had been responsible, notably The Ascent of Man. Only once had he been tempted to leave the corporation's enveloping womb. In 1967 he was part of the consortium that won the ITV contract for his native Yorkshire and he could have gone to Leeds as director of programmes. In the end he decided he was a BBC man at heart.

Once engaged on a project, Singer would force it through,

elbowing any opposition aside. One of his colleagues described him as a junior version of Robert Maxwell, the press tycoon. As a channel controller he was a fount of good programme ideas, as well as some bad ones. A controller with too many ideas of his own is not an unmixed blessing for programme makers, because he tends to give short shrift to ideas conceived by his subordinates. In many people's view – though not his own – Singer lacked an aptitude for organisation and the non-creative skills required by a managing director. He found it hard to keep his hands off programmes. In his radio post it was impossible for him to have any direct role in the end product, for the BBC's strict hierarchical tradition ruled it out. From time to time he would vent his frustration by walking to Marylebone High Street and slipping into Radio London, the BBC's local station for the capital. In that much smaller and less formal set-up he could visit the studio and feel that, for a while at least, he had his hands back on the business end of broadcasting.

During his spell as managing director of radio, the most difficult matter he had to handle was the reduction in the number of BBC orchestras and the resulting strike by musicians, causing the cancellation of many of the 1980 promenade concerts. He believed he had dealt with it triumphantly. Others blamed him for what they saw as a clear disaster.

* * * *

The BBC's orchestras are an integral part of its image. They hark back to the forties and fifties when radio was paramount, when the way to spend an improving evening at home was to sit by the wireless and hear a concert. Orchestras were assumed to be staffed by genteel folk wearing dinner jackets or long dresses – the kind of people at whom BBC programmes were for many years directed. Even the light orchestras and dance orchestras played nothing risky, nothing to excite the passions, nothing to make listeners start with surprise. It was as though they were specifically instructed to play background music for people doing the ironing, when a shock or jolt could be dangerous.

By 1980 it was common ground among almost everyone except the musicians that the BBC had too many orchestras in relation to its need. There were eleven, ranging from four full symphony orchestras to the more intimate London Studio Players. Several attempts had been made to reduce them to a number consistent with the BBC's need for live music, but all had foundered on the rock of the musicians' resistance. The Musicians' Union is an engaging body with a flair for public relations, frankly exploiting the fact that most of its members are genuinely modest and diffident, cultured and well-meaning, adept at winning the support of influential figures. But that does not mean that its leaders are any the less skilled at bargaining.

Hand in hand with the orchestral excess went a long-standing agreement restricting the hours in which the BBC could play gramophone records – the so-called 'needle time'. This meant that although listeners would have preferred to hear recordings of pop singers performing their latest hits, they often had to make do with, say, the Midland Radio Orchestra playing an ersatz version of a hit song, with an unknown performer singing the lyric. The success in Britain of Radio Luxembourg and the pirate radio stations, some operating from ships in the North Sea and playing records virtually non-stop, showed that people greatly preferred the 'real' thing on record to an inferior version broadcast live. It also meant that a generation grew up with an image of the BBC as a prim, stuffy organisation compared with the dashing buccaneers on the high seas.

In 1968, during one of the periodic bouts of concern over whether the BBC was wasting its resources, Lord Hill and the governors appointed McKinsey Brothers, an American firm of management consultants, to inquire into its organisation. The investigators produced two detailed reports recommending, amongst other things, the concentration of financial responsibility in a small number of managing directors, supervising their own budgets. McKinsey's people were manifestly bemused by the haphazard nature of the corporation's organisational structure. Yet of all the examples of waste that they located during their researches, they were most horrified by the staff orchestras. For a report that was supposed to be largely technical, to do with cost accounting amd answerability for expenditure, a disproportionate amount of space was given to the orchestras. They represented such a blatant case of profligacy that the consultants were scarcely able to believe it.

The first illogicality was Radio 3. With its insatiable demand for classical music (most of it live, because of the needle time agreement) this minority channel was grotesquely expensive to maintain in terms of cost per listener. Attracting no more than 2 per cent of the radio audience, it swallowed 28 per cent of programme costs. Each listener cost £1.10 per annum on Radios 1 and 2, £4.90 on Radio 4, but £34 on Radio 3. The BBC spent at least £2.5m a year on employing more than 500 staff musicians, plus a training orchestra and mumerous freelances. The musical output was 230 hours a week, of which, under the agreement, only 82 hours could be recorded.

'The needle time agreement is essentially a restrictive practice not conducive to improved productivity,' said the report. It recommended that the BBC should switch its emphasis from maintaining house orchestras to helping support independent orchestras.

That view was reflected in a BBC pamphlet issued in July 1969 called 'Broadcasting in the Seventies'. This was to prove one of the most important documents in radio's post-war history, for it established today's pattern of 'generic' broadcasting, with four national radio channels each catering quite rigidly to a specific range of interests – pop music on Radio 1, sedate light music on 2, classical music on 3, current affairs and drama on 4. This departure from the Reithian philosophy of providing a varied range of cultural experience on each channel had effectively been forced on the BBC by the success of the pop pirates. The new formula was put into effect soon afterwards with success. But amongst musicians there was resistance to the pamphlet's observations on music output, which echoed McKinseys' view that the corporation had more orchestras than it needed for the quantity of music broadcast.

'The licence fee is supposed simply to finance broadcasting,' the report pointed out. 'How far should it sustain a level of musical patronage beyond the immediate needs of broadcasting?' The aim should be to increase the use of gramophone records and reduce the employment of musicians, including the standing orchestras, to nearer what was really needed. The specific proposal was to keep five of the eleven orchestras, employing 279 musicians, and to disband three, with a strength of 104. That left the fate of three open to negotiation with bodies such as local authorities that might agree to share some of the cost.

The Musicians' Union organised a lobby to oppose the plan, arguing that the BBC, as the country's largest musical patron, had responsibilities that went beyond servicing its own programmes. It should also contribute to keeping the music profession healthy for the benefit of the nation as a whole. If it languished, the quality of British music would suffer, including that broadcast on the BBC. But it was not the logic of their argument that won the day for the union, nor their threat to strike if the BBC went ahead with the cuts – it was their ability to tap the support of friends in high places. Lord Goodman, then chairman of the Arts Council, said he believed the orchestras should be maintained. Goodman persuaded his friend Harold Wilson, the Prime Minister, to use his influence on Charles Curran, the director-general, to leave the orchestras as they were. Wilson told Curran that if he did not disband any orchestras, their cost to the BBC would be taken into account in determining the next increase in the licence fee. In the Commons John Stonehouse, the Postmaster-General, urged the BBC to re-examine the proposals. Most of the press came out against the cuts. Faced with such pressure, Curran capitulated. In August it was announced that the TV licence fee would go up from £6.00 a year to £6.50 – an increase that was supposed to include an element for saving the orchestras. Although Curran was not satisfied that the provision was adequate, he abandoned the rationalisation plan.

The second McKinsey report, delivered in 1970, returned to the subject at greater length. It pointed out that live orchestras cost three times as much as records per hour of air time. 'The BBC is expected to subsidise the music profession beyond its requirements but gets no government subsidy for doing so.' But McKinsey hectored in vain. The threat to the orchestras was to subside for a decade, until Aubrey Singer was made managing director of radio.

Singer does not like to see things drift. It offends him. A practical man, devoted to making programmes, he is outraged when union regulations or petty bureaucracy conspire to thwart his doing it in the most effective manner. In his years as a television producer and administrator, he would occasionally provoke the antagonism of union representatives when he accused them of making his job tougher by sticking inflexibly to restrictive rules. In the end, he would normally concede their point because his priority was to get the programme made. But he resented having to go along with what he saw as blackmail, and he blamed weak senior management for allowing it to happen. When he reached the top, he had no intention of letting the unions walk over him. That was why one of his first resolves on becoming managing director of radio was to bring about a final solution to the problem of the orchestras.

The opportunity came when, at the beginning of 1980, the BBC launched one of its periodic efforts at cutting costs. The initial announcement of the economy drive said that services would have to be cut between 5 and 8 per cent but there would probably be no redundancies. Yet when the plans were put to the unions in February, they involved the loss of 172 staff jobs for musicians. This time, five orchestras would disappear – two more than at the last attempt – including, most controversially, the Scottish Symphony. John Morton, the general secretary of the Musicians' Union, walked out of the meeting where the management unveiled the proposal. From that moment the two sides were inexorably on course for a showdown.

Singer was determined that this time there would be no backsliding by the Beeb, and to ensure that the policy was sustained he insisted on handling the dispute personally. In public statements he maintained such a firm line that he was accused of being high-handed and unwilling to negotiate. The accusations were justified, or at least the second one was. He was not going to negotiate if it meant surrendering as abjectly as Curran had done ten years earlier. During March and April he held four meetings with Morton and his colleagues, but did not budge. He repeatedly told Morton that the decision was one that had to be taken for the sake of good management. His job was to make economies and this one would save half a million pounds a year. Morton, a comfortable-looking man with a mild manner that masks a determined professionalism, scoffed at the argument. What, he wondered, did Singer, the programmes man, know about management? Before becoming leader of the Musicians' Union, Morton had been head of the department of management at Solihull College of Technology. He could teach Singer a thing or two about management, he taunted.

Singer was not to be moved by such personal attacks, which would become more severe as the dispute progressed. You did not rise so far in the BBC hierarchy without developing a tough hide. He spoke constantly of 'grasping the nettle' of the orchestra cuts. He further offended the union by characterising the musicians as ageing and their music as old-fashioned. He told Morton that redundancy notices would be issued to the unlucky 172 orchestra players in May. The union held a ballot of the membership that resulted in a majority on a scale of five to one for a strike if the notices were issued as planned. They were. The strike was called for Sunday, 1 June. When Saturday Night at the Mill ran on to past midnight, Kenny Ball and his Jazzmen refused to play the closing music. Next morning ceremonial pickets were mounted at Broadcasting House, accompanied by striking musicians playing 'Colonel Bogey'. They called their scratch band Aubrey's Nemesis.

The strike was an object lesson in public relations – a lesson from the musicians on how to present a case to the public, and a lesson from the Beeb on how not to. For the strikers, the impromptu performance outside Broadcasting House set the tone. When BBC concerts were cancelled, the musicians would play outside the venues for the benefit of passers-by. The permanent pickets at Portland Place were high-spirited. No attempt was made to stop people entering the building, but leaflets were handed out, some mildly abusive of Singer. The pickets wore lapel buttons reading KEEP MUSIC LIVE and SAXINGA (try saying it). Early in the strike Singer, an enthusiastic globe-trotter, visited China on the BBC's behalf. The strikers eagerly exploited the chance to contrast that apparent extravagance with his insistence on the need for musical economies.

On the evening of a debate on the strike in the House of Commons, the union chartered a boat on the Thames. An orchestra of 55, chosen from more than 600 volunteers and conducted by Anthony Hopkins, played Handel's Water Music as they drifted past the Palace of Westminster, although the river police made them move to the opposite bank to comply with the ban on demonstrations outside Parliament. Typical of press reaction was a comment from the *Daily Mail,* a paper not often sympathetic to strikes: 'The sweet serenading of striking musicians has so far done nothing to soothe the savage bureaucratic breast of the BBC. . . If these harmonious strikers alert the nation to preserve the best of British broadcasting, then their defiant puffing and fiddling will not have been in vain.'

But the savage breast of the Beeb, in the person of Aubrey Singer, showed no sign of being soothed. It had been clear from the beginning of the strike that unless it was settled reasonably rapidly it would prevent the July opening of the Henry Wood Promenade Concerts, among the most popular events of the London summer. The BBC, which runs them, liked to boast proudly that the concerts had never been suspended, even in wartime. Singer, though, was determined that the threat to the 1980 Proms would not be allowed to force his hand. At a press conference on 17 June he said: 'We are not going to do the Proms at the sacrifice of not going through with our intentions.' He added that he could detect no light at the end of the tunnel, and that the only way for the dispute to be resolved might be by one side grinding down the other. 'But I know which way round it is going to be.'

In public at least, Singer was getting full support for his firmness from the BBC's governors and management. When the veteran conductor Sir Adrian Boult wrote to *The Times* suggesting that the Proms should go ahead as usual but not be broadcast until the strike was over, he received a reply from Sir Ian Trethowan, the director-general, underlining the corporation's determination to go through with the cuts. While welcoming Sir Adrian's initiative, Sir Ian wrote: 'You may rest assured that we share your concern about the Proms, although I'm afraid our over-riding consideration must be the BBC's very severe financial problems, from which none of our activities can be exempt.'

Privately, though, there were many in the BBC who resented Singer's bull-in-a-china-shop tactics. Senior officials in the music department had personal friends among the musicians; and because the reduction of orchestras would diminish the department's function, they were opposed to it on professional as well as personal grounds. One music producer, Dr Robert Simpson, resigned, and explained his reasons in a letter to *The Times*: 'I can no longer work for the BBC without a profound sense of betrayal of most of the values I and many others believe in; and its management includes elements whose authority I cannot accept without shame.'

Doubts about Singer's tactics went higher. Michael Bett, the director of personnel, had joined the BBC in 1977 from industry. As a professional personnel manager, he deplored the head-banging school of industrial relations. Although Singer insisted on leading the negotiating team, Bett was an important part of it. In private discussions with the musicians, in Singer's absence, Bett thought he detected a way of making progress – but just as he saw that glimmer of hope, Singer appeared at another press conference pledging that the BBC would not give an inch.

Bett was furious. He railed at Singer and accused him of bungling on a spectacular scale. He expressed the same view to Trethowan and Sir Michael Swann, due to retire as chairman at the end of July to make way for George Howard. Swann, married to a musician, had some sympathy for the union's case. He phoned Singer and told him the strike had gone on long enough. The trouble was that he was not sure Singer was flexible enough to bring about a settlement. Swann advised Trethowan that if he wanted to see any progress made he must take Singer off the case, leaving it to Bett to make the running.

The first night of the Proms on 18 July was duly cancelled and the musicians scored another publicity coup by organising an alternative series of concerts conducted by such luminaries as Sir Colin Davis and Sir Charles Groves. The original plan was to stage them at Alexandra Palace, but when that was ravaged by fire they were switched to Wembley Conference Centre. The Commons Select Committee on Arts and Education met to consider the dispute. Trethowan, responding to Swann's advice, decreed that the BBC case should be put by Bett and that Singer should not be allowed to appear. His deputy Douglas Muggeridge sat in instead. The committee recommended referring the matter to ACAS, the government arbitration service, and appointing Lord Goodman as a mediator.

On 23 July, after twenty-seven hours of negotiation, the outline of a settlement was reached. The number of musicians made redundant was nearly halved, from 172 to 90: they would go freelance and the BBC would guarantee them at least two-thirds of their earnings for five years. Three orchestras were still to be closed, although the Scottish Symphony would be saved. The musicians who stayed on were awarded pay increases of between 19 and 24 per cent. In a ballot, the musicians voted overwhelmingly to accept the deal and on 7 August the Proms belatedly got under way, with twenty of that season's fifty-seven concerts lost.

Both sides believed they scored a victory. The union certainly saved more jobs than Singer would originally countenance and achieved reasonable terms for its members made redundant. The strike itself was a morale-boosting and at times an inspirational exercise. The union compiled a video from TV reports. Officials who helped organise the action still watch the tape emotionally and nostalgically, like a batsman re-living a test match century.

As for Singer, despite being sidelined in the final stages of the dispute, he is convinced that without his stubborn stand the BBC would never have achieved anything like the savings it did, and might still be running eleven orchestras. He is probably right, although many in the BBC and the musical establishment blame him for souring the formerly cordial relations between the corporation and its musicians. Barrie Hall, publicity officer for Radio 3 until 1980, was critical of him in his book *The Proms and the Men who Made Them,* published the following year. Singer considered taking legal action against Hall and his publishers, George Allen and Unwin, but was advised that he stood little chance of success. He contented himself with ensuring that the book was not sold in BBC bookshops and received no publicity over the air. Radio London nearly slipped under his net but an interview scheduled with Hall on one of its programmes was hurriedly cancelled with no proper explanation.

* * * *

Singer was sensitive about his image because the time was

approaching for big changes at the top of the BBC. Trethowan would resign in 1982 and although Milne was the obvious favourite for the succession, the governors were certain to want a contest. As managing director of an output service, Singer was of equal rank to Milne. He must have an outside chance. But even if he did not get the top post, he wanted to make sure that he was given his second choice, managing director of television. And to secure that, he had to win the support of the man who had become chairman just as the musicians' strike ended, the patrician Lord Howard.

Howard had been a governor since 1972, so he had been able, from his own observation, to form conclusions on how to tackle his new job. Among the things he had decided was that the chairman could usefully adopt a higher public profile than had been to the taste of Swann, who preferred to operate unobtrusively. This visibility should not be confined to Britain. The chairman, Howard believed, should make frequent trips overseas, both to see how broadcasting was organised elsewhere and in his capacity as the ultimate head of the external services, which command such a wide and enthusiastic audience in so many distant lands. It was only right to give those loyal listeners the chance to meet the man responsible for the service, and to give himself the chance of hearing their views on it at first hand. As it happened, Howard was fond of foreign travel, so he was able to fulfil the self-imposed requirement without feeling it to be too much of a sacrifice.

So when Howard heard that Singer was going to pay a second visit to China in May 1981, he decided to go with him. The purpose of the trip was to discuss a proposed tour by the BBC Symphony Orchestra, but in the gaps between meetings the schedule did allow time for sightseeing. Howard was a keen antiquarian and wanted to visit some of the Ming tombs not normally accessible to tourists. Of the thirteen tomb sites, only two are open regularly, but Howard received permission to look at some of the others. 'Two fat men on the Yangtze' was how unkind colleagues described the expedition, when Singer returned home and showed them his colour slides. They could laugh, but for Singer the trip was valuable not only as a cultural experience. It enabled him to forge a friendship with Howard that would stand him in good stead when the time came to lobby for a new job.

He had no more than the faintest hope of becoming director-general but went through with the interview in any event, taking the opportunity of giving the governors his views on some of the philosophical issues of broadcasting. He even wrote a long paper on what he would do as DG, and circulated it to the board. All this was primarily aimed at establishing his credentials for the post he more realistically coveted.

Soon after Milne's appointment as director-general was confirmed, he and Trethowan sat down with Howard to discuss the composition of his senior management team. Milne proposed that Cotton be made managing director, television (MD-TV) and that Singer, who had been in his radio job for three years and was due for a move, should be appointed deputy director-general, with a special brief for overseeing developments in direct broadcasting by satellite (DBS). There had in the last two or three years been great excitement about this new technology, which would ultimately enable many TV channels to be beamed direct into people's homes using cheap individual receiver dishes. The BBC had tentatively agreed with the government to be responsible for programmes on a British satellite but many problems remained unresolved, chiefly who would pay for the service and how, and what programmes would be beamed from the sky. Milne believed that a member of the board of management should take responsibility for this complicated new development and proposed Singer, partly because of his experience in making science programmes.

Singer resisted. He believed that deputy director-general, though a superficially seductive title, was essentially a non-job. To wield any power, an executive must have specific control over a section of the organisation and its staff. As for satellite developments, the managing director for television could easily take care of those: indeed if you removed from him that element of future planning, you were slicing away a substantial part of the job. To appoint a separate managing director, he argued, would be to expend too much of the corporation's management resources on what was still a highly speculative venture.

Howard and the governors did not accept that argument but in allocating the positions they did take protocol into account. Singer, as a managing director already, was senior to Cotton and entitled to have first choice of jobs, all other things being equal. Although the principle of Buggins' Turn had never been applied systematically in the BBC, there was something to be said for it as a device for resolving difficult appointments. If Singer did not want to become deputy director-general, he ought not to be forced into it. So, against Milne's wishes, Singer was made MD-TV and Cotton MD-DBS. The new director-general did not have his friend in the precise slot he had envisaged, but he did at least have him on the board of management.

Singer had won his way. All the same, this turn of events irritated him, partly for hierarchical reasons. He liked Cotton but resented his having drawn level with him in seniority. Though they were not still in a race for promotion – both would be too old to succeed Milne if he served his full six years – it meant, to put it at its crudest, that Singer would no longer have the authority to tell Cotton to pipe down. Many colleagues felt privately that despite (or perhaps because of) his reputation as a raconteur, Cotton talked too much, and often to little effect. Singer's fear was that questions relating to satellite television would henceforth dominate management meetings, not because of their relative importance but because the gregarious Cotton was responsible for them: and this would mean paying too little regard to terrestrial television, the bread and butter, the here and now.

That, in Singer's view, was precisely what happened when Cotton joined the board. One of the most ferocious rows between Singer and Milne came after a meeting with the board of governors, dominated by a long discussion on satellites initiated by Cotton. Singer interrupted to make the point that the television of today was more important than pie in the sky. There were, he declared, serious inadequacies in present programming. That was what they should be turning their minds to, not this space-age technology that might or might not develop as they expected. Milne, who does not like to expose management differences to the governors, remonstrated with him angrily. Undaunted, Singer followed up the stormy meeting by writing a *samizdat*, circulated privately to a few senior colleagues, criticising the whole satellite project. He said it was doomed to failure unless there was serious thought about the programmes to be beamed from space. He called it a 'Concorde film projector in the sky'. When the DBS directorate had been established, a committee, including both Singer and Cotton, was set up to consider programming, but Singer pointed out that it had never been convened. The document further irritated Milne, who thought Singer was simply pursuing a grudge against Cotton.

A second blow to Singer's authority, this time a double one, came not long after the Cotton appointment. Like several jobs at the senior levels of the BBC, that of director of programmes comes and goes. Its duties are ill-defined and the TV service does not suffer noticeably when the position is not filled. Often it is revived to provide a berth for an executive who cannot for the time being be placed elsewhere. Milne held the post when Trethowan was MD-TV, but when Milne took over as MD he did not press for his old job to be filled. The word at TV Centre was that he wanted to be his own director of programmes. If you have two channel controllers and a managing director, what is a director of programmes for?

Singer felt the same. He was therefore much put out when Milne told him that Brian Wenham, controller of BBC2, was to be made director of programmes. Not only that, but a brand new post of director of resources for television was to be established. The first holder of that would be Michael Checkland, formerly controller of planning and resource management. Both men would have a seat on the board of management.

Singer saw these appointments as a significant dilution of his power and he said as much to Milne. 'What do you want me to do?' he asked at a rancorous meeting in the new director-general's oak-panelled office at Broadcasting House. 'If I take a decision on programmes I offend the director of programmes and if I take a major resource decision I cut across the director of resources. What you've done is to deprive me of any executive responsibility.'

Milne smiled fleetingly. 'That's right,' he agreed. 'You're to preside over it.' Singer did not think that a satisfactory answer but there was nothing he could do. He surmised that Milne's real motive was to increase his own influence by diluting the power of those just below him. Divide and rule: the imperial tradition.

* * * *

Despite the discouraging omens, Singer was able to begin his new job with a palpable success, although not before going through another harrowing time with the unions. In January 1980, the Independent Broadcasting Authority heralded something new in British television. They invited tenders for a national commercial station to go on the air at breakfast time, between about 6 and 9 a.m. In the United States, breakfast television was an established part of the day's viewing pattern, but it had never been tried in Britain, apart from a half-hearted experiment in Yorkshire. (Among the reasons for this hesitancy were the difficulties anticipated in getting agreement with the unions to work at such unsocial hours.) The IBA received tenders from eight prospective consortiums and on the last Sunday of 1980 announced that the contract would be awarded to TV-am, a group led by Peter Jay and David Frost and including such well-known TV faces as Anna Ford, Angela Rippon, Michael Parkinson and Robert Kee.

The BBC had to decide how – indeed whether – to respond to the IBA's initiative. There was no compelling reason to do anything. The corporation had survived this long without breakfast television and there were other gaps in their schedule, notably in the afternoon, that might be thought to command a higher priority. What is more, it was in the midst of one of its triennial campaigns for a higher licence fee, arguing that it could scarcely afford to fund the existing level of broadcasting. If these pleas of poverty had any real foundation, it was surely perverse to consider opening up an extra three hours of television a day. One man who saw this clearly and felt it strongly was William Whitelaw, the Home Secretary. He privately urged George Howard not to allow the BBC to compete with TV-am. 'Your enemies will use it against you,' he cautioned sagely.

But that argument did not appeal to Howard's competitive nature, or that of the BBC's senior executives, especially the ultra-competitive Singer. Still running radio, he was not then directly responsible for the decision, but when it came up in the board of management he was among the most vociferous hawks. Ever since ITV began, the BBC has felt a compulsive drive to compete on every front, fearful that if it gives the independent companies a clear run in any sphere, its legitimacy as a comprehensive national broadcasting service will begin to be eroded. It is seen as a test of virility. That was why the BBC insisted on pressing ahead with plans to expand local radio in the 1970s, despite the arguments advanced even by some governors that this was one area that could be left clear for commercial interests. Now, faced with the strong recommendation from the board of management that they should establish their own breakfast TV programme to rival TV-am, the governors ignored Whitelaw's warning and succumbed readily to this corporate chauvinism.

When he was still in his radio job, Singer was much taken with the idea of radiovision, meaning broadcasting a programme on radio and television simultaneously. An early suggestion for breakfast television was to adapt radio's successful early-morning programme Today for that purpose. The television service opposed the hybrid concept, aghast at the thought of the compromises it would involve. When Singer moved to Television Centre he switched loyalties and supported his new service. Pure television it would be.

Ron Neil, a talented Scottish current affairs producer, was assigned to launch the programme, to be called Breakfast Time. The studios at Lime Grove were converted to a topical programmes unit housing Breakfast Time, the early evening Nationwide and the later Newsnight on BBC2. An advanced newsroom computer and a graphics system were introduced, and because the £500,000 cost could be split between the three programmes, the management were able to convince themselves that they were not being extravagant. Frank Bough, the popular presenter of sports programmes, was chosen as host, along with Selina Scott from Independent Television News. TV-am was to be launched in February 1983. The BBC's plan was to get its rival show on the air a couple of weeks ahead of that.

First, though, the unions had to be tackled. Despite his track record over the musicians' strike, it fell to Singer to negotiate a deal that would allow Breakfast Time to be produced without huge extra payments to staff. With 150 extra jobs to offer, he would have been in a strong bargaining position were it not that he and his management colleagues had convinced themselves that the launch date was of the essence. They believed they needed to start the programme in advance of TV-am if it was to have a chance of competing successfully. That ruled out the kind of war of attrition Singer had waged on the musicians.

The union chiefly involved was the Association of Broadcasting Staffs (now part of the Entertainment Trades Alliance). After months of negotiation, the discussions were stalled over extra payments of several hundred pounds demanded by the union for its members. Tony Hearn, general secretary of the ABS, went to Television Centre for what were to be the final talks. In the light of his experience with the musicians, Singer decided it would be politic to absent himself from the meeting, leaving Bob Pugh, then controller of personnel for the television service, to lead the BBC side. The meeting began in the morning and extended into a handsomely catered lunch, exploiting the resources of the BBC's wine cellar. But no progress was made on the business under discussion. Pugh was not offering as much as Hearn thought he could get, given the management's self-imposed time constraint. As 4 o'clock approached, Hearn rose from the table and, announcing that he had better things to do, returned to his Central London office.

When he arrived he was told there had been a number of urgent calls, all with the same message: Singer would like to see him back at TV Centre. Hearn was met in the reception area by an agitated Pugh. 'I ought to warn you Tony,' he said, 'Aubrey is in one hell of a temper. Don't let him upset you. If it goes badly come back and see me. He really is mad.'

Thus warned, Hearn took the slow lift to the sixth floor and was ushered into the large and comfortable office where Singer sat behind the expanses of his desk. Where the union leader had expected to find a gruff bulldog, snarling and baring his teeth, Singer assumed the benign role of a spaniel, rolling over and waiting to be tickled.

'Tony, you like a good cigar, don't you?' was his opening sally. Hearn admitted he did, and when the ceremony of conflagration was completed Singer fixed him with a sad and weary gaze. 'How much money do you bloody want?' he asked. Hearn told him. Singer agreed. The meeting was over before the cigar had diminished by more than half an inch. Outside, the worried Pugh was convinced that the brevity of the interview could only mean a breakdown in negotiations. 'Don't worry,' Hearn told him. 'You'll get your programme.' He smiled and took another puff on his cigar. He had won by recognising that, to an old TV hand like Singer, the show must go on; that was what mattered.

And so it did, at 6 a.m. on 18 January 1983. It was an immediate and surprising success, attracting nearly 2 million viewers at its peak quarter-hour. From the very beginning Ron Neil achieved a relaxed ambiance, dressing the amiable Frank Bough in casual sweaters and ensuring that nothing too thought-provoking was offered to bleary-eyed viewers. The advance promotion for TV-am suggested it would concentrate on hard news and analysis. 'News-reactive' was the phrase concocted to describe it. Neil and the BBC strategists decided to aim for the end of the market that might resist too much earnestness at dawn. Their target viewers would be readers of the *Sun* and *Mirror* rather than the *Guardian* and *The Times*. Although a reversal of the popular image of the comparative roles of the two channels, it proved a canny decision. For when TV-am made its debut on 1 February, the viewers quickly decided they preferred the BBC's more easy-going version. After a couple of weeks Breakfast Time was attracting four times as many viewers as the commercial offering.

Singer and his colleagues were pleased as punch. They beamed – smirked, even – as they discussed the programme's success, achieved in the face of largely pessimistic predictions by the press. It was not their business to worry about the catastrophic effect of the unbalanced ratings on their commercial rivals. Within weeks, TV-am's City backers had ousted Peter Jay, who was soon followed by most of the presenters and senior programme people. It took TV-am nearly a year to move sufficiently down-market to catch up with Breakfast Time and ultimately overtake it.

A bizarre dispute between Singer and the board of governors, a few days after the launch of the breakfast programme, was hardly grave enough to spoil his satisfaction. But in retrospect it was an ominous part of a pattern of increasing interference by the governors in programme matters that had not formerly been thought appropriate for their attention – a trend that would culminate in the multiple crises of 1985.

The matter that bothered the board was the astrologer, the rotund and outgoing Russell Grant. Ron Neil, aiming to give Breakfast Time something of the appeal of a tabloid newspaper, decided to introduce a screen version of the astrological column, one of the tabloids' most popular features. Grant was already a well-known television figure, and he purveyed his hocus-pocus with an arch ebullience that viewers found fun to watch. But the governors hated it, especially the chairman George Howard. He thought it wrong to give the BBC's implicit seal of authenticity to such blatant nonsense masquerading as genuine information and prediction. It would surely offend the religious susceptibilities of many viewers. Why not instead do something like Thought for the Day on radio's Today programme, in which men and women of a number of different beliefs retail uplifting anecdotes? Alasdair Milne disliked the astrological spot, too, and if left to himself would have acceded to Howard's suggestion. But Singer resisted stubbornly. He supported Neil's decision to hire Grant and it was clear that the viewers liked him. It would be absurd to drop such a popular feature. As for Thought for the Day, the trouble with that kind of spot, as BBC radio had found, is that once you have launched it there is no way of withdrawing it without provoking squeals of protest from the religious lobbies. You are effectively locked into it for ever. The governors reluctantly gave way and the astrologer survived.

* * * *

The second current affairs innovation of 1983 was 60 Minutes, a magazine programme that replaced Nationwide in the old Tonight slot around 6. In contrast to Breakfast Time it was an unmitigated failure and abolished after nine months. Interference by the governors was an important cause of its demise, and for that reason it is worth examining in some detail.

Oakley Court is a grim, rambling Gothic-style hotel, built in the 1920s by the Thames west of Windsor, a couple of miles past the racecourse. With more than ninety bedrooms and plenty of meeting accommodation, it is the sort of place BBC executives find convenient for weekend brainstorming sessions, away from the diversions of the office.

In August 1982 most of the senior TV executives concerned with current affairs were summoned to a weekend meeting there by Alasdair Milne, still working himself into the job of director-general. The others included Singer, Wenham and Christopher Capron, who had the previous month succeeded John Gau as head of current affairs. The specific purpose of the meeting was to discuss the future of Nationwide – or more strictly what was to replace it, since the prevailing view was that it had no future. Roger Bolton, then editor of Nationwide, was there, too. Capron had moved him from Panorama in an attempt to beef up the early evening programme, which had gained an unenvied reputation as a repository of winsome trivia – most notably a filmed item about a skateboarding duck that quickly became a standing joke, used to make the point that television current affairs had lost its seriousness of purpose.

Nationwide had been running since 1969 and was showing its age. The idea had been to co-ordinate regional with national coverage of current affairs by having a single network programme in which the regions were allotted twenty minutes for their own news and current affairs segment. This imposed on the programme a rigid framework that became more and more irksome. It began with the national news at 5.40, an eccentric time whose only virtue was that it was five minutes earlier than the news on ITV. At 6 came the regional section, followed by a return to network current affairs for the last twenty minutes. One weakness of the formula was that the final segment would often contain follow-up material on stories that had been in the 5.40 bulletin, but they were separated by the regional items. It lacked logic.

Bolton's first attempt at rescuing Nationwide was to bring in as its presenter David Dimbleby, a figure of substance far removed from the skateboarding duck image. But the change was too abrupt and Dimbleby's earnestness sent many viewers scurrying into the less demanding embrace of the independent channel. Dimbleby could see it was not working and left, allowing the programme to drift back into more comfortable ground. Whatever programme replaced Nationwide, it would have to include at least as strong a regional element. The BBC regions have always been conscious that the ITV companies, based locally, have a more distinct regional identity than the BBC. While there is not much they can do about that, they would certainly protest loudly if their position were made weaker by cutting the time available for their own programmes.

If the three elements of Nationwide were to be retained, the sensible way of organising them would be to have the two network segments – news and current affairs – alongside one another, with the regional opt-out before or after. The snag was that the regions thought it important to keep their news at 6. Short of a major upheaval in the evening schedule, there was no way they could keep that spot and allow the two national segments to run back-to-back. You could not start the programme at 5.20 – too early – or let it run until 7, then considered too late.

At Oakley Court the decision was taken to risk regional wrath and put the national news on at 6, followed by the network current affairs. This meant regional news at 5.40. Mike Alder, controller of English regional television, had his doubts but the other regional representative, Stan Taylor from current affairs in Scotland, seemed to approve. A more significant doubter was Brian Wenham, shortly to take a seat on the board of management as director of programmes. He thought the regional news should come after the more important national news. It seemed a natural order of events. And he also wondered aloud whether self-contained current affairs magazine programmes in the early evening, the direct descendants of Tonight, were not out of date. Might it not be better to have a more straightforward account of the day's events at that time, called the news, but done in a less formal style than the main news at 9 o'clock?

The traditional BBC divide between news and current affairs was narrowing all the time as the news bulletins carried more analytical reports. The remaining distinction between the two was as much a matter of bureaucratic in-fighting, with Lime Grove battling to maintain its identity, as of any real programme need. Take the case of Newsnight, the highly-regarded late-evening programme on BBC2. That was a combination of news and current affairs and it worked well. (Wenham, as controller of BBC2, had originally fought hard to keep Newsnight off his channel. Now that it had become a prestige programme he seemed content to count it among his jewels.)

The Oakley Court decision soon ran into predictable opposition. In all the English regions there are regional advisory councils made up of fifteen members whose role is to ensure their local concerns are known to the BBC. The three national regions – Scotland, Wales, and Northern Ireland – have national broadcasting councils and are disproportionately powerful because they also have their own governors on the board. Regional controllers therefore have the machinery to exert powerful pressure on the centre. With the threat, as they saw it, of the down-grading of their evening bulletin, they rallied the troops.

Such was the resistance to the change that Milne sent Wenham round the regional and national councils to try to sell the plan. He was an odd choice because of all the executives at Oakley Court he had harboured the most doubts about it. He reported back that the shires were adamant. By this time the three national governors were also expressing disquiet. Capron was all for standing firm against the special interests but Milne gave way and the decision was reversed. In any new arrangement, the 6 o'clock opt-out would remain sacrosanct.

Nationwide was still to be scrapped, though, and for many months the senior TV executives could not decide how to replace it. What they finally agreed on was a programme with the same elements as Nationwide but better co-ordinated, more slickly presented and using the computer graphics that were being deployed to such good effect on Breakfast Time. The new programme would be called 60 Minutes – a name borrowed from CBS television in America. One of its gimmicks was to have the sets in the regional studios built to appear identical with the London set used for the network portion of the programme. This, it was felt, would help the three parts achieve some sort of unity. You would scarcely notice the joins. (Only Southampton was excused from this edict. A new studio had just been built there, and to scrap it in favour of the approved design would have been unacceptably profligate.) The ill-starred programme had to survive persistent sniping from the regions before it reached the air. Having won their point about keeping the local news at 6, some regional controllers were still not satisfied with the format. They could not be blamed for being so concerned, because that time slot represented the largest potential regular audience for their own programming. Doing well in it against the commercial opposition was important for the stations' morale.

On 23 May Milne wrote to all regional controllers outlining 60 Minutes, stressing that it was designed to serve the whole network and calling for their co-operation. But one controller, the chubby and outgoing Patrick Chalmers in Glasgow, sought to wash his hands of the whole enterprise and originate his own programme for the forty-five minutes following the national news. In a memo to Aubrey Singer, he noted that the Scottish ITV companies had local magazine programmes during that time and were winning the fight for viewers. If he could challenge them on level terms and increase the BBC audience, that advantage might spill over into the rest of the evening's schedules.

Constitutionally he could have got away with it had he insisted. Alistair Hetherington's self-sacrifice on the altar of autonomy had not been in vain, for the governors, under pressure from the broadcasting councils, had come to accept that the national regions should have more independence. But there was not much enthusiasm for that view in the board of management, who feared that if the Scots were allowed to opt out of 60 Minutes the Welsh and the Northern Irish, for the sake of their *amour propre,* would feel obliged to follow suit. So heavy guns were brought to bear on Chalmers to dissuade him from breaking ranks. 'Remember Hetherington' was the dire warning given him by Brian Wenham when they argued about it over the phone. Singer replied to his memo in a pompous and frosty note in which he constantly referred back to Milne's note of 23 May as the fount of the proposal's legitimacy, like an old-time evangelist quoting holy scripture. In the seven paragraphs of Singer's memo, the phrase 'the DG's note of May 23', or marginal variations on it, appeared eight times.

Reading the uncompromising document in his Glasgow office,

Chalmers interpreted it as Singer throwing his weight about, not brooking any challenge to his authority. He guessed that if it had been left to the less excitable Wenham, Scotland might have been allowed to go its own way. He was wrong, but the fact that he held that view was a tribute to the diplomatic skills of Wenham, who had in fact drafted Singer's memo. Chalmers did not give way until he received a visit from Milne in person. On 5 July, a grey Tuesday, Milne stopped in Edinburgh on the way to a meeting of the board of governors in Nairn, on the Moray Firth. He called on Chalmers in the BBC office there. 'You have the right to opt out,' the director-general told the controller, 'but I would like you to take 60 Minutes and give it every chance to work and succeed. So all in all, boy, stay with it and if in three or four months you still have a mind to opt out then you can look at it again.' Chalmers gave way and they celebrated with a dram of whisky.

Having used his personal authority to solve the dispute, Milne nearly reopened it when, announcing the triumph at a press conference the following day in Inverness, he referred to Chalmers' view on Scottish autonomy as 'eccentric'. He had hurriedly to assure the bruised controller that the adjective had been taken out of context. Sassenachs might have used the same word about the DG's behaviour the following night at Brodie Castle, where the governors, the board of management and the Scottish Broadcasting Council were having a banquet. After dinner the guests were made to hear Milne, wearing a Gordon kilt, play two traditional airs on the bagpipes, which lasted so long that Alan Protheroe, the diminutive Welsh assistant director-general, was sent out for emergency supplies of whisky half way through.

* * * *

David Lloyd, a producer from Newsnight, was assigned to prepare the launch of 60 Minutes, due at the end of October 1983. Wenham, Capron and Alan Hart, controller of BBC1, took a close interest in his progress. The first decisions to be made by the four men were about the presenters. Because the programme would be like Nationwide in so many respects, it was important to choose fresh faces with qualities as far removed as possible from those of the soothing former presenter, Sue Lawley. Influenced by the success of Breakfast Time, they decided to pitch this programme, too, at the level of the tabloid press; so they looked for tabloid people.

They poached one of the original Breakfast Time team – Nick Ross, number three in the early morning hierarchy to Frank Bough and Selina Scott. The Jamaican Beverly Anderson had deployed a pleasing informal approach in Channel 4's Black on Black. Sally Magnusson, daughter of Magnus Magnusson of Mastermind, had a charming Scots accent that might mollify the lingering resentment north of the border at being saddled with the show. But the trio were young and the two women were short of on-screen experience. Lloyd felt strongly that they needed to be balanced by someone older. It was all very well banking on youth, but there were millions of viewers who would appreciate the calming presence of a more mature figure. Frank Bough played this avuncular role on Breakfast Time. Searching for an older person who understood tabloid-style journalism, Lloyd thought of Desmond Wilcox.

After his spectacular departure as head of features three years earlier, Wilcox had begun his rehabilitation by making a series of fine network documentaries for BBC Scotland. He still had a sneaking suspicion, though, that there was a vendetta against him at the BBC: his proposed thirteen-part series on the Jews had been cut to three programmes because neither channel controller was prepared to find the money to finish it. Wilcox was therefore greatly surprised when Lloyd, a slender and ascetic figure, went to his house in Kew and invited him to join the team.

Lloyd spoke persuasively, but Wilcox was sceptical. When the producer outlined the shape of the programme, Wilcox remarked that it seemed so like the old Nationwide that he wondered why the name had been altered. Why not simply continue the old programme with Lloyd as its new producer? When things went wrong in Fleet Street the custom was to fire the editor, not the paper.

Lloyd described his programme as a new concept, a seamless robe where the joins between the regional and national sections would be invisible. It would be uniquely flexible. Decisions on

length and running order would be made in the control gallery
while the show was on the air. If there was an interview that
turned out compelling, it could be run for as long as twenty
minutes and the rest of the programme scrapped. If it was boring
it could be cut after two minutes.

Wilcox wondered whether his invitation had been approved by
Milne. It had. Milne was always upset when senior people left for
reasons unconnected with their ability, and he was glad to give
Wilcox the chance to bounce back. His one reservation was not
that Wilcox was too old, but that his screen manner was perhaps
a bit dated, redolent of the 1970s rather than the 1980s. In the
last decade presenters had become more jaunty and off-hand.
Wilcox's air of earnest concern might jar with the flip brightness
around him.

Wilcox had his doubts, too, and expressed them to Alan Hart.
Aside from the question of his suitability, he was also keen not to
jeopardise the series of documentaries he was making for BBC1.
The channel controller was insistent. 'We're awfully short of
grown-ups in the BBC at the moment,' he confessed. As for the
documentaries, he would be happy to schedule them for a later
date than first envisaged. 'Must I do it?' Wilcox asked him.
'Nobody can force you,' Hart replied. It was the deadly approach
Milne had used with Chalmers. Wilcox, after nearly twenty years
with the BBC, recognised it as code for 'It would be in your
interests to do it'. Hart, after all, had the power of life or death
over his documentary series. Not wishing to risk displeasing his
patron, he agreed.

60 Minutes was an overnight disaster. Wilcox sat at the
presenters' desk looking shifty, as though he would sooner have
been somewhere else – as he most surely would. Beverly
Anderson was still more ill-at-ease. What were supposed to have
been the invisible joins were clumsy in the extreme: modern
technology made them more obvious, not less. Wilcox did
nothing to increase his popularity with a harassed Lloyd when he
compared the links between segments with noisily shunting milk
trains at Crewe in the middle of the night. A seamless robe? More
a poorly sewn patchwork quilt.

'Give it time', was the first line of defence, as adverse
comments from the press and viewers began to come in. But as

Christmas approached with no sign of real improvement, Milne and Wenham began to ease towards the view that the humane course of action would be to recognise that the programme was a flop and put it out of its misery promptly. By now, however, the current affairs people at Lime Grove, initially scornful of the project as a flimsy compromise, had become committed to it. They persuaded the board of management more than once to allow an extra few weeks to see whether it would take off and fly. When each deadline came and went with no miraculous recovery, it was extended a while longer.

Wenham did not believe himself responsible for the debacle. One day Peter Foges from the New York office was visiting TV Centre and went to see him. After their talk Wenham invited Foges to accompany him to Lime Grove.

'I'm going to lower the morale of the current affairs department,' he confided.

He did no less. When he arrived, all the key people in the department, from Capron down, were waiting for him.

'60 Minutes is a bad programme and it's yours,' he fumed, pinning the blame specifically on Capron for both the original idea and its execution. It was an uncomfortable meeting. Travelling back to TV Centre afterwards Wenham asked Foges: 'Do you think I lowered the morale enough?'

'You did a great job,' was the reply.

Capron's and Lloyd's first scapegoat was Desmond Wilcox. The press regarded him as fair game since his spectacular resignation from Kensington House, and as the husband of Esther Rantzen he was good headline material. Much of the newspaper criticism of 60 Minutes was centred on him. That, combined with his failure to achieve the customary sureness of touch, undermined his confidence. This in turn made him look still more uncertain and dithering, the worry deepening the lines on his face. Viewers attributed it to his age, which stood out glaringly because he was surrounded by youngsters.

It fell to Alan Hart to break the news to Wilcox that it would be better if he left the show. Having initially been reluctant to join it, he might have been expected to welcome the invitation to leave, but that fails to take into account any performer's natural reluctance to be saddled with the blame for a failure that is not entirely – or indeed mostly – his fault. He felt he had been poorly treated all along. As a sop, Hart agreed to bring forward the documentary series that had been postponed when Wilcox joined 60 Minutes a few months earlier.

The show did not improve after his departure. Sarah Kennedy, the pert presenter of ITV's Game for a Laugh, joined the presenting team in February, but by then Wenham and Milne had decided in their own minds that the project would almost certainly have to be abandoned. Milne's incautious promise to Chalmers gave them little scope for manoeuvre. The four months were up and they had to be able to tell the Scottish controller that relief was at hand, that he did not have to take up his agreed option of providing his own alternative to 60 Minutes, because the plug was about to be pulled on the programme nationally. Christopher Capron and David Lloyd fought a rearguard action for it, not because they felt committed to the format but for territorial reasons. They believed, rightly, that in any replacement the current affairs element would be down-graded in favour of news.

What emerged from the ashes was something very like what Wenham had originally envisaged. With the failure of 60 Minutes, he and his management colleagues were now in a stronger position to tell the regions and their governors that it was no longer realistic of them to insist on their right to keep the local news at 6. They had to swallow regional pride for the sake of solving the BBC's early evening crisis. The new formula would be a half hour of national news at 6 o'clock that would still include some current affairs input, followed by the regions' own news and current affairs at 6.30. (An exception was made for Wales, where the local programme was placed before the 6 o'clock news, for technical reasons connected with the Welsh-language bulletin on Channel 4; later Northern Ireland followed suit.)

It took until June 1984 for all the ends to be tied up, governors mollified and relevant appointments made. Ron Neil was put in charge of the new package, and Lloyd replaced him at Breakfast Time. As a protest against the loss of the early evening current affairs slot, journalists at Lime Grove went on strike for twenty-four hours. But the new Six O'Clock News went on the air as planned in the autumn, presented jointly by Sue Lawley and

Nicholas Witchell. It was a critical success, even if the viewing figures were much the same as for 60 Minutes.

The failure of the highly touted show did much damage to the BBC's self-confidence and reputation at a vital time, coinciding as it did with the Thorn Birds controversy and the beginning of the campaign for an increase in the licence fee. In a letter to Lime Grove staff explaining the withdrawal of 60 Minutes, Wenham wrote of a 'basic design fault' in the programme. In fact the basic fault went back further than that, to the very structure of the BBC's decision-making apparatus. Lobbying from the regions had led the board of management to base a new programme on a series of fudged compromises that went against their professional judgement. The incident showed how the corporation's elaborate system of reference upwards and across, of checks and balances, although notionally a model of responsive democracy, can adversely affect the quality of programmes. The issue was essentially the one that was to explode much more controversially a year later: how can the governors exercise influence over programmes without getting involved in the evils of censorship and political control?

One man who would have been greatly concerned with such issues was Aubrey Singer; but he was no longer obliged to worry about them. For that February, in the midst of the 60 Minutes fiasco, he was summarily booted from the BBC in a way that was ruthless even by the corporation's own standards.

* * * *

Alasdair Milne enjoys the outdoor life. He plays tennis and golf and indulges in the gentlemanly pursuit of shooting. Aubrey Singer is equally fond of the sport and they used occasionally to kill pigeons together until 1981, when they decided to take shares in a pheasant shoot near Hungerford in Berkshire, in a syndicate of twelve. Singer likes the idea of shooting – it is a pleasant social occasion and above all has style – but he does not do it very well. Milne calls him Kalashnikov Singer, after the Russian rifle.

On Saturday, 7 January 1984, Milne left his house in Holland Park shortly after 7 to pick up Singer from his West Kensington flat, for a long-arranged day's shooting. The day had started damp but as they sped west on the M4 in Milne's BMW the sky soon brightened and after they reached the Berkshire Downs there were some good spells of sunshine. It was mild for the time of the year. They shot until about 2 p.m., then broke off for a highly convivial lunch. It had been an average day's sport – about 100 pheasants killed. After lunch Milne and Singer piled their share of the bag into the boot and climbed into Milne's car for the drive back.

As they reached the motorway, the only thought that disturbed Singer's peace of mind was that Milne, beside him, was driving too fast. He usually did and Singer rather wished he wouldn't. It was uncharacteristic for a man in such a responsible position and with something of a dour reputation to take his and his passengers' lives into his hands every time he sat behind the wheel. No doubt he knew what he was doing. Anyway, the combination of the morning exercise and the excellent lunch would soon make Singer dozy, blunting the alarm. . .

His musing was interrupted by a question from Milne that shattered his composure:

'Have you ever thought of taking premature retirement?'

He had, as it happened. He was now 57 and by BBC rules would have to retire at 60. But he did not feel anywhere near ready to stop working. He had often thought, idly and unspecifically, that what he would really like to do would be to spend his last active years at what he enjoyed and did best – making programmes. Maybe a year before he was due to retire would be the appropriate time to launch into something like that; but so far his thinking had been tentative. One point he was clear on, though: the initiative would come from him. He was shocked and hurt that it should come from his friend.

'What do you mean?' he asked. 'You mean go in the autumn?'

'No, before that,' Milne replied. But he added that it should not be in the next month because he was about to go off to India for three weeks and wanted Singer to stand in for him.

When Singer arrived home he told his wife Cynthia the news and reminded her of a conversation the previous November. Singer had just learned that he was going to be awarded the CBE in the New Year honours list and had told her cynically: 'You wait, now I've got the CBE they'll have me out within a week.' The timing was almost exactly right, for the conversation with Milne on the way home from the shoot took place six days after the award was announced on 1 January.

It was a ruthless firing and some of Milne's closest confidants told him so when the story came out.

'That was cruel, wasn't it?' asked William Carrocher, the man who had taught him Gaelic and whom he had just appointed chief press officer at Television Centre.

'Don't be impertinent, boy,' was Milne's half-serious reply.

Stephen Hearst, special adviser to the director-general, compared it with the fall from power of a Soviet leader.

'A bit like the Kremlin, surely?' he suggested. Milne winked.

* * * *

Milne was not motivated by a desire to get his own back for the reverse Howard had inflicted on him over Singer's appointment two years earlier. He had to make changes at the top because the performance of BBC Television, in terms of both ratings and critical acclaim, had declined alarmingly during 1983. The year had begun well enough. The second ITV channel, Channel 4, had been introduced at the end of 1982 and had been declared an instant failure by critics and viewers. In January, the BBC's Breakfast Time had been an unqualified success. But then came the dithering and eventual calamity of the early evening current affairs programme; the expensive series on the history of the theatre and a bad ratings beating in the autumn when ITV led their schedule with an American adaptation of Herman Wouk's *The Winds of War*. It had been Wenham's decision, as director of programmes, not to compete with that by scheduling a popular show against it; but Singer was in charge and had to share the blame.

A more serious development, as far as ratings were concerned, was that Channel 4 had by now found its feet and was chipping away at the audience for BBC2. Nobody thought that the BBC should try to share the audience equally with ITV: commercial programming, free from the onerous sense of responsibility that lingers with the BBC from its early days, is bound to be more popular. But when their share began to slip towards 40 per cent, firm action was required. Wenham had already made his first approach to Michael Grade in Hollywood. If Grade did eventually agree to come, Milne thought it unlikely he would work well with Singer, who would in all likelihood see him as a threat to be suppressed. Bill Cotton was a friend of Grade's and could be expected to work with him to pull up BBC1's ratings.

A further factor was that Stuart Young had replaced Howard as chairman in August 1983, so Singer could no longer count on the support of his Chinese travelling companion. Young is an accountant with little previous experience of creative extroverts like Singer: Cotton's confidential approach comes closer to what he is used to. Young shared Milne's doubts about Singer's ability to organise and motivate a body as large as the television service. Although Young did not initiate Singer's dismissal, he raised no objection when Milne told him of his plan. He agreed that action was urgent, because 1984 would see the start of the BBC's always contentious campaign for an increase in the licence fee. To justify its claim on the viewer's purse, it was important that it should be in a more competitive position against ITV by that time.

On the Monday following the shooting party, Singer's first act was to engage the services of a firm of lawyers specialising in high-level redundancy cases. His second move was to raise with Milne again a matter that had been discussed on and off in Television Centre for some time. A committee had been established to see whether the BBC should set up its own semi-independent film production company modelled on Euston Films, which had been responsible for the ITV hit series Minder. It was thought this would give more flexibility in raising finance for joint productions and marketing them than is the case with wholly in-house production. Singer told Milne that he would like to be considered as managing director of this company when it was formed. Milne replied that the scheme might never get launched. Having established that the BBC had not yet registered the name, Singer did so himself. Next time the subject came up between them, Singer told Milne proudly: 'You are now talking to the chairman, managing director and office cat of White City Films.'

Having established his own independent production company, Singer and his lawyer made it the central point of their termination negotiations with the BBC. In essence, they persuaded the corporation to fund his new company by commissioning programmes for the next five years and paying in advance for their development. On top of that, he was given a five-year consultancy contract – which already took him beyond the normal age for retirement. In addition he was able to take with him, to his new home-cum-office in Chiswick, some of the computer and video equipment he had amassed at the Beeb.

But before he left he would enjoy his final fling, his three weeks as acting director-general. As Gerald Mansell had found during the Carrickmore row in 1979, the absence of a director-general does not prevent public controversy breaking round the head of the BBC, indeed it often seems to encourage it. (The Real Lives fracas in 1985 confirmed that perverse phenomenon.) On this occasion, Singer had to parry the initial hostile barbs about The Thorn Birds, screened just before Milne went away. He also became involved in another union dispute, this time over the weekly publication *Radio Times*. Since before Christmas the London printing and distribution of *Radio Times* had been disrupted by industrial action by the union SOGAT '82 at Robert Maxwell's British Printing and Communications Corporation. Singer had been keen to join with Robert Maxwell and take tough legal action against the union but Alan Protheroe (assistant DG) and most of the board of management maintained that the dispute was nothing to do with the BBC and they should leave Maxwell to sort it out. Stuart Young agreed with the Protheroe view and was not impressed with Singer's arguments. Had the decision not already been taken that Singer should go, Young might have been urging it on Milne before long.

The plan was that Singer should make an orderly exit some time in March. Inevitably, there was a leak and the *Guardian* published news of his departure on Friday, 17 February. The official announcement of his going, and his replacement by Bill Cotton, was made six days later. In traditional fashion, he was offered an exotic foreign trip as a sop. Given the dismal February weather, Barbados was suggested but Singer had more distant places in mind than that: Burma and Thailand. He left on 1

March and was back in time for his investiture at Buckingham Palace on the 20th. On the 23rd, Milne organised a farewell dinner for him at Television Centre. Singer's speech was quite funny, fairly standard for events of that sort, but it still succeeded in infuriating Stuart Young. Along with travellers' tales about Bangkok and the Irrawaddy, Singer made some points about the future of the BBC and television in general.

'Whilst there can be no doubt that BBC Television is a national asset,' he remarked, 'it is not the national asset that it used to be. Three channel dominance has been exchanged for four channel parity without the funding to give us the primacy among equals that we once had.' He made the argument that was to become familiar over the next twelve months in the debate on the licence fee: that Channel 4 had shown the way for the future by operating 'on the economics of the market place rather than relying on economies of scale'. And he added: 'In the end, there has to be an end to expansion within the organisation. Risk-taking needs to be hedged out to points of real responsibility.' That could have been put down to a new independent producer rooting for his corner, but what annoyed Young was the homily Singer addressed to him personally during his farewell remarks to his colleagues. He quoted John Kenneth Galbraith: 'Ageing in the organisation occurs when excellence is regarded as that which is already there.' Young interpreted that as a veiled criticism of Milne, and was furious. By now he was heartily glad to see the broad back of this turbulent executive.

* * * *

Having righted the first of the appointments he had been unhappy with when he became director-general, Milne, with the enthusiastic assistance of Bill Cotton, proceeded to deal with the second. Alan Hart, unlike Singer, had already spent a respectable period of time in his job. Three years is considered the optimum term of office for the controller of a channel, and Hart, at BBC1, had exceeded that by six months. After the long negotiations to secure Michael Grade's services bore fruit on 24 May, a way ought to have been found to move Hart on with some dignity. But time was short. Because Grade had to tell his Hollywood employers of his decision, it was virtually certain that the story would break from that side of the Atlantic if it was not announced quickly. Hart had not been informed of any of the initial approaches to Grade, and Cotton only gave him a hint of what was to come a few days before the negotiations reached their conclusion. When the announcement was made, on 30 May, Hart was on holiday in Greece. No new role had been agreed for him, so the press could only be told that he would be found a job in the television service. In the event, the best that could be found was a new post as special assistant to the director-general, responsible for looking at the regions and for relations with the European Broadcasting Union. It was something of a come-down after controlling the main TV channel, but Hart kept a stiff upper lip, never allowing himself to express the disappointment he must have felt.

Others were less restrained. Paul Fox, a former controller of BBC1 himself, had some fun at the Beeb's expense. Asked to comment by *The Times,* he said:

'It is interesting that the BBC can be quite such good butchers. It shows that the BBC is absolutely ruthless when it wants to achieve its aims.' And another ITV executive, who asked for anonymity, agreed with him:

'People think that Michael is coming from the brutal business of American television to work in the gentle pastures of the BBC. What they do not realize is that there is nothing so brutal as the BBC at the moment when it is able to get rid of its managing director and controller of BBC1 within the space of a few months.' Nobody at the BBC minded this very much. If you are about to launch a campaign aimed at demonstrating your efficiency, a reputation for ruthlessness may be no bad thing.

Grade himself, interviewed by phone from Los Angeles, was not forthcoming when asked what he planned to do when he took over on 1 September, but he was at pains to point out what he was not going to do. Despite having a name associated primarily with light entertainment, he would not take the corporation as far down that road as some commentators seemed to believe.

'I hope you will understand that I am not too populist,' he said defensively. 'Ratings are important but they are not the most important thing. It would be very, very easy to go in and push the

Joe Cummings

The man most likely. The young Alasdair Milne in his days as editor of Tonight (*BBC*); and as seen by cartoonist Joe Cummings (*Sunday Times*) at what should be the pinnacle of his career − but as director-general he is under assault from snipers.

(*Top left*) The BBC's founding father and first director-general, Lord Reith (*BBC*), and (*Top right*) Sir Hugh Greene, his most influential successor (*BBC*). (*Below*) Lord Hill, the first of the truly 'political' governors, who forced Greene out (*Camera Press*); and newsreader Robert Dougall symbolising the traditional BBC virtue of low-key reliability (*BBC*).

BBC buildings are scattered all over central and west London. The three most prominent are (*Top right*) Broadcasting House, the art deco monument in Portland Place (*BBC*); (*Below*) Bush House in the Aldwych, home of the External Services (*BBC*); (*Bottom*) Television Centre at Shepherds Bush (*BBC*). A new radio complex is to be built alongside Television Centre at White City.

(*Top left*) Aubrey Singer, victim of a dramatic firing by Alasdair Milne, initiated while they were on a shooting trip together (*The Times*). (*Right*) Lord Swann, as chairman, ordered Singer to be removed from the negotiations to end the 1980 musicians' strike (*Universal Pictorial Press*). (*Below*) Striking musicians serenade MPs from a boat on the Thames (*Press Association*).

(*Above*) John Gau, barred from promotion to controller BBC1 because of the Carrickmore incident (*BBC*). (*Left*) The skateboarding duck, symbol of the inconsequential image of the early evening current affairs programme Nationwide (*BBC*). (*Below*) Presenter Beverly Anderson on the set of 60 Minutes, the short-lived successor to Nationwide (*BBC*).

(*Top left*) Paul Fox left the BBC because he thought he would not be made director-general (*Yorkshire Television*). (*Bottom left*) Donald Baverstock's fortunes never recovered from his departure from the Beeb in 1965 (*Sunday Times*). (*Bottom right*) Brian Wenham, resident intellectual, whose chance of becoming director-general receded with the appointment of Michael Checkland as Milne's deputy in 1985 (*BBC*).

(*Top*) Bill Cotton climbed doggedly to the Board of Management in a career largely parallel to Milne's (*BBC*). (*Below*) Desmond Wilcox, Esther Rantzen and daughter in an idyllic domestic scene of the kind that infuriated some of their colleagues and fuelled moves to oust Wilcox in 1980 (*BBC*).

Michael Grade, brought in to rescue BBC1 in 1984 (*BBC*). (*Below*) EastEnders, the soap opera that got the BBC back to the top of the ratings. It was initiated before Grade's arrival but his clever scheduling ensured it maximum audiences (*BBC*).

How much of the BBC's output would you describe as laughable?

We British, renowned the world over for our sense of humour, don't actually have one.

We have dozens.

What may be a rollicking rib-tickler to one will leave another stony-faced.

For every man or woman who enjoys a good belly laugh, there is another whose delight is a mischievous snigger, and another who is content with a wry smile.

So when it comes to producing comedy for 50 million viewers, we can't hope to please all the people all the time.

And we don't try.

We endeavour, instead, to please all the people at different times.

Let your eye roam the page and you'll see what we mean.

It shows but a small selection of our comedy offerings in both past and future months. But it does demonstrate the breadth of tastes we cover.

From Alf Garnett, the world's biggest bigot, to Les Dawson, one of the country's biggest comics. (That's what his tailor told us anyway.) Some you probably love. Some you possibly loathe.

If the antics of the Yellowcoats at Maplins leave you cold, you may well crease up with Messrs. Smith and Jones.

If the Black Adder isn't to your taste, then Del boy in Only Fools and Horses may be just your cup of Rosie Lee.

And as for the Krankies and Kenny Everett, well, they clearly divide the nation into two opposing comedy factions.

We suspect, however, that there is less argument when it comes to Open All Hours.

For 6 weeks it has been the most popular programme on the television screens of Britain.

But so what?

You might well consider it puny when compared with the waspish ditties of Ms. Victoria Wood.

That, sir or madam, is your prerogative.

All we can do is employ the talents of Britain's best writers and performers to bring you the broadest possible spectrum of comedy.

The plain fact is, making people laugh is a funny old business.

But it's one that we at the BBC take very seriously indeed.

The BBC

The finest broadcasting service in the world.

(*Top left*) Douglas Hurd criticized the mini-series The Thorn Birds and later became Home Secretary responsible for the BBC (*Camera Press*); (*Top right*) publicity still from The Thorn Birds (*BBC*): (*Bottom left*) Professor Peacock, who headed the committee looking into alternative ways of financing the BBC; and Alastair Hetherington (*Bottom right*), member of the Peacock committee and former BBC controller in Scotland (*both Universal Pictorial Press*).

(*Top left*) Stuart Young, Mrs Thatcher's choice as chairman, did not behave in quite the radical way she expected (*BBC*); (*Top right*) Leon Brittan, Douglas Hurd's predecessor as Home Secretary, urged the BBC not to show the Real Lives programme including an interview with an alleged IRA leader (*City Syndication*); and (*Below*) the governors who initially complied with the request, posing in the lobby of Broadcasting House (*BBC*).

The Real Lives crisis. (*Top*) Alasdair Milne assures journalists waiting outside Broadcasting House: "I'm in charge." (*Stefano Gagnoni*). (*Below*) BBC journalists picket Television Centre in August 1985, during the one-day strike in protest at the temporary ban on the programme (*Stefano Gagnoni*).

ratings up virtually overnight by going down market, but you just would not do that.'

Whatever remedy he had in mind, by the time he took up his post the BBC was in still greater need of it. For, during the three months it took him to move from Los Angeles, the critics' sniping, the first shots in the licence fee war, was beginning to build into a persistent barrage.

Chapter 6

TOMORROW'S WORLD

BEING PROVED right is seldom a defence against being made a scapegoat. It was ironic that Aubrey Singer should have been elbowed out of the Beeb just as events were confirming his prognostications about the less than wonderful new world of satellite TV. By 1984 it was apparent that the BBC's long-term problem was not going to be solved by magic beams pulsating from a chunk of electronic wizardry in the sky. And it began to look as though those many hours of bewildering technical discussions at board meetings, ploughing through voluminous documents, had been wasted.

In the past, technical innovation had proved the saviour of the BBC, assuring it of a regularly growing revenue base without the need to go cap-in-hand to the government every few years. Throughout the 1950s, as television ownership grew, revenue from TV licences increased faster than inflation. When most people owned a set and saturation loomed, along came colour television to begin a new cycle. More and more viewers were prepared to pay the higher licence fee to enjoy colour pictures. But by the end of the 1970s that area of growth, too, had slowed, until the annual increase in BBC revenue nowhere near kept up with galloping costs. The result was bitter rows every three years, as the BBC put in claims for fees that the government felt were excessive.

The search began for a fresh technological advance that

viewers would pay extra for without complaining. The most recent development, the video recorder, provided no revenue for the BBC and merely increased the competition for audiences, giving viewers the chance to use their screens to watch films and programmes that were not being broadcast at that moment – time-shifting, in the jargon of the trade. The government were keen to develop cable TV systems in areas of high population, using co-axial or fibre-optic cables that could carry more than thirty channels. Some cities already had a primitive version of cable TV, based on wiring that had originally been laid for radio transmission between the wars. Extending the system and making it more sophisticated would mean diluting the BBC's potential audience without offering any obvious scope for raising revenue unless the corporation decided to run its own cable operation. Howard and the governors decided against that option early on, arguing that by definition cable served communities even more restricted than local radio – a field that the Beeb had already been criticised for entering by those who thought it should concentrate on maintaining its national profile rather than reaching down for segmented audiences.

It seemed in the second half of the 1970s that satellites would be the answer to the corporation's prayer. In a fixed orbit in space, 22,300 miles above the equator, geostationary satellites move at the same rate as the earth spins, and thus their position in relation to the earth remains constant. They will pick up TV signals and bounce them back so that they can be received over a wide area by anyone with the necessary saucer-shaped aerial, or dish. They had been hovering on the horizon (figuratively, at least to begin with) since the Russians first sent one up in 1957. In the 1960s television companies began to use them to send pictures from far-flung parts of their operation to their headquarters, whence they were relayed to viewers by conventional means. The use of satellites led to enormous improvements in the speed and quality of transmission of news reports and live sports coverage from overseas. Until their introduction, rolls of news film generally had to be carried physically from all over the world to the TV company's headquarters.

In the 1970s, satellites began to be used for feeding material into America's developing cable TV systems. The local cable operator would equip himself with a dish up to 20 feet in diameter. In it he would pick up signals from stations such as the subscription movie channels and Ted Turner's Atlanta-based Cable News Network. These were bounced from what have come to be known as low-powered satellites, to distinguish them from the newer high-powered versions. Their use has now spread to cable systems in Europe. So long as the dish needed to receive the low-power signals remained large and expensive, there was no prospect of using satellites to transmit programmes economically to individual sets, except in large hotels or blocks of flats – and that was illegal in Britain until 1985.

The high-powered satellite needs less elaborate ground equipment. Technicians are confident that in the near future signals could be received from it on smaller dishes, not much bigger than a gramophone record, which could be fitted inconspicuously on roofs – or even indoors – for only a few hundred pounds. The Direct Broadcast Satellite (DBS) would have a far wider range than the low-powered models, covering the whole of Britain and much of Western Europe. A third variation is the mid-powered satellite, which can be used for direct broadcasting with reasonably compact dishes, though over a narrower geographical area. Its advantage over the high-powered version is that the initial investment is significantly lower.

In 1977 the World Administrative Radio Conference assigned DBS channels to the nations. Britain, like the other European countries, was allotted five. In 1981 Kenneth Baker, the enthusiastic minister responsible for information technology, invited applications for the first two of the permitted channels and encouraged the BBC to make a bid. The government's motive was not solely to increase the range of in-home entertainment offered to the populace: the satellites could be used for sophisticated military communications, too. His notion was that the technology could be developed cheaply, on the back of broadcasting. But not everyone in Whitehall was as convinced as Baker that the BBC should get involved. William Whitelaw, who as Home Secretary had ministerial responsibility for broadcasting, privately urged caution on his friend George

Howard, the chairman; as he had on the matter of breakfast TV. He was unsure whether either would turn out for the best,

Howard and Ian Trethowan, the director-general, were both excited by the prospect and determined that the BBC should get a large slice of the new opportunities available. Here at last was the next generation of television that could solve the BBC's cash problems as the introduction of colour had temporarily done. It would have to be financed differently, though. Unlike colour, this was not an innovation that would dramatically and obviously alter the nature of the service offered and thus justify a new scale of licence fee. As far as the viewer was concerned, programmes beamed from the sky would look exactly the same as those delivered by the conventional means. There was one technical improvement in the offing that could only be introduced on a large scale from satellites – high-definition television, a wide-screen picture made up of 1,125 horizontal lines instead of the present 625. But that was some way in the future and it was open to question whether the difference in quality would be sufficient to persuade people to invest in expensive new viewing equipment to receive it.

At least until these high-definition pictures became available, satellite operators would have to rely on distinctive programming to persuade viewers to subscribe to their service. In the United States, cable companies were finding that people would pay a modest subscription to a channel whose schedule was based on first-run feature films, although the demand had not been as great as some of the more optimistic pioneers had hoped. Still, the BBC management were convinced that, with their unrivalled programming experience, they could come up with a package attractive enough to lure sufficient subscribers to cover the cost and earn a surplus that could help fund the terrestrial services as well.

The initial calculations, based on a subscription of some £20 a month, were extremely encouraging. Although the cost of renting the satellite would be steep, the forecast was for a profit of £50m-£60m a year by 1988. Trethowan thought there would need to be just one more licence fee increase in 1984 before the BBC could freeze the fee and absorb inflation through the growing revenue from the satellite, perhaps supplemented later by a premium licence fee for high definition TV. David Webster, the high-powered director of public affairs on the board of management, was packed off to New York as the corporation's first overseas-based director, with the assignment of looking into how subscription TV worked in the United States, as well as keeping an eye on satellite developments. Howard was intrigued by the technological aspects and digested all the fat reports from Webster and the engineering people, enabling him to discuss DBS with impressive authority at board meetings. Since few of the governors had the time to read so widely, they mostly deferred to his bullish judgement of the prospects.

The lure of big profits was not the only consideration. Perhaps still more significant in the long term was the 'what happens if we don't' argument. Since its creation, the BBC's priority has been to preserve itself and sustain its *raison d'etre* as the central pillar of British popular culture. It seeks to do this not solely to legitimise its claim to licence revenue, but because it feels it to be its proper role. In the 1950s the Beeb fought ferociously against the introduction of commercial television, rightly calculating that it threatened a serious erosion of the BBC's position. It lost the battle but after a few rocky years recovered its composure and, under Hugh Greene, became a vigorous limb of the duopoly of public broadcasting, continuing to set standards of excellence, even if it was generally the minority channel in terms of audiences. While it ran two channels against ITV's one, it was able to dominate the medium, at least in a cultural sense. The arrival of Channel 4, scheduled for 1982, would alter the balance marginally but, viewed from the perspective of 1981, there were no grounds for believing it would undermine the BBC fatally.

Satellite and cable television were threats on a much larger scale. In some American cities viewers are offered a choice of thirty and more cable channels. It is true that they are not all competing equally. Some broadcast in minority languages and others are devoted to community access, drawing insignificant audiences in relation to the total. It is also true that the three major American networks, broadcasting conventionally on airwaves, continue to share the great majority of the national audience among themselves. But they do it by ruthlessly devoting almost the whole of prime time (7.30 to 10 p.m.) to popular, undemanding programmes, chiefly comedy and crime series. Since the networks have immeasurably greater resources than the small cable operators, they can afford the best popular programming and are therefore practically invulnerable to attack from cable stations plumbing the lower depths of public taste.

All the same, canny tycoons such as Rupert Murdoch were investing enthusiastically in satellite operations both in the United States and in Europe. If they could identify limited audiences prepared to pay an economic rate for the fare they offered, they did not necessarily need to compete viewer for viewer with the mass networks. In 1983 Murdoch bought Sky Channel, a British company beaming films and old TV series to cable systems across Europe. In the United States in the same year he launched Skyband, a satellite-to-home service that, according to his company's annual report for that year, he hoped would be operating within months. As it turned out he had been over-optimistic and was forced to postpone the enterprise indefinitely, taking a loss of some £20m. But it was clear that the setback was only temporary. Murdoch or someone else would be broadcasting by satellite direct to individual homes before many years had passed.

If the BBC found itself competing with a couple of dozen cable and satellite channels as well as with ITV, it would have to choose between two equally distasteful courses of action. Either it could hold on to its audience share by copying the American networks and excluding in prime time any programmes with pretensions to a serious purpose; or it could decline to enter the competition and, continuing with the present mix of programmes, content itself with a greatly reduced percentage of the available viewers. Either way it would forfeit much of its influence and weaken its case for maintaining its privileged status as the sole beneficiary of the licence fee. If it took the popular route there would be renewed and possibly irresistible pressure for it to accept advertising. Yet if, by determinedly keeping to the Reithian high road, it reached, say, fewer than a quarter of viewers, it would be difficult to argue that the entire population should continue to pay for it.

As the pros and cons were thrashed out at board meetings, the governors became convinced that there was only one way of avoiding that Hobson's choice: the BBC would have to run at least as significant a segment of satellite television as it did here on earth, enough to dictate the terms of competition. Howard saw it as an extension of the corporation's responsibilities under its charter. 'It is surely not surprising', he wrote to *The Times*, 'that the BBC should seek to be in the forefront in developing new services to the public.' Governors and management decided to make a bid for both the available channels, on the assumption that by doing so they would be certain of getting one. To his management colleagues who expressed reservations about whether the BBC could cope with both, Trethowan winked and said it would be politically impossible for a government devoted to free enterprise to give them a monopoly. The independent companies, or some other private consortium, would certainly be awarded a share in the satellite.

So no doubt they would, had they put in a bid. But speculating with your own rather than with public money is a powerful deterrent to making rash commitments. The independents did their sums and failed to come up with such favourable forecasts as the BBC had produced. The most powerful argument against the project came from Colin Shaw, the former BBC secretary, then director of television at the Independent Broadcasting Authority. Like Aubrey Singer, he wondered what people were going to pay £20 a month for. Films? A substantial segment of the potential audience had videos, and could hire first-run movies for £1. Shaw felt that neither the BBC nor the IBA were equipped to deal with satellites. He advocated the establishment of a separate cable and satellite authority, with the role of the BBC and the independent companies confined to supplying programmes. He persuaded his colleagues at the IBA to stay well out of it: so in March 1982 the BBC, as the only serious bidder, was awarded both DBS channels.

If the reluctance of anyone else to get involved gave Howard and Trethowan pause, this was not reflected in the vigour with which they promoted the new project. Their 1983 annual report sported a dramatic colour picture of a DBS satellite on the cover and some confident prose inside. In 1981 the corporation's charter had been extended until 1996 and revised so as to give it the right to take part fully in the development of satellite technology. The report spoke of the 'tonic effect' of the revision and added: 'We were encouraged when we were given permission to provide two DBS services, which we hope to have on air in 1986.' It noted the plan for the satellite to be provided by United Satellites (Unisat), a consortium of British Telecom, British Aerospace and GEC-Marconi. One of the DBS services would be a subscription channel while the other would be known as Window on the World: there was no amplification of that cryptic sobriquet. The report suggested that the cost of the dish aerial, with the converter needed to enable existing sets to receive satellite transmissions, would be around £250. There were even detailed instructions on siting the dish:

> Suitable locations can be ascertained by observing the position of the sun at 3 p.m. British Summer Time in mid-October (when it will be in the same position in the sky as the satellite); it will be possible to receive the signals at any position which is not in shadow at this time, although obviously aesthetic and practical considerations will be taken into account. . . Since this type of aerial will be heavier than a conventional multi-element television aerial and will be subject to greater wind forces, caution must be exercised when fixing at any height, such as to a chimney stack.

Those warning cautions served to give solidity to a project that still, to the general public and even to some professionals, appeared insubstantial, a castle in the air rather than a piece of sophisticated hardware in the sky. The following year's report was just as optimistic, reporting the formal creation of the DBS directorate on 1 January 1983. Christopher Irwin, head of Radio Scotland, was made general manager of the satellite project and Gunnar Rugheimer, an affable Swede who for years had been in charge of television programme acquisition, was made controller of DBS acquisition and programming. There were to be two satellites launched in 1986, possibly on the space shuttle. One would be the operative one and the second a spare. A third would be kept on the ground as a reserve. There were more details about the two channels: the subscription one would be based on feature films, while the second would 'offer a more general service'.

Not long after the directorate had been established, the

euphoric mood evaporated. Although the IBA had by now been persuaded to take an option on the third and fourth DBS channels, the BBC's own financial projections began to look ever more alarming. This was chiefly because the cost of the satellite was soaring even at the very earliest stage of its development. The government, keen to use the project to boost British technology, were insisting that the contract with the United Satellites consortium should be honoured, even though cheaper and equally effective satellites were being developed in the United States. From New York, David Webster was bombarding the governors with opaque technical reports. He was now recommending that the BBC should consider using a lower-powered satellite. It would not have such a wide range and would need more expensive equipment to receive the signal, but the capital cost would be much lower. Forbidden by legislation to use any part of the licence fee to fund satellite developments (not that there was any to spare), the BBC was faced with having to borrow heavily to fund the project, saddling itself with steep interest payments.

Stuart Young, who succeeded George Howard as chairman in August 1983, is an accountant, and was badly shaken when he looked at the financial prospects for DBS. Chairing his first meeting on 4 August, he was given new projections showing that, far from making tens of millions of pounds in profits by 1988, the project would not break even until 1993 at the earliest. In talks with the Home Secretary, Leon Brittan, Young failed to get him to budge over who should provide the satellite, and was told there was no chance of the present Cabinet, bent on cutting government expenditure, agreeing to chip in with any contribution towards the cost. His stubbornness on those two points fuelled the suspicion that the government were trying to develop British satellite technology at someone else's (the BBC's) expense. 'There are many calls on the taxpayer and there are many things that we should be doing,' Brittan explained in a television interview. 'I don't think this (DBS) is one of them.'

As a last resort, Young and the governors decided to see whether they could share the initial development cost with the IBA and other interested parties. It was a bitter pill for the board of management to swallow. They had always taken their rivalry with the commercial channel very seriously indeed, partly out of genuine conviction of the BBC's superior standards and integrity as a broadcasting organisation, and partly because emphasising competition is a well-tried device for raising staff morale. To have to bed down with the opposition – worse, to seem to be pleading with them to snuggle close beneath the sheets – was embarrassing and humiliating. But it was better than the alternative of pulling out of celestial television altogether.

On 7 August 1984, Alasdair Milne took the chair at an unusual meeting at Broadcasting House. He had invited representatives of the fifteen ITV companies and five other firms not connected with television production. The aim was to form a consortium to get the satellite launched and beaming. The BBC would continue to be the largest stakeholder, providing half the investment. The ITV companies would stump up 30 per cent between them, with the remaining 20 per cent divided between the five 'third force' companies, the largest slice of that going to the electrical and entertainment conglomerate Thorn-EMI. As bait for the commercial TV companies, they were offered the prospect of their regional franchises being extended beyond the normal period if they agreed to join in.

The meeting ended with agreement in principle on the formation of what came to be known as the '21 Club'. As a result of that agreement the Home Secretary appointed a Satellite Broadcasting Board to regulate the venture. It included three governors of the BBC and three members of the Independent Broadcasting Authority. Chairmanship of the new body would alternate between the chairmen of the BBC and the IBA. In announcing the new arrangement, there was no trace of the bullish confidence that had accompanied the launching of the original DBS scheme less than three years earlier.

There remained serious doubts whether it could ever be operated economically, especially since the government, while continuing to refuse to put any start-up money into the project, still insisted that the costly Unisat satellite had to be the vehicle for transmission. Although Unisat had now scaled down their original plan to make three identical satellites and would settle for two, the price had risen to £463m. A rival consortium, Britsat, had come up with an estimate of only £338m, but the government were opposed to it because it employed American technology. The new partners were also worried that their licence was for only for ten years: by the time it expired they might only just be starting to make a profit.

The BBC's annual report for 1985 reflected this more subdued mood. Although it had gone to press before the Club of 21 had formally been created, the report mentioned that preliminary discussions were under way to make the DBS services a joint venture. 'Whether operated by the BBC or independent companies they will be run on a commercial basis.' The 1986 start date had slipped to '1987 or 1988'. And the report delivered this sober warning:

> During the first few years of DBS – the period during which relatively few people will have the equipment to receive its services – it is highly vulnerable. The sums of money involved are very large. Not only is there the cost of the satellite system itself: even more expensive is the cost of programming and of suitable receiving equipment. In the course of investigating and planning the development of DBS for the United Kingdom the BBC has been primarily concerned to identify these basic costs and to establish what price the market will bear. . . If the UK is to pioneer this important new distribution technology it must be sure that the market is developed in a sensible and orderly way, in order to contain the risks involved within realistic bounds.

Writing in the *Listener* in October 1984, Sir Ian Trethowan revived David Webster's notion of using a cheaper, lower-powered satellite, at least to begin with. Since leaving the BBC in 1982, Trethowan had been working part time as an adviser to Thorn-EMI, a member of the 21 Club. He argued that it was important to begin satellite transmission quickly, otherwise the British DBS would be pre-empted by other services that would be starting well before the end of the decade. Although these services would not be aimed specifically at Britain, they could certainly be picked up here. If the 21 Club rented space on an existing low-powered satellite and beamed its programmes chiefly to cable systems, it could begin earning revenue in a year or two and use it to help finance the high-powered DBS later.

The cause of lower-powered satellites was boosted in May 1985, when the government eased the laws restricting reception from them. It had previously been illegal to tune into any of the programmes emanating from the three foreign satellites that included Britain in their reception area. The new rules abolished that restriction on SMATV (satellite master antenna TV), meaning that anyone willing to spend around £2,000 on a dish aerial and a new receiver could watch what they liked. While uneconomic for most homes, such an investment would be feasible for institutions, hotels and apartment buildings and would provide damaging competition for the proposed DBS. The cost of renting a channel on a low-powered satellite was less than £2m a year, compared with some £60m a year for DBS.

Meanwhile scepticism grew about whether the programmes offered by the satellite channels (whether high-powered or low) could be attractive enough to persuade people to pay £20 a month for them. David Plowright, managing director of the commercial TV company Granada, said:

> I think people talk a little glibly about the attraction of movies. Most people in the feature film industry know they're lucky if they get 12 box-office successes a year. The appetite of an all-movie channel on DBS or anywhere else is a lot greater than that, probably for up to 150 films a year. So the chances are you'd get a lot of very bad films. . . We may start with a movie channel but I would see the likelihood of the 1990 equivalent of Dallas being up there with the movies as well. Beyond that, it will be a box office of the skies. . . It could be a star wars battle of circulation implications rather than ballistic missiles and, in those circumstances, I don't hold out much hope for the quality of the programmes.

Surrounded by such publicly stated doubts about the viability and desirability of high-powered satellite TV, small wonder that the 21 Club was short-lived. The Satellite Broadcasting Board had commissioned two reports on its prospects and both made gloomy reading. The estimated capital cost of Unisat had now risen to some £600m. If it went ahead, the new service would need 3 million subscribers before it could begin to make a profit – about double the break-even figure for the cheaper Britsat scheme. Using the Unisat hardware, it was unlikely that the consortium could make any money at all during its ten-year licence term. As much as £300m could be lost in the first four years. In June 1985, the decision was formally made to abandon the British satellite project, at least in that form. Both the 21 Club and the Satellite Broadcasting Board were disbanded. It did not mean the end of DBS or the BBC's involvement in it, but with the government still insisting on the uneconomic Unisat there was no realistic alternative to abandoning that particular project, while keeping an open mind about fresh initiatives into financially feasible space technology. One idea was that the BBC and the independent companies should join forces to lease one of the two proposed English-language channels on the French DBS, due to begin broadcasting in 1986. Most of Britain would be in its reception area. The Irish government, too, were planning a satellite that would cover parts of the eastern United States as well as Europe. And now Unisat was dead, a way might be found to breathe life into the cheaper Britsat.

All these were possibilities, but they were some way from the grandiose plans of just three years earlier, by which the BBC, with its two celestial channels operating by 1986, would have achieved a dominant position before the independent companies had been able to start competing. The 21 Club had set a precedent. Any future involvement by the BBC in these new areas of broadcasting was likely to be as part of a consortium of commercial companies. It would not be playing the central role envisaged by George Howard (who died at the end of 1984, a few months before the total collapse of the project he had been instrumental in initiating).

The BBC had lost face. Where Howard had seen the project as a means of shaking the dust off the corporate image and striding towards a shiny high-tech future, the reverse had been achieved. The dithering uncertainty, the setting of deadlines and then pushing them back, had reinforced the very reputation he was trying to live down, that of an incompetent institution steeped in the past but pretending unconvincingly that it was pioneering the future. Rather than sustaining the Beeb's position as the lynchpin of British popular culture, the satellite venture now seemed likely to hasten its descent into being just one of a clamour of voices competing for attention. In the nineteenth

century, when rival medicine men would clash in the emerging
settlements of the American West, victory would invariably go to
the salesman with the liveliest patter and the most robust larynx,
not the one peddling the best medicine.

Howard knew that as well as anyone. Part of the reason for his
desire for a major BBC role in DBS was his fear of cable
television. Both systems had the power to increase greatly the
number of options open to viewers. If the BBC were not to be
allowed a major voice in cable, it was important to stake a claim
in the alternative new system of home delivery of programmes.
In 1982 he said:

> If there is unregulated cable and pay-per-view, public service
> broadcasting would have its financial base eroded. ITV's
> advertising difficulties would increase and people who were
> getting their entertainment on cable would be likely to say: 'Why
> pay the licence fee?' . . . From our point of view, unregulated
> cable and pay-per-view would make life very difficult, not
> immediately but in the nineties.

In the three years since Howard's warning, the 'cable revolution'
beneath the ground had been proceeding as slowly as the DBS
project in the skies. It had begun with just as much hope and
fanfare in 1982, when the Hunt Report had provided a blueprint
for a Britain wired up with high-technology 'interactive' cable
that allows two-way communication. It would carry not just
television programmes but services such as home shopping and
banking and possibly a visual telephone. The hope was that 4
million homes would be wired up by 1990. The Department of
Information Technology, headed by the optimistic Kenneth
Baker, sought applications for franchises and by August 1983
had received thirty-seven, mostly from consortiums of local
people combined with big names in the electronics industry, such
as Thorn-EMI, Rediffusion and British Telecom. In November,
Baker allocated the first eleven licences, some of them in parts of
cities where there was already an old-fashioned cable system,
others in areas so far untouched.

The government insisted that the cables must be of the most
up-to-date kind and buried underground. The old-fashioned
cables had, for the most part, been strung from house to house
like early telephone wires: sometimes unsightly but much less

expensive than having to dig up miles of road. But as with DBS the government, although insisting on the highest technical standards, doggedly refused to put any public money into the project. Wanting the services to be strictly local, Baker placed a limit of 100,000 on the number of homes served by any single cable operator. The contracts were limited to twelve years – not long considering that some believed it could take up to nine years to start making a profit. But the worst blow to the nascent industry came in March of 1984, when the Chancellor of the Exchequer, Nigel Lawson, abolished capital allowances in his budget. This meant that the cable operators, obliged by the terms of their licence to invest in an expensive infrastructure, could no longer write it off for income tax purposes. This greatly extended the time they could expect to wait before receiving any return on their investment,

For these reasons, the first eleven licence-holders were inordinately slow in getting their new cables installed. By May of 1985, eighteen months after the award of the franchises, only two of the eleven projected systems were operating, in Swindon and Aberdeen. Although in July 1984 the licence period was increased from twelve years to fifteen, a number of the franchise-holders were having second thoughts. In October Rediffusion, the largest owners of existing low-tech relay systems and the successful bidder for the Guildford contract, sold out its entire cable interest to the newspaper publisher Robert Maxwell. The optimistic initial forecast of 4 million cable homes by 1990 had to be halved. When the second batch of licences came to be awarded, most of the large national companies had dropped out of the bidding, leaving the field to local business people.

By the summer of 1985 only 140,000 British homes were wired for cable, and nearly all of those were on the old low-tech systems. In Swindon, the first of the high-tech areas, the results were disappointing. The total of subscribers was still in three figures, representing less than an eighth of the number of houses within range. And there was an unhealthy rate of 'churn' – viewers not renewing subscriptions when their initial contracts expired. At that stage, then, George Howard's fears about competition from cable looked a long way from nearing reality. But that did not mean that the BBC could relax and get on with making its programmes. For the greatest threat now to its survival lay in the same Government philosophy that had persuaded ministers to stand firm against subsidising developments in satellite and cable. Not only would there be no *new* Whitehall money for the broadcasting industry but the Conservatives were looking questioningly at the traditional means of funding the existing service, the licence fee. If 1985 was a sobering year for the apostles of the new technology, it was to be an utterly deplorable one for the defenders of the old faith at Portland Place.

Chapter 7

POINTS OF VIEW

EVER since the BBC was created, politicians have sought to exercise more influence over it than the management and governors have been prepared to concede. Lord Reith set the tone during the 1926 General Strike, when he refused to give Winston Churchill the freedom of the airwaves. During the Second World War the BBC naturally had to submit to Whitehall's emergency powers but eleven years later, during the Suez crisis, it insisted, against the government's strongly expressed wishes, on allowing air time on both the home and overseas services to people who represented the significant domestic opposition to the landing of British troops. Coverage of politicians themselves has always been one of the most tendentious areas, for obvious reasons. Of the numerous disputes over allegations of bias against individual public figures or their parties, one stands out, and is worth examining because it has similarities to what happened over Real Lives in the summer of 1985.

The row over Yesterday's Men has become more than a *cause celebre*. Until Real Lives it was regarded as a benchmark providing object lessons and precedents for the conduct of relations between the BBC and the political parties, as well as between the BBC's governors and management. The Annan Committee on Broadcasting blamed the 1971 furore for what they saw as the 'palsy' and 'feebleness' afflicting the BBC's current affairs output in the mid-1970s. 'At all levels in the BBC,' their report observed, 'the row over this unfortunate episode was blamed for the caution, lack of direction, touchiness and unsteadiness in the current affairs output.' Following the unexpected Labour defeat in the 1970 election David Dimbleby, who had succeeded his late father Richard as one of the BBC's weightiest political commentators, had an idea for a programme examining what it felt like to be ousted suddenly from office. He wanted to find out from former members of the government whether they suffered withdrawal symptoms, what activities they were pursuing to fill their newly loosened schedules and to make up the shortfall in their income.

He put the plan to John Grist, the peppery head of the television current affairs group, who was not at all keen. He had no political objections: he merely thought it sounded boring. But Dimbleby was persuasive so Grist assigned him a producer – Angela Pope – and gave him the go-ahead to find out whether senior Labour politicians would co-operate. The response was tepid. None of the ex-ministers refused outright to take part but they were so wary as to make Dimbleby doubt whether they would talk frankly enough to make the programme interesting. He went back to Grist and suggested scrapping the idea – but now it was Grist who was keen to see it completed. He made the point that once Labour politicians were aware the programme was being mooted, they would interpret its abandonment as a politically motivated scheme to deny them publicity. He knew from long and sometimes bitter experience that politicians can detect conspiracy in almost anything, especially if it is connected with broadcasting and their public image. So he urged Dimbleby to go ahead with the programme.

Later Grist was to look back ruefully at that decision, for his prospects of rising to the top of the BBC hierarchy were destroyed by the eventual row over Yesterday's Men. He knew more than most about quarrels with politicians, for he had clashed with all the main parties during the thirteen years – from 1957 to 1970 – when he was responsible for the BBC's coverage of the party conferences. It is a thankless job. Politicians look on their annual conferences as celebrations of themselves and their triumphs, and resent critical reporting that suggests less unanimity than is contrived on the platform. Grist's disputes with Labour leaders had tended to be especially bitter. Two stood out. At the 1962 conference, interviewer Kenneth Harris accused George Brown, then deputy leader to Hugh Gaitskell, of leaking to the press details of party discussions on joining the European Community. Grist would not apologise and when Gaitskell retaliated by refusing to be interviewed by the BBC Grist threatened to announce the fact on the programme. The next day, to Grist's annoyance, the BBC apologised formally.

A few years later Harold Wilson, then Prime Minister, was incensed because Grist, during a party conference, arranged for Robin Day to interview Clive Jenkins, the left-wing union leader who opposed the party line on entry into Europe. Marcia Williams, Wilson's secretary, summoned Grist to the Prime Minister's hotel room very late one night. Grist, always firm in his conviction that the BBC should be sturdy in resisting pressure from the political parties, took an uncompromising line. 'If you want to change the relationship between the BBC and the government,' he declared pompously, 'no doubt you will introduce legislation to do so.' Wilson told him not to be silly and the matter blew over.

Wilson quarrelled frequently with the BBC about what he saw as anti-Labour bias. Peeved about coverage of the 1966 election, he refused to give a BBC reporter an interview in the train to London from his constituency at Huyton. This history of antagonism was running through Grist's mind as he persuaded Dimbleby that, in spite of his reservations, Yesterday's Men should go ahead. Indeed, Grist began to worry not about Labour but about Conservative reaction. If fifty minutes were to be devoted to a programme about the opposition, would the government not demand equal time? So he initiated what turned out to be an anodyne survey of Edward Heath's first year in office, to be screened on the following night. The difference in tone between this and the caustic Yesterday's Men only added rancour to the subsequent controversy.

Dimbleby and Pope began recording the interviews in the spring. One important fact they purposely withheld from the politicians was the title of the programme. They judged – and they were right – that it would suggest a flippant approach, provoking some of the subjects to reconsider their decision to take part. When the name was finally revealed it compounded the ex-ministers' anger over the affair, not just because it was personally insulting but because it ironically echoed the theme of Labour advertising in the 1970 campaign, where the phrase 'Yesterday's Men' had been applied to the Conservatives. (Huw Wheldon said later that it was akin to making a programme about doctors and calling it 'Quack Quack'.) To make matters worse, the background music was an irreverent song specially commissioned from The Scaffold, a Liverpool pop group. The victims were not told about that, either.

Dimbleby interviewed Wilson late one May afternoon in his room at the House of Commons. The ex-Prime Minister had been keen to co-operate, even agreeing to be filmed reading an appropriate lesson at his local church in the Scilly Isles: 'To everything there is a season and a time . . . a time to live and a time to die.' The interview began well enough with general discussion around the programme's theme. Then Dimbleby asked what he claims was an innocent question about Wilson's book of memoirs. He referred to reports that the opposition leader had been paid between £100,000 and £250,000 for the work by the *Sunday Times* and asked him, he thought genially, whether the money had been 'a consolation to you over the year' since the election.

It was soon clear that he had touched a raw nerve.

'I would not believe any of the stories you read in the press about that,' Wilson answered. 'My press handling over a long period of time has been one of rumour. If they got the facts they twisted them – anything personal. If they did not get the facts they invented them. So we can dismiss that from the case right away. I got a fair, I think a fair compensation for what I wrote.' Dimbleby, undaunted, pressed ahead and asked him to confirm the exact payment.

'Why do you come snooping with these questions?' Wilson snapped, and inquired whether Edward Heath, the Conservative Prime Minister, had been quizzed similarly about the source of funding for his ocean yacht. Then he added angrily: 'This last question and answer are not to be recorded. . . If this film is used or if this is leaked there will be a hell of a row.' Joe Haines,

Wilson's press officer, reinforced the threat with a warning to Pope that her professional future could be harmed if word of Wilson's outburst reached the outside world, or if any part of it appeared on the screen.

There *was* a hell of a row but it took time to come to a head. The day after the interview Haines rang John Crawley, just promoted from editor of news and current affairs to a new post as chief assistant to the director-general, responsible for exercising his editorial functions. Crawley gave what Haines took to be an unequivocal promise that the offending segment would be excised from the programme before it was screened.

When Dimbleby learned of Crawley's undertaking he was furious. Like many broadcasters – indeed like Grist – he was of the decided opinion that responsible journalists should not be swayed by political pressure. He and Crawley exchanged intemperate memoranda, the favoured means of communication at the Beeb. Dimbleby suggested that Wilson's pressure was akin to blackmail and that Crawley had caved in too readily, possibly damaging Dimbleby's reputation and career as a result. Crawley replied that he thought the questions were misjudged and should be excised. Moreover he found Dimbleby's memo offensive, as he presumed it was designed to be. He decreed that the tape should be cut at the point Wilson had suggested.

Such bickering between on-screen personalities and backroom officials is not uncommon at Television Centre. Producers and administrators regard Dimbleby and his like as 'talking heads' who know less than the true pros about what really makes good programmes and who, in an ideal world, would simply do as they were told. The on-screen stars are aware of this attitude and naturally resent it. It encourages them to assert themselves on what they see as points of professional principle.

Yet the internal squabble was as nothing compared with the conflict between the BBC and the Labour Party, which had by now broadened to embrace the programme as a whole and not just the Wilson episode. It brought to the surface the latent feeling among politicians of both parties that broadcasters lacked a proper respect for their calling. Here was the BBC, which had never won an election in its life, arrogating to itself the right to make snide insinuations against the nation's properly elected legislators, in the guise of a serious current affairs programme.

The dispute came to a head on the evening of 16 June 1971 – the day before the programme was to be broadcast. A year after the general election, Harold Wilson was giving a party in his Commons room for the BBC's technical people who had assisted in making Labour's election broadcasts. Sir Charles Curran, the director-general, was there, and soon became involved in a noisy argument with Wilson. Other guests formed a circle round them, listening with fascination. Wilson was seeking cancellation of the programme, on the grounds that he had never signed a contract to appear on it. (BBC lawyers were of the opinion that this gave him less rather than greater power in the matter.) Failing that he wanted a change in its title, then the elimination of the one remaining question relating to the money for his book and of photographs of his three houses, included to suggest that he was a man of some wealth. There was talk of libel writs, lawyers and injunctions.

Curran made no commitment to Wilson before hurrying off to Television Centre in Shepherd's Bush, where he, with the chairman Lord Hill and Huw Wheldon, managing director of television, were due to host a dinner for some visiting Americans. It was far from being a relaxed meal. Wilson's staff had been inciting the other politicians on the programme to protest. Although none of their interviews had contained an incident as blatant as the question to Wilson on money, it did not take much to persuade his colleagues that their precious dignity too was at risk. Anthony Crosland, for instance, complained that the BBC had taken a picture of his house with washing hanging on the line outside. He, James Callaghan, Roy Jenkins and Richard Crossman put in calls to Television Centre, as did the formidable Lord Goodman, who often acted as Wilson's legal adviser. Curran had constantly to abandon his knife and fork and go to the phone. Wilson and Goodman would have liked to bring Lord Hill into it, but the chairman decided that at this stage it was a matter for the executive and prudently made himself unavailable.

Before long the evening began to degenerate into low farce. Grist and Desmond Taylor, who had in March succeeded Crawley as editor of news and current affairs, sat at Television Centre waiting to talk to Curran as soon as he could politely abandon his Americans. The result of all the telephoning was an agreement that Curran should go to visit Goodman after dinner at his flat in Portland Place, a few hundred yards from Broadcasting House. It would have helped if Curran could have seen the programme before the meeting, but Angela Pope had taken the only available tape home with her. He did manage, with difficulty, to contact John Crawley, on a Finnish cruise ship at Leningrad, to learn exactly what he had promised Joe Haines in March.

Curran and Wheldon jumped into a BBC car and on the way picked up Paul Fox, controller of BBC1. They sped towards Goodman's flat, until it dawned on them that they did not know his exact address or phone number. Alighting from the car into the cool June night, they used cigarette lighters to check the names by the doorbells of likely looking houses. It was a pathetic little scene. Here were the three most important men in BBC television, the most powerful cultural medium in Britain; yet they were insufficiently worldly to have ensured that they knew the address of this prominent lawyer before setting out to see him. After a while, recognising that their unorthodox scrabbling might attract the attention of the constabulary – especially since they were in the close vicinity of the Chinese embassy – they retired to Broadcasting House and made a plaintive appeal for help to Grist, standing by at his Lime Grove office.

It is not an easy matter to find an ex-directory number or address at any time of day, let alone after midnight. Grist battled in vain with a conscientiously unbending ex-directory supervisor. Finally somebody remembered they had a friend who knew a client of Goodman's in the West Country. He was contacted, divulged the address and the meeting took place in the small hours. Goodman repeated the three demands Wilson had made at the Commons party earlier in the evening. Curran said he would discuss the matter with the chairman and governors, due to meet later that morning at Television Centre.

The 10.30 meeting of governors was preceded at 9.30 by a session of the finance committee, comprising about half the full board. Hill thought it would be a good idea if they saw the programme before their discussion. It was not convenient to wait until the full board had assembled because the tape was needed for a press screening, already delayed from 11 a.m. to noon. So only those governors on the finance committee, and others who arrived early, had a chance to see it before it went out on the air.

It is an article of faith among BBC theologians, reinforced by the Yesterday's Men debacle and much later by Real Lives, that governors should not preview programmes. If they approve them in advance, it is argued, they will be unable objectively to judge complaints from the public afterwards. On the other hand if they were to ban a programme cleared by the director-general, they would be declaring a lack of confidence in their senior executive. This goes to the heart of the contradiction inherent in their dual function as masters in their own corporation and protectors of the public against it.

The keeper of the corporate conscience on these matters is the BBC Secretary. His functions are to compose the minutes of board meetings and act as the chief conduit between the governors and the management. The holder of this pivotal office in 1971 was Colin Shaw, a slight, precise man with the wholly appropriate bearing of a deacon. He warned Hill that by watching the film in advance he would be 'setting a precedent' – one of the most alarming suggestions you can make to an official at the BBC, as in the civil service. Hill, not easily alarmed, said he knew that but would do it anyway. In the agonised internal discussion of the dispute in the ensuing months and years, this abstruse point of procedure took on as much significance for the BBC mandarins as the politicians' actual complaint.

At their subsequent meeting the governors – those who had not been in time for the screening as well as those who had – decided to cut the one question that had remained in the script from the original three about the money from Wilson's book. Otherwise the programme could be screened as it was. Some years later the Annan report commented that when Hill refused to ban the programme, 'politicians may have wondered whether they had appointed an admiral who habitually turned a blind eye when the Admiralty made a signal.'

By now tempers had reached such a heat that there was no chance of the Labour Party allowing the issue to rest there. Haines had attended the press screening and was horrified by what he saw. He said that Dimbleby's and Pope's original stated intention of making a serious programme about the Opposition amounted to 'carefully calculated, deliberate, continuous deceit'. And although the question about the money Wilson earned from his memoirs had been deleted, there remained the suggestion that in writing the book he had exploited his prime ministerial access to official documents.

Lord Goodman was still making threatening sounds. By a coincidence, he was to be a guest that afternoon – Gold Cup day – in the BBC box at Royal Ascot. Huw Wheldon was supposed to be the host but, because of the continuing controversy, he asked Paul Fox, a racing enthusiast, to get dressed up in topper and tails instead. The weather had been kind throughout that year's Ascot meeting – plenty of sun but not uncomfortably hot. Goodman, though, had no time to enjoy the sun and was generating for himself all the heat he needed. Arriving late, he found numerous messages awaiting him. He spent most of the afternoon on the phone, although he managed to break away for long enough to back the Gold Cup winner, the 2-1 favourite Rock Roi, before hurrying back to London early. Someone at the BBC might have paused at that point to reflect that you should never tangle with a lawyer on a winning streak. (Some days later the horse was disqualified following a positive drug test, but successful backers were not required to return their winnings.)

Yesterday's Men was duly aired on 17 June, after a last-minute screening for the BBC's own lawyers. The removal of the questions about Wilson's money infuriated Dimbleby and Pope, who insisted that their names should be deleted from the credits. But one allegation did remain in the linking commentary: 'Only Harold Wilson became richer in opposition by using his privileged access to government records to write his memoirs.'

In the press the next day the lobby correspondents, briefed by Haines, wrote colourful reports about the anger of Wilson and the others who had been interviewed. Dudgeon was high and rising. To make matters worse, somebody at the BBC had leaked the transcript of the bits of the Wilson interview that had been excised. The opinion of the press, always ready to weigh into the BBC, was that the politicians had been treated shabbily. *The Times* published an especially magisterial leading article:

What was disturbing about it was that its attitude towards

politics was utterly trivial, the attitude of the gossip column or the political novelette. . . (It) unfortunately treated politics as though all politicians were motivated purely by a personal appetite for power. . . (There was) no serious discussion of the significance of any political issue. . . The leading Labour politicians were all treated as though the great questions of public affairs played no part in their lives, and were mocked by a pop song to make 'good television'. . . Ambition and money are not the only motivation of human life, surely not even at Television Centre. This view of political affairs is, to put it frankly, the view of immature young people. . . It is much more dangerous to trivialize than ever it is to criticize politicians.

(The author of this editorial, William Rees-Mogg, became vice-chairman of the BBC ten years later and as such played a key role in the Real Lives dispute.)

In the following week's *New Statesman* Richard Crossman, one of the participants, reflected the view of his colleagues when he wrote of 'the deliberate fraud by which the politicians were persuaded to take part and . . . the even greater fraud by which fragments were snipped out of the interviews they gave and juxtaposed in order to convey a false impression of what they had meant and even of what they had actually said.'

The governors met in emergency session the evening after transmission. Had they not seen the programme in advance they could have issued a statement mildly criticising misjudgements, and felt that they had thus disposed of their responsibilities. As it was, Hill thought the only course was to establish an internal inquiry. Not surprisingly, when its report was published in July, the inquiry largely vindicated the programme and its makers, using detailed statistics to prove, at least to the authors' satisfaction, that it had achieved a proper balance in selecting which segments of the interviews to include. This served to revive the Labour Party's hostility. Haines was active in the lobby again, inspiring more press stories about the row. Goodman wrote to Hill demanding a public apology over the suggestion that Wilson had misused privileged documents. The apology was duly made the following month.

People at the BBC agree with the Annan Committee's conclusion that the ferocity of the argument inhibited further experiments in innovatory coverage of politics and politicians. When television began it was the custom to treat politicians with extreme deference, scarcely asking any but the blandest of questions. A broadcast interview was an opportunity for ministers and opposition spokesmen to make statements, not to be cross-examined by reporters. During the sixties the restraints had been eased, partly under the influence of William Hardcastle's pioneering radio programme 'The World at One'. Tough questions on political topics came to be acceptable, although by some politicians only with reluctance. Still taboo, however, was any attempt to delve into the personal aspects of their jobs, carrying as it does the risk of denting their carefully nursed dignity by presenting an image of them in terms other than their own. In Yesterday's Men, Dimbleby and Pope were challenging that tradition. Because of the resulting fuss, nobody again made any sustained effort to make politicians look foolish until the 1980s, with the satirical puppet show Spitting Image – and that was on ITV.

BBC tradition demands that a public drubbing of this nature requires a scapegoat. The two leading contenders for the role were Crawley and Grist. Partly because of his frequent squabbles with politicians, Grist already had a reputation as a testy, difficult character, gifted but troublesome. He had served as assistant head of current affairs to Paul Fox – a relationship that seldom makes for a cordial association. When Fox was made controller of BBC1 in 1967, Grist was his heir apparent but was not confirmed in the job straight away. When he was offered it Sir Hugh Greene told him candidly that he had not been first choice. Alasdair Milne, who had left the corporation in 1965, had been approached but turned it down (preferring to wait until the job he really coveted, controller in Scotland, became vacant the following year). And Grist was never on close terms with Greene's successor, Charles Curran.

Humiliation by promotion is practised in a number of British institutions. The most obvious example is the elevation to the House of Lords of politicians who have become an embarrassment to their party in the lower chamber. The equivalent at the

BBC is either to be put in charge of the regions or to head the most important of the overseas outposts in New York. Grist did both. For his career to have stayed on track, he would have expected to be shifted from head of current affairs to controller of a channel – like his predecessor Fox – or to some other senior position in news and current affairs, or even become a member of the board of management. Instead, very soon after Yesterday's Men, he was promoted to controller of the English regions, based in Birmingham. It is a post of importance and responsibility, involving much travel inside England, but since its establishment in 1969 it has never been regarded as one of the Beeb's glamour jobs. In 1978 he was moved to New York, certainly glamorous this time; but a long way from the corporate centre of power. In 1981 he retired early from the BBC.

At the beginning of 1972, six months after Yesterday's Men was screened, Wilson was a guest at a governors' lunch. The purpose of the invitation was to repair relations with the opposition leader. It succeeded up to a point. Wilson, though still feeling himself the victim of a great wrong, spoke less acerbically than some of the governors had anticipated.

'The hatchet is buried,' one of them observed afterwards. 'But the place is still marked.'

* * * *

After Labour was returned to office in 1974, senior figures at the BBC wondered whether Wilson and his colleagues would try to wreak revenge. The appointment of the Annan Committee could have been a first move in that direction – although its broad and vague terms of reference made it a less obvious threat than Peacock a decade later. In July 1978, with James Callaghan now Prime Minister, the government published a White Paper on broadcasting that took account of some of Annan's suggestions. For the most part it was uncontroversial, but one provision caused a quiver of apprehension at Portland Place: it was proposed to introduce an extra layer of authority between the BBC governors and management, in the shape of three service management boards – one for television, one for domestic radio and one for the external services. Their members would be appointed by the Home Office and would take over the governors' role in the direct management of the BBC, thus removing the contradiction between their twin functions exposed by the Yesterday's Men affair. The idea had more merit than the BBC's reaction to it suggested.

> The public must ask whether the government's proposals are the right way of creating more accountability and diversity while safeguarding the BBC's independence (said the corporation in a statement issued just after the White Paper was published). The proposals raise many difficult questions and would appear to lead to more bureaucracy. The insertion of Home Office appointees could cause confusion in executive authority and in the role of governors and could lead to a danger of increasing government intervention in the content of programmes. It would be a pity if the search for accountability and diversity weakened the ability of the corporation to fulfil that particular independent role which is endorsed within the White Paper itself.

So far as the BBC management are concerned, the contradiction inherent in the governors' position is usually an advantage in that it inhibits them from interfering in programme matters except in extreme cases. Stripped of most administrative functions they would in all probability intervene much more in the areas of responsibility that remained to them: it was simple human nature. Moreover, if they no longer had the power to appoint the heads of the three output services, they would feel less obliged to stand by programme decisions. The proposed boards would certainly have proved an irritant to the BBC by making them subject to a second set of government-appointed watchdogs, whose political complexion could change with every election.

Whether the Labour cabinet would have persisted with the plan had they won the 1979 election is uncertain. Merlyn Rees, the Home Secretary, did not seem swayed by Lord Swann's strongly expressed arguments against it. The BBC, in any event, made no attempt to hide its relief when the proposals fell by the wayside with the Conservatives' victory. The introduction to the 1980 annual report reiterated that Labour's changes would have been 'profound, and to our minds perilous'. It continued patronisingly: 'We did not believe those threats arose from ill will so much as from an insufficient understanding of the corporation's governing and managerial mechanisms, even among its friends and admirers. Nevertheless the apprehensions they aroused were not assuaged until after the end of the year under review. The financial problems remained.'

At least one member of the board of management believed that this defensive, whining reaction was a mistake. Michael Bett, the thoughtful director of personnel, wrote a memo to David Webster, director of public affairs, criticising that section of the report. The BBC's endless self-defence, he wrote, encouraged antipathy. 'We often behave as though we're under siege and the great British public is lucky that our vigilance keeps at bay the erosion of our independence from government control. Nobody loves a moaner. . . We should admit we have warts and are doing our best to eradicate them.' Bett left the BBC not long afterwards, having failed to alter that basic attitude.

* * * *

In one respect, therefore, the arrival of Margaret Thatcher's Conservative administration came as something of a relief after the threat posed by Labour. There were, however, reasons for trepidation. Shortly before the 1979 election Mrs Thatcher had been a guest at a luncheon of BBC editors, where she railed at them for what she saw as anti-Conservative bias, as well as for their coverage of Northern Ireland. Her Cabinet was dominated by radical Tories who questioned the workings of the establishment and the consensus politics that sustained it. The BBC exemplified much of what they distrusted about the system – an unwieldy, self-sustaining, self-satisfied institution that by its nature could hold no clear, decisive views on contentious issues but was devoted to fudge, compromise and endless tolerance.

All the same, relations with the new government were helped by William Whitelaw, the Home Secretary, being sympathetic towards the BBC and its view of the arms-length relations it ought to maintain with Westminster. Whitelaw believes in consensus politics and recognises the value in a democracy of bodies that seek to accommodate the entire spectrum of mainstream views. He saw it as his role to protect the BBC against threats from the wilder right. Often, as in the case of Carrickmore, that involved urging the corporation to make concessions to back-bench critics so as to pre-empt any more damaging assault.

Ian Trethowan, director-general for the first three years of the Thatcher administration, shared Whitelaw's philosophy. Following Carrickmore, the two men managed to avert any serious clashes between the government and the Beeb for nearly two years. On occasion Trethowan would act inside the BBC to head off broadcasts that might provoke the hostility of MPs, most notably in the E. P. Thompson affair during the summer of 1981. Thompson had been tentatively invited to deliver the Dimbleby lecture, a prestigious annual televised event named after Richard Dimbleby. The lecture came under the auspices of the reorganised documentary features department, successor to general features, where a year earlier Will Wyatt had taken over after the departure of Desmond Wilcox. It was Wyatt's job – along with Eddie Mirzoeff, one of his senior producers – to secure a speaker to deliver the lecture in November. Thompson, a Marxist historian, had been making news as a supporter of unilateral nuclear disarmament for Britain – a cause that, to the government's consternation, appeared to be gaining ground. He had sound academic credentials and it seemed a lively, topical notion to approach him. He delivered a synopsis of his intended remarks which, while not specifically advocating unilateralism, dealt with the dangers inherent in the Cold War and the arms race that went with it.

Alasdair Milne, managing director of television, had approved the approach without consulting Trethowan. The director-general did not hear about it until early in the summer, and insisted that Thompson must not be allowed to deliver the lecture. However subtly the disarmament issue was approached, Trethowan was sure Thompson would get his message across unmistakably, and was equally sure that the government would be furious. When news of Trethowan's decision was leaked to the press in August, the BBC sought to maintain that Thompson had never formally been invited to lecture but was merely being sounded out on the possibility. This defence was not plausible enough to prevent supporters of nuclear disarmament from accusing the BBC of censoring anti-establishment opinion. Wyatt compounded the embarrassment by making another informal approach, this time to Edward Heath, the former Prime Minister who made no secret of his dislike of Mrs Thatcher. He was to speak on the gap between the developed and the developing world but Trethowan vetoed that too, ostensibly because Heath was a friend of his and he thought people might draw unworthy conclusions. The series of embarrassments ended with the lecture being postponed for a few weeks and finally delivered by Dr Garret Fitzgerald, the former (and subsequent) Prime Minister of Ireland.

By banning Thompson before the government had time to make a fuss about the invitation, and by soaking up the opprobrium himself, Trethowan had diverted a potential new assault on the Beeb by Thatcher and her supporters. But any credit points he might have thought he was accruing in Westminster counted for little when the Falklands war began. Argentina invaded the Falkland Islands, a British colony in the South Atlantic, in April 1982. A task force was sent to sieze the islands back, and from the moment that British lives became endangered the BBC was under pressure from government supporters to go virtually on to a wartime footing and bar from the air any expression of doubt or opposition to the military action. The corporation had withstood such pressure over the potentially graver Suez crisis in 1956, but in the intervening twenty-six years attitudes had become less tolerant.

Coverage of the actual fighting was strictly controlled from the start by the Defence Ministry who, because the disputed islands were so inaccessible, enjoyed an effective monopoly of transport and communications arrangements. Strict censorship was used to stifle reporting and pictures of the worst British casualties, for fear that too much exposure to the horrors of war would lower the morale of the British public and reduce the level of popular support for the military action. Defence chiefs believed that the failure of the United States intervention in Vietnam had been caused partly by the demoralising impact of the extensive and horrific coverage of the fighting on television. They were determined to rule out any such effect in this war.

On the home fronts, both in Britain and Argentina, no such logistic restrictions on coverage could be applied. The BBC's first instinct was to behave as they would in relation to any other news story, giving fair weight to all sides of the argument. But from the start, the board of management recognised that even-handedness would be controversial. On 6 April, the day after the British task force sailed, Alasdair Milne expressed his fears at the weekly meeting of news and current affairs producers. (The minutes of these meetings during the Falklands crisis were leaked to the Glasgow University Media Group and a selection of them published in their 1985 book *War and Peace News.*)

Milne, due to succeed Ian Trethowan as director-general that August, said the BBC would come under pressure to conform to the national interest, as it had during the Suez crisis. The difficulty was to define the national interest. While they should be careful about military and diplomatic matters, they should report fully the arguments in Britain over the government's actions. That was part of what provoked the anger of government supporters the following month, but they were equally furious about the coverage given to the Argentinians' view of the conflict in despatches from Buenos Aires. Argentinian spokesmen were allowed to explain their country's claim to the islands and there were pictures of anti-British demonstrations. Worse, because no film from the task force was reaching London in the early days of the fighting, the only war coverage was Argentinian material beamed by satellite from Buenos Aires. A few days later Richard Francis, the former director of news and current affairs and now managing director of radio, made the much-criticised comment that the widow of Portsmouth was no different from the widow of Buenos Aires. In a speech to the International Press Institute he added: 'We are not in the game of patriotism.'

But the BBC was quickly forced to assert that it was not in the game of neutrality, either. If you accepted the government view that Britain was fighting a crusade for national honour, then it was incumbent on the national broadcasting organisation to fall into step. On 6 May Margaret Thatcher told the Commons that reports on radio and television treated the claims and assertions of both sides as equal and were not presenting the British case forcefully enough. In a speech that same evening, George Howard, the chairman, responded that the BBC could not be neutral as between Britain and the aggressor, but the criterion for news coverage was whether it helped viewers and listeners understand what was going on. 'Coupled with that is a determination that in war truth shall not be the first casualty.' And Ian Trethowan wrote to the Conservative MP John Page declaring that the BBC was not neutral 'but one of the things that distinguishes a democracy like Britain from a dictatorship like Argentina is that our people wish to be told the truth and can be told it however unpleasant it might be'.

Milne put it like this in the 1983 annual report:

> When the nation is forced by the act of an aggressor to take military action in its interests, there is no question of the BBC being neutral; the Argentines did not think we were – witness their immediate jamming of the Latin American services. Nor has the BBC or its staff ever been short of patriotism. Those who made charges of that kind during the Falkland conflict might now care to reflect that in a parliamentary democracy truth is paramount.

He wrote those words in the wake of the most searing introduction to office that a new director-general has ever had to endure. As the long build-up to the war in April ended with the arrival of the task force in the Falklands and the loss of British lives, pent-up emotions began to spill over. It was an unfortunate piece of timing that only four days after Thatcher's remarks in the Commons, Panorama devoted itself to a discussion of domestic criticism of the Falklands operation in an edition provocatively entitled: 'Can we avoid war?' Conservative MPs were furious. Sally Oppenheim, a former junior minister, called it an 'odious, subversive travesty'. Back-benchers began to wonder whether there were any emergency powers the government could invoke to bring the Beeb to heel. To forestall any such suggestions, and to enable the party faithful to let off steam, Whitelaw urged Geoffrey Johnson Smith, chairman of the Conservatives' media committee, to invite Howard to meet the committee in the Commons.

Wednesday, 12 May, had been a pleasant late spring day with bursts of warm sunshine, and George Howard was feeling in a vigorous and confident mood as he set out from Broadcasting House in the early evening. Trethowan was visiting America so Howard took Milne with him, believing the experience – the 'blooding', in his countryman's term – would do him good. Whether or not it did him good, the events that evening in Committee Room 13 certainly showed Milne that the broadcasters' view of their role and performance was distant from that of politicians.

It was already hot in the room when they arrived and Howard was obliged to begin mopping his brow even before the 122 MPs present launched their assault. By the time the hour-long meeting was over, his shirt and handkerchief were wringing wet. The MPs wanted him and Milne to apologise for the Panorama programme, describing it as an abuse of the corporation's freedom. Howard's reaction did not help. Instead of being conciliatory, he tried to lecture the MPs on the responsibilities of broadcasters. 'He treated them as a Whig grandee would treat his retainers,' said one who was present. But if he expected them to react by doffing their caps and acceding gracefully to his arguments, he had gravely misread their mood. The sounds of anger spread to other parts of the Commons and even to the House of Lords at the far end of the corridor. As lobby correspondents and excited MPs swarmed near the committee room entrance, committee members came out and gave them lurid eye-witness accounts. 'There is blood and entrails all over the place,' said one. 'Everyone is roasting them alive.' When Howard maintained that it was the BBC's function to report all views, Winston Churchill, grandson of the wartime leader, said: 'We did not see fit to give equal time to the Goebbels propaganda machine.'

The two victims finally emerged, looking drained; but Howard was still unwilling to climb down. He told the waiting reporters that he had refused to apologise and that the Panorama edition had been 'misunderstood'. Whitelaw hurried from the meeting, put his arm on his old friend Howard's damp shoulder and said to Milne: 'Come on, my boy, you have to have a drink. It had to happen, you know.'

Trethowan, returning from America, was appalled when he heard about the blood-letting in Committee Room 13. He quickly arranged to appear before the back-benchers himself the following week, to try to repair the damage. It was the kind of situation he excelled in, calling on the smooth, mollifying skills he had acquired in his years as a lobby correspondent and television interviewer. Without conceding the point of principle that Howard had maintained so doggedly, the director-general was able to convince the MPs that the BBC was not neutral, but was performing its allotted function loyally and conscientiously. Their mood was not, in any case, as excitable as it had been the week before. Far fewer of them turned up and those that did felt slightly sheepish about their previous excesses.

While Trethowan did not recant, he did appreciate that the BBC's coverage of the war would have to take account of the emotions expressed by the back-benchers, which, he was sure, were shared by most viewers and listeners. On 18 May he told news and current affairs producers that the BBC's reporting had to be 'sensitive to the emotional sensibilities of the public'. With the public's nerve endings raw, the best yardstick was 'the likely general susceptibility'. It meant, in effect, that the BBC was not free to pursue a line that diverged to any significant degree from the jingoism that the government's information machinery was encouraging. Its editorial independence could be exercised only within defined limits – and one of the factors that defined them was Parliament's responsibility for setting the licence fee.

Whitelaw's instinct had been sound. The almost public mauling inflicted on Howard and Milne had performed a useful function both in terms of the BBC's future handling of war news and for its cathartic effect on MPs. The corporation's patriotism was never seriously questioned again. Very soon the reports from the correspondents with the task force began flowing regularly, and those from the BBC men were as vividly supportive of the British troops as everyone else's. The British victory was reported with a level of enthusiasm appropriate to a major national triumph. But the incident none the less had its long-lasting effects. When the future of public broadcasting became a subject for discussion and decision in the ensuing years, Conservative MPs felt no obligation to leap to the BBC's support.

* * * *

In 1983, in the aftermath of the Falklands, the Conservatives won a convincing general election victory. Relations between the government and the BBC remained at a tolerant level until the end of January 1984, when an edition of Panorama was devoted to allegations that some extreme right-wingers, former members of racist groups, had been selected as Conservative parliamentary candidates and that twenty-four of them had been elected as MPs. The programme was inspired by Young Conservatives worried at the rightward drift in the party, but the charges in it were vigorously denied by John Selwyn Gummer, the party chairman, and by the MPs named, some of whom sued for libel. (The last of the cases was dropped early in 1986.) Those Conservatives who regarded the BBC as being a nest of 'pinkoes' saw this as another piece of evidence to support that view. Milne stood by the accuracy of the programme and was left to reflect that no broadcasting organisation aspiring to serious journalism can avoid offending the political parties. The dilemma was that one of those parties always controlled the level of BBC funding and recommended appointments to the board of governors. Milne and his colleagues recognised that this left them vulnerable. But they remained convinced that, despite the drawbacks of the licence fee and the possibilities of political control inherent in it, any alternative financing system would only make things worse.

Chapter 8

QUESTION TIME

THE BBC and its programmes are part of the fabric of our lives. Day in and day out, they present us with experiences that are marvellous, appalling or commonplace. That is one reason why they are a regular and simple target for comment and criticism in the press. The other is the reputation the corporation won for itself in the first twenty-five years of its life as a repository of impartiality, good taste, sobriety, responsibility and the other virtues that were then thought to make up the national character. When iconoclasm came into fashion in the decades following the Second World War, the pompous BBC was among the more obvious icons to assault. Hugh Greene did a lot during his years as director-general to change it into a less stuffy institution, but the old 'Auntie BBC' image was too useful a stereotype to be abandoned by people seeking to mock the establishment. Because it provides so constant a target, it is hard to pin down when any particular campaign against the corporation begins. But it is not misleading to identify The Thorn Birds debate, sparked by Douglas Hurd's criticism of the mini-series, as the start of the increasingly noisy discussion about the BBC's future that ran throughout 1984 and into 1985.

On 19 February 1984 the *Sunday Times* had as its main 'Focus' feature an article headlined BBC AT BAY. It included a summary of a leaked document, written by Brian Wenham, director of television programmes, reporting a discussion of The

Thorn Birds at one of his weekly programme review meetings. Every Wednesday a few dozen of the most senior television executives – heads of department, controllers and managing directors – gather in a basement room at Television Centre to discuss the previous week's output. The cynical say the meeting's most important function is to settle scores, with one programme chief tearing holes in a rival's output; but most of those who attend take it seriously and find it useful. For some it is the highlight of the week. (Desmond Wilcox used to be one of the most enthusiastic participants and his comments were generally constructive: when he was trying to negotiate a new, diminished role during his dramatic final days as head of features, his right to continue attending programme review meetings was among his priorities.)

The discussions are meant to be confidential and outsiders are not admitted to this weekly ritual. The leaked memorandum referred to the meeting at which The Thorn Birds had come up. According to Wenham, it turned into 'an hour-long debate on Whither BBC Television'. In between much routine moaning about poor morale, and money spent on Breakfast Time that could have been devoted to other programmes, some important wider points were raised about the relation between the BBC and its commercial rivals. The central dilemma was identified – that the BBC is expected to justify its monopoly over the licence fee by producing programmes of responsibility and artistic merit but at the same time competing with ITV for the mass audience. That was feasible when the BBC had two channels to ITV's one, but on level terms, with two channels each, it had to be accepted that ITV would have the edge in terms of ratings. And as soon as the BBC tried to do something about this, by screening The Thorn Birds, then it was attacked on grounds of artistic merit.

It seemed an insoluble dilemma; which it is, for it springs from the contradiction built in to the British system of public service broadcasting. Once that is recognised, logic suggests that the system itself is in need of radical reform – but it is a rare BBC bird who can be persuaded to consider that possibility. They respond that the corporation has been responsible for most of what is excellent in British television and radio and, if left to get on with it in peace, will produce more of the same in the future. A temporary decline in standards and morale, caused by many factors, is no reason to dismantle the entire structure.

At the programme review meeting Wenham did not challenge that article of faith. He attributed much of the malaise to the financial arrangements:

> Government has willed the ends – that of a four-channel TV system, with IBA having a monopoly of advertising monies and BBC having a monopoly of licence money. But government has not, however, willed the means, which in my view means that the monies available to each side should be more closely related than they currently are. If not, what will surely happen will be a drift towards a 3½ or three channel system, with effort and variety simply having been switched from the public sector to the private.

What Wenham meant was that the licence fee would have to be increased substantially. The BBC's licence income that year was just over £700m, compared with ITV's revenue of nearly £1000m – and the BBC had the additional expense of its national and local radio services. (Not the external services, which are funded by a direct grant from the Foreign Office.) To equal the revenue of commercial television, the fee to the 15.5 million licence payers would have to go up to £65 a year, the figure the BBC would in fact be seeking from the government.

An opposing view was expressed in the same *Sunday Times* article by Tim Brinton MP, a former broadcaster who is chairman of the Conservative Party's media committee. He suggested cutting the fee to £30 from its then level of £46. 'That way you would force the BBC to concentrate its resources on just one very good TV channel. This might well be the best solution for the BBC against the new cable and satellite technologies.' He added that the television and radio services should be separated, sport on television should be funded by sponsors and advertising taken on the two most popular radio channels, Radios 1 and 2. (He has since modified his view on advertising.)

The BBC has always resisted with fervour the notion that it should concentrate its resources on providing high-quality programmes to the educated middle class, leaving the popular lower ground to the commercial companies. It calls that 'ghetto television', the ghetto being the living-rooms of the highly cultured minority. As a dreadful warning, it points to the Public

Broadcasting Service in the United States, funded partly by the administration and partly through appeals to the public. Because of its chronic poverty, it can afford to make few programmes of its own, buying instead from the BBC (and to some extent from the British commercial companies). And because of the constant need for funds, its programmes are interspersed regularly with appeals for contributions, as irritating in their way as commercial advertisements. PBS provides no challenge in terms of ratings to the three large American networks, although it has a loyal minority following.

It is not the only example of a poor-relation public television service unable to compete with the commercial networks. In Australia, Canada and, to a lesser extent, West Germany, the same applies. In all three countries advertising supplements the licence revenue. These are potent spectres for the BBC to raise in its bid to justify its insistence on competing at all levels – head-to-head quiz games, breakfast television, darts – in an attempt to win a respectable share of the audience.

The Annan Committee on Broadcasting, reporting in 1977, found that the BBC had taken the spirit of competition too far. In its evidence the corporation had claimed for itself almost uncanny skill in fine-tuning, declaring that 'BBC programmes do not need to be more popular than is necessary to gain and hold 50% of the audience.' The committee commented:

> We appreciate that the BBC feel that they must obtain a reasonable share of the television audience in order to justify the licence fee and that the producers themselves want large audiences for their programmes. But competition seems to have become so ingrained in the BBC that an uninstructed public might be forgiven for believing that the main concern of the BBC's schedulers is to do a piece of major no good to ITV. . . The main objective of BBC Television should not be to gain and hold 50% of the audience: it should be to provide interesting and entertaining programmes which will amuse and enrich the experience of large numbers of people.

The committee aired some more radical criticisms, too, and made a perceptive analysis of the change in broadcasting in the middle years of the century. Much of it remains so relevant that it could have been written this year and not nine years ago:

> We sensed that all was not well with the BBC. There has been a subtle change in its ethos. The old loyalty to public service broadcasting, so clear in the days of Reith or Haley, has diminished.

In those days nobody doubted that culture reflected the assumptions of Oxbridge.

> But once commercial television was introduced . . . loyalty to the ideal of public service gave way to loyalty to the ideal of professionalism. . . The new spirit is much more managerial. . . Although there are still instances of the old arrogance, the complacency of which the Beveridge Committee complained has vanished. The BBC today sees itself as beleaguered, pressurised, lobbied and compelled to lobby. . . In recent years there have been both criticism from outside the corporation and discontent within. The BBC has been attacked for being too monolithic, too impervious to criticism from within, too thin-skinned and arrogant in response to criticism from without and too inept in its dealings with pressure groups, Westminster and Whitehall. It is accused of being top-heavy in management, extravagant in its day-to-day operations, slow in decision-making and of strangling itself by its own bureaucracy. . . The charges cannot be brushed aside. The BBC seems to us to have shown some loss of nerve which is partly the cause and partly the result of this barrage of criticism. Its sense of direction has weakened. The question we have to resolve is whether . . . it should continue in its present shape at all.

Some members of the committee thought the BBC should be split into two, with separate organisations running television and radio. The majority agreed with the corporation's own view that the very size of the BBC gave it 'that influential place in the life of the country which is the best guarantee of its independence'. They did, however, suggest hiving off the local radio stations. Like all the other bodies that until now have examined the corporation's financing, they recommended sticking with the licence fee system, ruling out either a direct grant from the government or funding by advertising revenue.

The question whether the BBC should take advertising has been debated off and on over several decades. In 1965 the Labour politician Tony Benn, as Postmaster-General the minister responsible for broadcasting, had proposed to his Cabinet colleagues that, instead of increasing the licence fee, the BBC should take advertising at least on the Light Programme (later to become Radios 1 and 2) and perhaps too on television. Part of his motive was to encourage the BBC to respond effectively to the newly established pirate radio stations. They fulfilled a clear demand for pop music that was unsatisfied by the Beeb. When news of the proposal reached the governors a few months later, there were threats of a mass resignation if it were put into effect. Benn countered by warning that the governors might be dismissed, but that raised questions about the royal prerogative and the plan was dropped, although the BBC had to accept the freezing of the licence fee at £5 for a year.

The Annan Committee's view on advertising has provided the standard intellectual case against it for many years. It is that if two rival television companies compete for the same source of revenue, the inevitable result is a decline in programme standards, specifically the virtual elimination of serious, demanding fare at peak hours. Those who support that argument point to the United States, where the three main networks offer a prime-time menu of back-to-back soap operas, detective series and trivial comedy. In the 1984/5 debate that stereotype of American television was challenged. It was argued that the programmes were not as bad as 'elitist' critics made out. With cable and satellite technology making dozens of channels available at once, there would always be something for more discerning viewers to watch.

Although the threat of advertising has been successfully fended off over the years, it never goes far away, usually returning to yap irritatingly at the corporation's heels when the licence fee is due to be renegotiated. In 1980 Margaret Thatcher, then the fairly new Prime Minister, went to lunch at Broadcasting House and asked Aubrey Singer, as managing director of radio, why he did not take advertising on Radio 1, the pop channel. He replied that if that flood gate were opened, the advertising would inevitably spread to Radio 2 the next time an increase in the licence fee was suggested, then to Radios 3 and 4, then to television. All British broadcasting would thus be subject to the 'ethos of covetousness'. That is not at all the kind of language calculated to appeal to a Prime Minister who regards covetousness as a perfectly proper motivating force. She asked Singer whether his soft suit and expensive watch had not been purchased through the same ethos. As a grocer's daughter, she sees nothing wrong with trade.

The conversation must have confirmed Mrs Thatcher in her belief that the BBC, one of the last of the great liberal institutions, was run by intellectuals with their heads in the clouds, quite out of sympathy with the kind of Britain she was trying to shape. Most such institutions exist in the worlds of scholarship or the professions, so their influence is limited; but the BBC has the direct access to the ears and eyes of the electorate that politicians envy. It is a rival power base to the government of the day and as such a potential threat to it.

Her chance to do something about it came when it was time to appoint a chairman of the corporation in 1983, to succeed Lord Howard. Sir William Rees-Mogg, former editor of *The Times* had been appointed deputy chairman in 1981 on the understanding that he would be in line for the succession. But in 1982 he had become chairman of the Arts Council and he clearly could not do both jobs. That left the way clear for the Prime Minister to choose Stuart Young, a North London accountant and the brother of David Young, one of her close political advisers, who was later made a life peer and a member of the Cabinet. It would be wrong, though, to suggest that she foisted Young on an unwilling Beeb. He had been a governor since 1981 and had impressed the board of management with his sympathetic grasp of broadcasting issues. In their reaction against Howard's excessively high profile, the professionals relished the idea of a lower-key figure. And at a time when the BBC's finances were certain to become a matter of contention, it might be a sound tactical move to have an accountant at the helm. Rees-Mogg, too, told Mrs Thatcher that Young should be her man. She needed little persuading. At the very least, someone of his profession would be unlikely to harbour ethical doubts about covetousness.

In 1984 it was Douglas Hurd, the junior Home Office minister who had inspired the furore over The Thorn Birds, who first indicated publicly that the government were not ruling out advertising as a future means of funding the BBC. In May he told the House of Commons that it would be 'foolish to stand here and say that the licence system would never be modified'. In an interview with the *Sunday Times,* published a few days later, he went further:

> The more variety of broadcasting there is, such as cable and satellite, the more tatty the present licence system looks. We have not ruled out any potential form for future financing, whether advertising, sponsorship, subscription, the separation of radio from television, or privatisation.

The only comfort for the Beeb came when he added:

> I am certainly not now considering any breakup of the BBC – it's pretty well immortal. There is no demolition squad out. At present the licence fee, despite all its imperfections, is easier to criticise than to replace. It is just that the more broadcasting competition there is, the more we must look to the long term and see how the BBC fits in.

The other papers, following up the *Sunday Times* story, took more notice of the first paragraph than the second. Both the *Sunday Mirror* and the *Sunday People* ran items in their late editions. TV LICENCE TO BE AXED? asked the *Mirror* headline, while the *People* did not even admit to the uncertainty suggested by the question mark, declaring trenchantly: TORIES TO SELL OFF BEEB – a headline based on Hurd's reference to privatisation. Gerald Kaufman, the shadow Home Secretary, accused Hurd of trying to wreck the BBC by prostituting its standards and diluting its integrity. A Home Office spokesman was forced to deny that the government had any plan to change the licensing system 'or to do anything dramatic'.

The denial did not deter the *Guardian* from reporting two days later that MINISTERS AIM FOR RADIO ADS ON BBC. The story said that ministers were 'privately advocating' advertising on Radios 1 and 2 to limit licence fee increases, but that advertising on television would be politically unacceptable. It added that these same ministers also had doubts about the future of BBC local radio.

The issue lay dormant over the summer but was brought back to life by a September article in the trade journal *Marketing Week*. The magazine had asked the advertising agency D'Arcy MacManus Masius to devise a workable plan for advertising on the BBC. The article describing the plan was written by the agency's media director, Rodney Harris, a quiet-spoken, rumpled, slightly donnish man who belies the suave, go-getting image of his trade. He began the article by pointing out that if the corporation began taking ads overnight, and sold air time on the same scale as its commercial rivals – six minutes in every hour – then the ITV companies would all go bankrupt. 'Quite simply, there is not enough advertising money to fund all UK broadcasting.' He therefore proposed a scheme for keeping the licence fee but holding it at £46 and paying for increased BBC costs by a limited amount of advertising on television, beginning at an insignificant level but increasing as costs rose and inflation reduced the value of the fee. The mathematics were based on the statistic that television advertising revenue grows at a rate of 6 per cent a year. For the idea to work, all of that increase would have to be channelled to the BBC, giving an extra income of £60m a year, 'enough to meet its 1985 and 1986 requirements without raising the licence fee or doing serious harm to ITV's profits.'

Because the shortfall between the BBC's income and expenditure would increase annually with a static licence fee, the amount of advertising it accepted would have to increase to take that into account. The agency calculated that for the first year it need only take 15 seconds per hour, rising to 30 seconds per hour in the second year, with further incremental increases. (The BBC later challenged that arithmetic.) The article went on to suggest that since independent television also undertakes public service broadcasting, in the sense that it is controlled by the Independent Broadcasting Authority, a case could be made for allotting some of the licence fee to ITV, thereby making its commercial breaks shorter and more valuable to advertisers.

It was a clever piece of special pleading, enlivened by a few merry swipes at the Beeb: 'It is part of that British Establishment that looks down on tradesmen, salesmen, commerce in general and advertising in particular. It is the perpetuation of this attitude that has helped reduce Britain's share of world and home markets.' Harris criticised the 'highly unsuccessful venture into local radio and the costly breakfast launch, both designed to keep up with the IBA'. And he made no secret of his principal motive, to end the ITV monopoly on television advertising and, through competition, bring down the cost of air time. The cause was taken up by Woodrow Wyatt, the maverick former Labour MP, in his column in *The Times*. He wrote:

> The BBC contends that if it were to rely on advertising it would have to lower the quality of its programmes – in other words make them more acceptable to more people – to attract advertisers at peak times. That argument is implausible because already at peak times BBC programmes are rarely more elevated than those on commercial TV. It all comes back to vanity. The people who run the BBC just don't like the idea of soiling their hands in the commercial world. Somehow they have got away with the idea that the public should pay a huge rising tax to maintain them in this privileged and gentlemanly position.

Alasdair Milne sprang to the defence of the Beeb in an article in *Ariel,* the BBC's weekly staff journal. First he dismissed Rodney Harris's assertion that BBC mandarins looked down on tradesmen, commerce and especially advertising, but he did it so arrogantly as almost to confirm the charge. 'That particular statement', he declared, 'is too silly to be worth discussing.' Answering the criticism of local radio and breakfast TV, he wrote: 'The BBC began local radio 20 years ago in the clear knowledge that this was a new service which would add a new dimension to British broadcasting. . . Just for the record, it was the IBA who followed.' As for Breakfast Time, at £15,000 an hour it was 'inexpensive television indeed'. Then he gave a succinct rendering of the corporation's case against advertising, which he was to reiterate often in the ensuing months:

> The fact that competition in this country is confined to programmes alone and that this competition makes for healthy, professional rivalry is the cornerstone of the British achievement: the case for the BBC competing for the same source of funding as the commercial sector has not been made. The argument for a pooling and splitting of licence and advertising incomes cannot be sustained. . . Our broadcasting system is delicately balanced and easily destroyed. A wholly commercial system would transfer the ultimate power of broadcasting decisions into the hands of men and women whose primary interest could not be the quality of broadcasting itself.

In any case, he did not believe that people thought the licence fee a burden: 'It must be one of the best bargains in the country.'

It was the first of many such articles and speeches that Milne and other senior BBC people would have to compose over the next months. It proved hard to get the tone right. The BBC labours under a disabling handicap when it comes to its own defence. If it does not respond to criticism it is accused of high-handedly ignoring the views of its customers, the licence-payers. Milne's instinct is to rebut attacks vigorously, point by point, but that provokes a different accusation – that the BBC is blind to its faults, unwilling to concede even that its opponents' case has any merit. That is unfair, but it is a fact that nobody in BBC management believes there is a better way of running British broadcasting than the one we have, and they point to the quality of the programmes on all four channels as proof. Every year, programmes of all kinds win dozens of international awards – as they should, seeing that the Beeb is the largest TV production house in the world.

Because they regarded the excellence of the system as self-evident, Milne and his colleagues were convinced first that any assertion to the contrary must be motivated by self-interest, and second that all they had to do to win the argument was to reiterate that truth on all suitable occasions. That proved not to be so. The difference between this debate and those that had accompanied previous licence fee negotiations was that this one had in effect been launched by a government philosophically opposed to the BBC's liberal values, so not sharing the basic assumptions on which the corporation rested its case.

But if Mrs Thatcher thought that her appointment of Stuart Young as chairman would be a means of steering the Beeb away from its traditional certainties she was to be disappointed, at least on the issue of the licence fee. He teamed up with Milne as enthusiastically as the director-general could have wished, presenting in unison with him the case against advertising and for a licence increase. For a time, until a little while after the licence level had been set the following year, it seemed as if the BBC had succeeded in capturing to itself another potentially troublesome chairman, as it liked to think it had captured Lord Hill in the early 1970s.

Following the Masius report a second advertising agency,

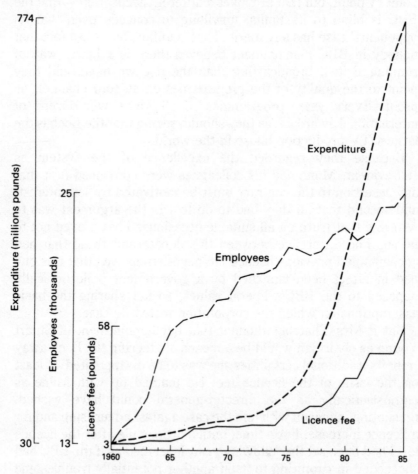

BBC Expenditure, licence fee income and number of employees, 1960–1985

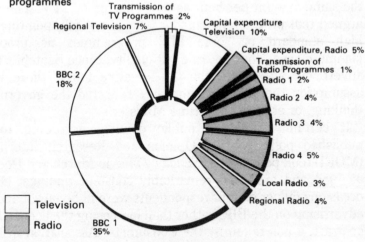

WHERE YOUR MONEY GOES

The TV licence pays for all BBC services – two TV channels, four radio networks, local radio and regional programmes

Transmission of TV Programmes 2%
Regional Television 7%
Capital expenditure Television 10%
Capital expenditure, Radio 5%
Transmission of Radio Programmes 1%
Radio 1 2%
BBC 2 18%
Radio 2 4%
Radio 3 4%
Radio 4 5%
Local Radio 3%
Regional Radio 4%

☐ Television
▨ Radio

BBC 1 35%

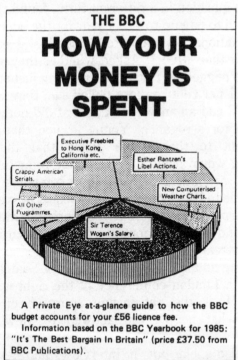

THE BBC
HOW YOUR MONEY IS SPENT

Executive Freebies to Hong Kong, California etc.

Esther Rantzen's Libel Actions.

Crappy American Serials.

New Computerised Weather Charts.

All Other Programmes.

Sir Terence Wogan's Salary.

A Private Eye at-a-glance guide to how the BBC budget accounts for your £56 licence fee.
Information based on the BBC Yearbook for 1985: "It's The Best Bargain In Britain" (price £37.50 from BBC Publications).

Pie chart showing how the BBC spends its money; and a spoof from the satirical magazine *Private Eye* (*BBC and Pressdram Ltd*)

Saatchi and Saatchi, carried out a similar exercise to show that the BBC should take advertising. They wanted it introduced gradually over all sections of broadcasting, growing eventually to the same amount per hour as now appears on ITV. The agency argued that programme standards need not fall, pointing to the high standard of some ITV programmes as proof that commercialism does not rule out quality. Since Saatchi's are the advertising agents for the Conservative Party, there was an assumption that this in some way reflected the government's thinking, or at least the Prime Minister's.

It certainly reflected public opinion, according to most published polls. Market Opinion and Research International (MORI) took polls for the *Sunday Times* in March and December of 1984 and produced remarkably constant findings. On both occasions 69 per cent of respondents were in favour of accepting advertising on the BBC rather than increasing the licence fee. (In contrast, a poll taken by the Consumers' Association in March, asking the question in a different form, found that people would be prepared to pay up to £75 a year for the licence.) On behalf of Masius, National Opinion Polls found still more support for advertising than MORI. Asked whether they would like to see the licence pegged, in return for enduring just one advertisement an hour, 77 per cent of those polled said they would.

The BBC had an answer to this that did nothing to temper its reputation for arrogance. Young argued that it had not been pointed out to the people polled that the acceptance of advertising would lead to an inevitable reduction of programme standards, as both BBC and ITV competed for the highest ratings so as to boost revenue. In essence, he was telling viewers that the corporation wanted to show programmes that were good for them and not to be forced by competition into showing the things they really wanted to see. It provided an easy pretext for an articulate ad-man like John Perriss of Saatchi and Saatchi to declare at a London conference of the right-wing Adam Smith Institute: 'It is the patronising approach of broadcasters in choosing what people are allowed to view that I find so terrifying.'

Young also spoke out, in interviews and newspaper articles, against the notion that advertising could be limited to a few of the

BBC's services, perhaps only radio. 'You can't be a little bit pregnant,' he asserted repeatedly, implying that once the seed had been planted it would inevitably turn into a child and then a fully-grown person. (A more earthy but rather more apposite metaphor along the same lines was deployed by BBC people privately: a woman who works as a whore on Mondays and Thursdays does not become a virgin on the other days of the week.)

In fact the case against partial advertising could have been made less emotively than that. Sir William Rees-Mogg put it crisply when it was raised at meetings of the board of governors. The main objection to advertising, he pointed out, is that it leads to lower standards. The main objection to the licence fee is that it compromises the BBC's independence by making it rely on a level of funding set by the government, and the method of collecting it in exchange for an official licence identifies the corporation as part of the government bureaucracy. Taking advertising to raise only part of its revenue would involve suffering both sets of drawbacks simultaneously. If advertising were to be introduced, it would have to be across the whole system. Colleagues on the board felt Sir William would have resigned had the government forced the BBC to accept limited advertising.

The BBC's insistence that advertising had to be total, if it were allowed at all, was sound tactics. The reason why the two advertising agencies were recommending that the corporation should go only partly commercial, at least to begin with, had nothing to do with fastidiousness or the protection of standards. It was based pragmatically on projections of future advertising levels. While a restricted expansion of the market would help advertisers by keeping rates down, it would still not create anything like sufficient demand to support four channels full time. If BBC1 were allowed to accept as many advertisements as the main ITV channel, neither could make money. Even taking advertisements on Radio 1 would jeopardise several commercial radio stations as well as local newspapers, as Young and Milne repeatedly pointed out.

The independent companies, too, could see the danger. David Plowright, managing director of Granada, expressed the view of

most of them in a letter to the *Guardian* in November. He said the
existing duopoly enabled the two systems 'to avoid damaging,
cut-throat competition for ratings and strive instead for a full
measure of audience interest, appreciation, programme originali-
ty and excellence.' He concluded:

> The BBC deserves a significant increase in the licence fee. It has
> set standards we in ITV have done our best to emulate. Both
> organisations want to grow, to expand the range of broadcasting
> to increase employment opportunities and to develop new export
> markets. They can do so without putting programme standards at
> risk which advertising on the BBC would surely do.

From the beginning, however, the financial argument was not
restricted to whether the BBC should or should not take
advertising. Other forms of funding were suggested that would
alter the structure of British broadcasting, based as it is on the
duopoly between commercial ITV and the publicly funded BBC.
Some of the most original ideas came from the ranks of the
independent producers, a new breed of serious programme
makers, mostly refugees from the BBC, who had multiplied
when Channel 4 was created as a market for their wares. Since
striking out on their own they have become apostles of
deregulation, in favour of a wider spread of control of the
airwaves, offering the independents a larger market and making
for increased cultural diversity.

In February 1984 David Elstein, an independent formerly with
Thames Television, wrote an article in *Television Today*
suggesting a system of subscription to BBC programmes. The
signals would be scrambled and could only be watched by means
of a decoder, which the BBC would sell at a price decided by the
market place. This would eliminate one objection to the licence
fee, that it has to be paid to the BBC even by people who mostly
view ITV. Under Elstein's system, people who watched only
those channels supported by advertising would not have to pay
anything for them. The drawback from the BBC's point of view
would be the risk of dwindling subscriptions when cable and
satellite greatly increased the number of channels available.

Another independent, David Graham, put forward a scheme to
lease most of the available channels (ten or more, once cable and

satellite are operating) to private operators, free of virtually all regulation. The revenue would be used to finance one or two public service channels, presumably run by the rump of the BBC. This would put the Beeb in precisely the position it dreads, abandoning the mass market and catering only to the cultured minority. The mixed schedule – where the heavyweight documentary is placed after a popular American series in the hope that inertia will persuade some people to stay switched on – is central to Beeb philosophy.

In their bid to destroy the duopoly and weaken the BBC, the independent producers have made odd bedfellows for the advertising lobby, whose motive is nothing to do with cultural diversity, just with maximising business. Critics of the campaigning independents maintain that if their proposals were put into effect the result would almost certainly be to hand over part of the British broadcasting system to those press tycoons – Rupert Murdoch and Robert Maxwell in particular – who have so far been unable to penetrate commercial TV to a significant extent, but who have important interests in cable and satellite. It is doubtful whether the producers of serious programmes, as both Graham and Elstein are, would find a receptive outlet in channels run by the barons of the popular press.

Such considerations do not bother the Adam Smith Institute, the think tank of the new Conservative right to which Mrs Thatcher and most of her ministers are allied. In May 1984 the institute published a leaflet called *Communications Policy* that suggested privatising the BBC by breaking it up into independent units operated in a similar fashion to the ITV companies, under a board of governors whose role would resemble that of the Independent Broadcasting Authority. Breakfast Time would be produced by a separate commercial company equivalent to TV-am, BBC1 would be financed by advertising, while BBC2 would take some advertisements and gain extra revenue from sponsorship, subscription and subsidy by BBC1. The news operation would be another separate unit, financed like Independent Television News by levies on the participating companies. Radio would be split along similar lines, with Radios 1 and 2 going commercial, Radios 3 and 4 surviving through subscription and sponsorship.

Although the government were philosophically sympathetic to these suggestions, Mrs Thatcher and her Home Secretary, Leon Brittan, planned no such radical reorganisation, at least not in the short term. Their immediate objective was to avoid too steep an increase in the licence fee and to ensure that the BBC was not being profligate with licence-payers' money. Allegations of BBC extravagance were commonplace in the press, with tales of expenses-paid junkets to the Far East by executives and their wives; directors' transatlantic trips by Concorde; ludicrous over-staffing of overseas news events such as American political conventions. Some of these accounts were exaggerated but in other cases the charges of extravagance were justified.

In an interview with *The Times,* published on 3 November 1984, Stuart Young admitted: 'If I had not been connected with the BBC I think, for the wrong reasons, I would have been attracted to the idea of advertising.' But having studied the matter he could see that the result of going commercial would be to have the schedules dictated by the advertisers, through the advertising salesmen. He agreed with the prevailing corporation view that the licence system, however flawed, was the best means yet devised for funding the BBC and giving it a reasonable amount of freedom from commercial and official pressures. His two concrete suggestions for improving things were matters of detail rather than principle: the licence base should be broadened by requiring a separate fee for each television set, rather than one per household, and by introducing a licence for car radios. Neither of those devices would have prevented a hefty increase in the fee the BBC would be seeking in the next settlement.

The licence had been set at £46 in 1981, to cover the next three years. The BBC adjusts its projected expenditure to take account of inflation, which meant that in the first of the three years it was spending at the rate of a £41 licence and in the last year, 1984-5, at a £51 rate.

In July 1984 Stuart Young and Alasdair Milne went to see Leon Brittan. The Home Secretary had already decided to delay any decision on the licence fee until the spring of 1985. He told Young and Milne that before setting the level there ought to be an independent inquiry into the BBC's efficiency, and whether it really represented the value for money that its management were fond of claiming for it. In political terms it was a sound idea. If the inquiry found in favour of the Beeb, Brittan could use it to deflect the criticism of Tory back-benchers if they thought the settlement too high. If it uncovered corporate profligacy, it would be a pretext for setting the fee low.

As soon as Brittan made the suggestion it was clear to the two BBC men that they had no alternative to accepting it, although Milne in particular was depressed at the notion. The BBC, he thought grumpily, must be the most closely examined organisation in the country. There were three internal inquiries under way even then. The corporation's own auditors, Deloitte's, were engaged in a long-term look in detail at all its operations; and there were specific investigations into the external services and two of the commercial limbs of the BBC – Enterprises, which sold TV programmes, and Publications, which produced *Radio Times,* the *Listener* and the books based on programmes. (Enterprises and Publications were merged in 1985.)

As a result of Brittan's suggestion, the accountants Peat, Marwick, Mitchell were asked to look at the BBC's cost-effectiveness and to suggest ways of improving it. They were to report in January 1985, a few weeks before the government would announce their decision on the licence fee. But the Beeb's formal request for a higher fee had to be in before the end of the year, so it would not take Peat, Marwick's findings into account.

* * * *

A fortnight before the BBC announced its claim for the new fee, a familiar ritual was played out concerning the one part of the corporation not affected by the licence negotiations. The external services at Bush House are financed directly by the Foreign Office, although they insistently plead their independence from government control. Their role is to make Britain's voice heard across the world; but from time to time – as in the Suez crisis of 1956 – they stand on the principle that paying the piper does not give the government an automatic right to call the tune. Despite that, it is realistic to assume that the people who decide the tone of coverage of contentious issues, and the range of comment permitted, are conscious of the need to keep their paymasters happy, or at least not actively disconsolate.

Every so often the Treasury calls for stringency in Whitehall and the Foreign Office is forced to make budget cuts. Invariably Bush House has to shoulder part of the burden. Some of the more recherche services – Swahili or Maltese, say – are curtailed or abandoned altogether. BBC executives complain about the muffling of our voice abroad, then sit back and await the by now well-drilled reaction. This habitually comes in questions in Parliament and a clutch of letters to *The Times* from well-travelled members of the establishment. Sometimes what the press calls the 'outcry' achieves its object and the cuts are modified.

On Thursday, 22 November 1984, Sir Geoffrey Howe, the Foreign Secretary, told the Commons that he would cut expenditure on the external services by 1 per cent. The BBC duly huffed and gave a warning that it might have to abandon its plan to restore the Caribbean and Sinhala services, axed in earlier cuts. And the protests did indeed come, in their familiar form – but significantly fewer than customary. Only a handful of letters in *The Times:* 'For millions of people all over the world the BBC overseas service represents the nearest they can get to the truth . . .' 'Truth can be a formidable international force, if skilfully used . . . .' 'The shortsightedness of the proposed cutbacks was made clear to me last week in Murmansk. . .'

Two explanations were possible for the apparent shortfall in outrage. Either fewer worthies were bothering to write to *The Times* or the newspaper was nowadays less ready to print the protests. Either interpretation should have triggered alarm bells at Broadcasting House as the governors and management limbered up for the tussle over the licence fee. For they signified that the BBC no longer had an automatic claim on the support of its traditional allies.

* * * *

On Wednesday, 12 December 1984, Stuart Young and Alasdair Milne told a press conference at Broadcasting House that the BBC was asking the government for a 41 per cent increase in the colour television licence fee, from £46 to £65 a year for the next three years. Pointing out that this came to less than 18p a day, Young called it 'remarkable value for all the BBC's television and radio services'. He added: 'The BBC has a demonstrably strong case for a fair and reasonable licence fee settlement based on value for money.'

Milne repeated the phrase that was to become central to the campaign: the TV licence was 'the best bargain in Britain'. He asked: 'What other major organisation in the country can offer to hold down its prices to 18 million customers for three years?' He explained:

> Our calculations must take account of advances in technology, the need to maintain programme budgets and the special inflationary pressures that affect broadcasting in the UK – forcing up, for example, the market rates for performers, writers, creative staff, feature films and sporting contracts. In return the BBC offers all of its existing services – plus some important but modestly budgeted new developments – at a guaranteed price for three years.

There was never any chance that the bulk of the press would accept Milne's and Young's evaluation of their claim as modest and justifiable. And in a remarkable intervention the Prime Minister, Margaret Thatcher, further spoiled its chance of being adequately reported. On the very day the claim was announced she let her spokesman, Bernard Ingham, drop a broad hint to lobby correspondents that she was in favour of the BBC taking advertising. She believed the Beeb was too big, over-staffed, extravagant and wrong to have undertaken breakfast TV and local radio. Early hints from Whitehall suggested that the Cabinet were thinking of a fee of £55 set for only a year, to give time for a review into advertising and other means of funding. The BBC's reaction was that this would be an inefficient compromise because it would rule out long-term planning.

A *Daily Express* editorial, moved to the front page for extra effect, summed up much of Fleet Street's view. SAY NO TO THE BBC it was headed, and it declared:

> This increase is not warranted. No increase is warranted. . . The BBC now makes almost as many headlines for its wastrel ways as it chooses to broadcast on other topics. . . Mr. Milne appears to think there is nothing wrong in using licence-payers' money to

pay for the lavish propaganda packs he showered on Fleet Street, justifying the proposed increase. . . Mr. Stuart Young says with mind-boggling arrogance that the issue of advertising is not part of the debate. . . It is high time Aunty's bluff was called.

The *Mail* accused the Beeb of being smug, the *Telegraph* said local radio could be axed and the *Sunday Mirror* called for the abolition of Breakfast Time. Not all the BBC's critics, though, went all the way with Mrs Thatcher on the question of advertising. The *Telegraph* was against it and so was the *Observer*. The editor of the *Sunday Times* Andrew Neil, in a signed article, suggested limiting the licence increase to £12 and supplementing the corporation's income with limited advertising on radio:

> It is hard to see how the BBC's great mission to uphold broadcasting standards and British culture could be thwarted by allowing advertisements on its pop music and light entertainment radio stations. . . 'Slippery slope' arguments are a familiar device of the British establishment when it comes to resisting inconvenient change.

Milne and Young pulled out all the stops to counter the critics and promote their proposal for a £65 fee. They appeared on as many of their own programmes as could be persuaded to accommodate them – Breakfast Time, radio's Jimmy Young show, the World at One, Tuesday Call, regional and local programmes. They wrote articles for any newspaper that would provide space. Young told the BBC's staff newspaper *Ariel* that it would take time for the message to get across, but that eventually the rightness of the claim would be properly understood:

> I think that when some of the hysteria dies down we will do what I believe we have to do – show the justice of the case, that our budget has been very well thought through and that the increase is justified. Since our figures are being or will be in due course confirmed by an independent professional firm, I am relatively relaxed.

If he was genuinely feeling relaxed he had no right to be, because he had unwittingly disclosed a contradiction in the campaign. In order to make the case for the £65 fee, the corporation believed it had no alternative but to bring the issue repeatedly into the public arena, banging its drum with fervour. Every time it did so, its critics felt constrained to counter what they chose to characterise as Beebish arrogance and self-satisfaction. So the hysteria did not die down, but was fed by the BBC's own stridency.

After Christmas the evangelism was supplemented by publication of a pamphlet called 'Why Does the BBC. . . ?' It provided answers to questions often put by listeners and viewers in letters and in the public meetings with senior executives held from time to time at centres across the country. In it was a table showing that the British licence fee was only the tenth highest in Europe and would rise only four places if the requested increase were granted. It repeated the familiar statistic that BBC programmes cost on average £34,500 an hour, compared with £50,000 an hour for ITV. And it included a statement by Young that presented succinctly the case for the BBC's universality. Answering the question: 'Does the BBC really need to compete for audiences?' Young declared:

> By keeping in touch with the majority through programmes like The Two Ronnies, Tenko and Last of the Summer Wine, we are able to keep faith with the minority. For if the licence fee continues to be seen as good value by the viewers of Top of the Pops, for instance, it will continue to fund the contribution that the BBC's orchestras make to the serious music culture of Britain.

The pamphlet did not include the specific question: 'Why does the BBC have to be one big organisation instead of a group of smaller ones?' Yet that was one of the main themes of a remarkable series of three leading articles in *The Times* in January 1985 – remarkable because it is unusual for *The Times* to write leading articles in series and because of the degree of indignation they provoked in the BBC.

The first appeared on Monday 14th January under the almost satirical headline WHITHER THE BBC? The immediate pretext was a private member's bill due to be presented in the Commons the following day by the Labour MP Joe Ashton, calling on the BBC to take advertising. (Most of Ashton's Labour colleagues disapproved of his bill. He was motivated not by sympathy for the advertising lobby but by concern for his poor constituents who found it a real hardship to pay the existing fee, let alone the one now proposed. The bill was defeated by 159 votes to 118, most of the support coming from the Conservative side of the House.)

In that first editorial, *The Times* made its position clear from the beginning: 'The BBC should not survive this Parliament at its present size, in its present form and with its present terms of reference intact.' It went on to discuss the nature of public service broadcasting: the question had until now always been fudged, allowing the BBC to evolve its own concept of a seamless robe, with no definable point at which entertainment ends and the public service begins.

> To the true disciples of Lord Reith, the meat and the pudding are both necessary parts of the same well-balanced meal; it is as much a component of the public good that the quiz show should be a suitable family treat as that the news programmes keep the electorate properly informed of world events. To the more cynical broadcasters, the role of the quiz shows is to bring in the size of audience necessary to justify a licence fee which comes from everyone who owns a television set regardless of whether he/she watches television or not.

The Times then set itself a list of questions about public service broadcasting and its funding that it would seek to answer over the next two days. It did so in a radical but well-reasoned way. The Tuesday offering looked at length at the argument that programme quality would suffer if there were any change in the method of funding the BBC:

> The government might consider critically the question of whether British television really is better than that of the Americans and the rest of the world. It would find much that is wrong with American television but that it does produce many fine programmes at no public expense. . . If it decided that Britain really can justify its claim to the best quality television in the world it should look at the cost of that quality and whether consumers really want to pay it. . . Suppose it were proposed that all cornflakes boxes have printed on them the works of Shakespeare. Would that mean we had the highest quality cornflakes boxes in the world, or would it mean that we were rather foolish?

The sting was reserved for the final editorial in the series, printed on Wednesday:

'The government should concede no increase in the BBC licence fee. Nor should it jump to an ill-considered conclusion that advertising be taken immediately on Radios 1 and 2 and BBC1. The future of British broadcasting requires rapid and radical enquiry first.' *The Times* then outlined what, in its view, the result of such an enquiry should be:

> Eight years ago Lord Annan's committee recommended a break-up of the BBC into its radio and television and local radio components. (It did not, as it happened.) The government should now prepare to go further than this. It should consider quickly the establishment of a new broadcasting commission to auction franchises that are currently held by the BBC. These franchises could form one or more than one of the services that the corporation currently controls. Public service criteria would be constructed and strictly enjoined upon the franchise holders, all of whom would be allowed to take advertising under as little regulation as the commission thought appropriate to the smooth establishment of the new arrangements.
>
> The licence fee would not be abolished. It would be held at its present level – or possibly lower – and used by the commission to ease the changeover and to fund the public services. The most important of these would be a news and current affairs service which would most likely be created out of the present BBC departments. This could be protected from political interference by a board of governors similar to that now employed for the BBC as a whole. . . In the next few weeks the government has the opportunity to begin the process of redefining public service broadcasting in a way that will ensure its survival for the 1990s and beyond. It should seize it with a will.

Alasdair Milne and the BBC management read all that with growing horror. *The Times* had for years been an ally of the BBC and of its paternalist attitude to culture. There had been much useful cross-fertilisation between the two organisations. Sir William Haley, one of the most respected post-war directors-general, had become editor of *The Times,* and his successor in that post, William Rees-Mogg, was now vice-chairman of the board of governors. In 1981 the paper had been bought by

Rupert Murdoch, the Australian press and television magnate. Under the terms of the purchase he was forbidden to exercise any influence on the editorial content, but *The Times* had nevertheless moved sharply to the right since the change of ownership, from moderate Conservative to something approaching Murdoch's own brand of right-wing radicalism – a philosophy he shared with the editor Charles Douglas-Home, the nephew of a former Tory Prime Minister.

Faced with this frontal assault from an erstwhile ally, the BBC chiefs searched for ulterior motives. Aside from his Australian TV interests, in 1983 Murdoch had bought control of a satellite television venture beaming programmes – mainly feature films – to cable systems in Britain and the rest of Europe. He had also bought a satellite company in America that would beam programmes to individual homes, although that project had suffered a setback. And in 1984 he launched an ambitious and ultimately unsuccessful bid for Warner Communications, the American conglomerate that has film and TV interests. (His successful bid for Twentieth-Century-Fox came later in 1985.) Murdoch, then, was no disinterested party in any discussion of the future of television. When his newspapers suggested auctioning off the BBC's franchises, could it be that they envisaged their proprietor as being among the more active bidders?

Milne's first public speech after *The Times'* leaders was at a dinner of the Cardiff Business Club on Monday 21 January. It was an impassioned defence of the £65 application, which was 'not a bargaining bid in an Eastern bazaar, but a responsible request for proper funding in the bracing, sceptical air of our democracy'. The BBC, he said, was suffering from the fact that it was in the public sector, and all public sector operations were now being viewed with the gravest suspicion. But if it were to supplement its revenues by accepting advertising, programme standards would be bound to plummet.

> Every seasoned television pro will tell you how easy it is to maximise audiences by exploiting the worst that is in us: women wrestling with one another in mud, the secretary's rival testimony about her boss as against the evidence presented by the wife – these are not fancies but programmes televised in other

countries. All that stands between us and that sort of calculation is civilisation itself. Often that civilised barrier is as thin as a wafer. We should not in a fit of temporary weakness make it thinner still. . .

We are thus united at the BBC, from top to bottom, in rejecting advertising as either an exclusive or partial means of financing our kind of public service broadcasting operation. We are united, not at all out of some toffee-nosed horror of the supposed vulgarity of commerce which a tiny advertising lobby seeks to ascribe to us, but out of the deep conviction that there ought to remain in Britain one sector of broadcasting in which programmes are not interrupted, one sector in which the number of listeners and viewers for a programme are not decisively important.

It was a powerful speech but essentially a defensive one. That point was made to Milne by Stephen Hearst, the veteran broadcaster who is now one of the director-general's two special advisers. He believed that the BBC was engaged in ideological warfare against the Thatcher/Murdoch right. 'All defensive ideological battles in the twentieth century have been lost battles,' he told Milne. 'You have to boot the ball back into your opponent's penalty area.' Historically the BBC has not excelled at that tactic. It has thought itself too big to bother. Hearst persuaded Milne that if the Murdoch press was laying into the Beeb, he should give Murdoch a taste of the same.

The director-general was due to make a speech to the TV and Radio Industries Club on Tuesday, 29 January. At his request, Hearst wrote him a paragraph responding to *The Times* leaders. 'Who is the more likely to serve the public interest?' he asked. 'The BBC or *The Times* whose recommendations if acted upon would have the practical effect of enabling its owner Rupert Murdoch to acquire some of the most valuable broadcasting action in the UK?' He went on to discuss the unrestrained self-interest of 'one or two fortune seekers' who saw a plum ripe for harvesting.

This unusual tactic succeeded in provoking a rapid response from *The Times* in the shape of another long editorial the following Saturday, 2 February, headed THE BBC AT BAY (the same headline as on the long *Sunday Times* article almost a year earlier). The pretext was the delivery that week to the Home

Secretary of the Peat, Marwick report on BBC efficiency, but it was apparent that the real motive was to strike back at Milne. The leader began by noting that the BBC had so far succeeded in keeping the battle to its own ground by channelling the discussion towards how much it needed to maintain its existing level of activity. It had not faced the question, put in the three editorials, whether a single organisation should continue to fulfil all its functions. After a swipe at Milne's suggestion that 'press critics could be acting only out of the crude self-interest of media rivals', *The Times* made a concrete suggestion: the establishment of a Home Office inquiry into the financing and structure of British broadcasting, and whether the monolithic BBC was the best model for the provision of necessary public services:

> If frequencies were eventually to be auctioned to regulated private companies, the BBC's many and various parts would have a head start to win their share of what Alasdair Milne calls 'some of the most valuable broadcasting action in the UK'. They would be in a still better position if their masters decided now to face the real arguments and to stop pretending that the Home Secretary's decision begins and ends with the present structure of the BBC.

Alongside the public debate, the BBC was putting its case privately to people who would be influential in determining the outcome. Members of Parliament are regularly invited in groups to Broadcasting House and Television Centre to see what licence-payers get for their money. Milne himself often goes to the Commons to talk to committees of MPs concerned with media matters. But his most potent lobbying weapon is his series of intimate weekly lunches with ministers, shadow ministers, trade unionists, editors and industrialists. These take place in the oak-panelled private dining room near his third floor office. The BBC is represented by Milne, his deputy (then Alan Protheroe) and Margaret Douglas, whose specific function is to oversee the corporation's relations with the political parties.

In the months before the licence decision was taken, scarcely any relevant politician had not been entertained at either one of these lunches or the grander affairs that follow governors' meetings every other Thursday. One week in April, after the new fee was announced, the guest was Charles Douglas-Home, editor of *The Times*. Milne was surprised to discover that, even at that stage, Douglas-Home was exercised about his January speech. The editor still felt wounded by the suggestion that *The Times'* view on the BBC's future had been motivated by the interest of its proprietor. 'You've done us a lot of damage,' he told Milne. The director-general responded that surely the BBC had been the more damaged, through having its very legitimacy challenged so vigorously in his newspaper's editorial column.

Douglas-Home was not content to let the matter rest there. He asked the 'independent' national directors of *The Times* (not truly independent because they can be appointed only with the agreement of the proprietor) to investigate Milne's suggestion that the editorial line may have been improperly influenced by Murdoch. They asked Milne to present evidence of this. He did not have any – and he had not in any event made a specific charge of collusion. 'The inference I drew from the paper's behaviour over the BBC seemed a reasonable one,' he wrote. 'But the editor's explanation was sufficient to lay my fears to rest.' In their pompously worded findings, printed in full in *The Times* of 19 June 1985, the independent directors declared solemnly: 'There is no case for sustaining any suggestion that the editor's independence has been threatened or impugned.'

Nobody was overly impressed with this magisterial but scarcely impartial judgement, which was thought to detract from the dignity of the newspaper rather than enhance it. The following week it published a letter from David Elstein suggesting that it should now print an article explaining how Murdoch's extensive media interests would be affected by the changes it recommended. No such article was forthcoming; but the incident did the director-general little good, either. For it reinforced the growing perception that Milne, foolishly trapped into writing a letter that could be interpreted as a retraction of his January remarks, was too unworldly for a job that more than ever required political acumen.

* * * *

While this drama and high comedy was being played out in the boardrooms and in the columns of the press, what was happening on the small screen? By the spring of 1985 Michael Grade had been controller of BBC1 for six months. It would be an exaggeration to report that he had taken up his post the previous September with a fanfare: but the event did provoke more fuss than is customary. He was photographed arriving at Television Centre bright and early on the Monday morning, sharply suited and parrying questions about his intentions. Commentators had been speculating as to whether he would prove the great populariser that his family name suggested. He and his supporters had countered that by pointing to the cultural programmes he had been responsible for at London Weekend, including the South Bank Show, a successful venture in the difficult area of finding a format for a TV arts magazine.

For his first few weeks at the Beeb he had kept his head below the parapet, finding his way around the confusing doughnut-shaped building. He was trying to identify those people Paul Fox had warned him against, the ones with whom contact should be avoided at all costs; and then to find people he could work with fruitfully. Among his first executive acts was a request for the home telephone numbers of producers: he liked to congratulate them instantly if he saw anything especially well done. Once he had got to grips with the people, he could start work on the programmes and the schedules. An early scheduling change produced rapid results. When he arrived there was a series called Tenko, about women in a Japanese prisoner-of-war camp. It played on Thursday nights to modest audiences. He switched it to Sunday and it moved into the top three in the BBC ratings.

Grade's first major public utterance came in November at a symposium of the Royal Television Society in Cardiff. As if to confirm to the audience, and to himself, that he had decidedly switched sides, he devoted some time to criticising ITV for trivialising its schedules by pushing serious programmes to non-peak times, and blamed the Independent Broadcasting Authority for allowing it. David Cunliffe of Yorkshire Television commented: 'He's had a head transplant down there at the Shepherd's Bush hospital.'

He also gave a few early clues as to his intentions. He would be buying fewer feature films for BBC1 and putting the money towards more home-grown films and mini-series; there would be more drama series and more half-hour comedy. But that did not mean abandoning the BBC's commitment to single plays – the most expensive form of television – and documentaries. And he made one headline-grabbing declaration of intent that served to modify his reputation of being primarily concerned with show-business values: beauty contests would no longer be seen on BBC television. 'They are an anachronism in this day and age of equality, and verging on the offensive.'

It takes a channel controller at least a year to begin stamping his personal imprint on the output, because for the initial months he is simply scheduling programmes initiated by his predecessor. So when Grade introduced his spring schedule in February 1985, the only part he could truly call his own was the timing. The main changes came in the early evening, after the national and regional news programmes. On two nights a week the 7 o'clock spot was occupied by East Enders, a new soap opera about working-class Londoners that had been three years in the making. Frankly modelled on Granada's Coronation Street, it was an instant ratings success. On the other three nights at that time Terry Wogan, the popular Irish radio personality, hosted a talk show.

The same month Grade revealed his rebellious streak by moving in on two well-entrenched programmes. Panorama, the venerable current affairs warhorse, had occupied the 8 o'clock position on Mondays for as long as anyone could remember. Over the years there had been desultory talk about shifting it to a later time, after the Nine O'Clock News, when the audience for serious television was assumed to be larger. But because it was such an institution, a symbol of the BBC's commitment to responsible journalism, the safe course had always been to leave it where it was. Grade is not a man for safe courses. Braving the clucking of Lime Grove traditionalists, who feared this was the first part of an attempt to downgrade Panorama, he moved it to 9.30. Criticism was stilled when the first ratings appeared: at its new time, it doubled its audience right away.

His other move proved even more controversial. The fantasy adventure series Dr Who had formed part of people's Saturday evening for twenty-two years. In 1984 Alan Hart had tried to change its timing to midweek, but public pressure was such that he kept it where it was. Work on a new series was due to start in

March 1985, but in February Grade announced its postponement until the autumn of 1986, to free money for other drama projects. At least Panorama does not have a formal fan club. Dr Who does and its members were outraged, worrying that the postponement could ultimately lead to outright cancellation. There was a suspicion that Grade had made this well-publicised gesture to impress on the Cabinet how grave the BBC's financial position was, as they neared a decision on the licence fee. He denied it and declined to bow to the pressure to reprieve the Doctor, pointing out that, although still watched by 8 million viewers, his figures were slowly declining.

There were other small controversies. Although he had declared his commitment to the expensive single play – another BBC totem capable of provoking passionately defensive tirades from the drama department – Grade said in March that the Sunday night Play of the Month was being suspended.

This came not long after the announcement that the corporation was paying £500,000 for an American mini-series based on Jeffrey Archer's novel Kane and Abel. Grade's last Hollywood job was as executive producer to that project, but the BBC pointed out that he no longer had any pecuniary interest in it. Taken together, these two incidents showed Grade shifting BBC1 towards more popular and accessible forms of drama, away from plays that, although artistically admirable, worked out at a formidable cost per viewer.

None of these squalls could compare with the thunderous storm over Dallas, the American soap opera that regularly figured in the BBC's top ten ratings with audiences of around 13 million. On Wednesday, 16 January, Grade called a short-notice press conference to announce that the next series would not be shown on BBC because Thames Television, the London weekday commercial company, had made a higher offer. Brian Cowgill, the boss of Thames, had that day signed an agreement with Worldvision, the American distributor of the series, to pay £54,000 for each episode, almost double the £29,000 the BBC was then paying. The BBC had declined to match the offer.

Grade and Bill Cotton were angry because Cowgill's deal broke a gentlemen's agreement between the two British channels not to push up the price of imported programmes by bidding for them competitively. This meant that once an American series had been secured for one channel, it stayed there for the rest of its natural life – a cost-saving ruse for the TV companies, although naturally irritating to the Hollywood distributors deprived of a free market for their goods. Occasionally such inter-channel agreements were broken – as when Grade himself had tried to hijack live soccer for ITV – but generally they stuck. Indeed in 1981 the ITV barons, when Grade was still among them, had been approached by Worldvision, who wondered whether they might consider making a grab for Dallas. They decided the price – then £30,000 an episode – was too high and it would not be worth the inevitable obloquy and the possibility of legal action by the BBC.

This time Cowgill had acted alone, without involving the other ITV companies. By doing so he succeeded in antagonising not only the BBC but also his independent colleagues. Paul Fox of Yorkshire and David Plowright of Granada declared petulantly that they would not screen the programme, and several of the other commercial companies were considering their position. Plowright was particularly irritated because that very week he had been urging the government not to increase the levy on TV companies' profits. The Dallas deal hardly supported his plea of poverty in the commercial sector. If Cowgill could not get his new property shown on the network, it would turn into a very expensive acquisition indeed. The Independent Broadcasting Authority joined the chorus of disapproval and Cowgill was summoned for a dressing-down by its director-general, John Whitney. At a higher level Lord Thomson, chairman of the IBA, warned Hugh Dundas, chairman of Thames, that the company might lose its franchise if the deal went ahead.

Petulance was the order of the day among BBC executives, too. At his press conference, Grade called the deal 'shabby and underhand'. And he threatened that he might retaliate by holding back the remaining sixteen episodes in the current series until the autumn, when Thames proposed to begin showing the new programmes. That meant addicts would have to start viewing the next series before they knew what had happened at the end of the last one.

Nobody thought Grade meant it: the tantrum would pass soon

enough. But it did not. The following week he cancelled the spring run of Dallas – and ensured that the protests were now diverted away from Cowgill's head and around his. The *Sun* ran three editorials urging him to think again, then began printing accounts of the plot lines viewers were missing. The *Sunday Times* fumed: 'For an organisation which keeps on trumpeting the virtues of public service broadcasting this is a disgraceful way to behave. If any private company acted with such disregard for its customers it would soon be out of business.' A councillor from Sheffield presented the Prime Minister with a petition, signed by 3,000 constituents, asking her to use her influence to get the series back on the air. A letter-writer in the *Daily Mail* recommended: 'Michael Grade should be sent back to kindergarten where his childish tantrums can be dealt with effectively,' and another said the incident negated the BBC's claim for an increase in the licence fee.

It was that last point that worried the board of governors. They told Milne that Grade's move was poorly timed in the light of the impending licence decision. Milne agreed. He had adopted a hands-off attitude toward Grade until now, on the ground that if you hire someone to put new life into a demoralised organisation, it makes no sense to cramp his style. But this had now become a public issue bearing on the BBC's central current concern. Milne called in Grade and told him that, while he appreciated the competitive urge that had led him to pull Dallas off the schedule until the autumn, it would now be politic to retreat and show the remaining issues. Grade chose a public forum for the climb-down. Terry Wogan, on the first of his series of talk shows on 18 February, announced that Dallas would return in March. Bill Cotton admitted sheepishly: 'We were taken aback by the strength of viewers' reaction to taking it off.'

The question nobody raised during the furore was whether the BBC should be in the Dallas business at all. The argument for the glossy American series is that they are professionally made, popular and much cheaper than anything comparable that the BBC could produce. They help justify the licence fee by achieving high ratings. They are watched by *Sun* readers, which is why the *Sun* devoted three leaders to them. But Dallas contains no public service element and there is something incongruous about the board of governors, whose minds you might assume to be on loftier things, solemnly debating when the remaining issues should be shown. It highlights the central lack of clarity about the governors' role and the wider uncertainty over whether the BBC should, after all, be going for the mass market. The fact that many of its popular programmes are interchangeable with those on the the independent channel does not help the Beeb's claim for support from public funds.

If the Dallas affair resulted in an embarrassing blow to the BBC's credibility, it did no good to Cowgill, either. His dispute with the other ITV chiefs simmered for six months and caused strains within Thames Television. On 12 July 1985 he resigned as managing director, attacking the 'cosy and dangerous accommodation' between the two channels on overseas programmes and saying that his decision sprang from the IBA's threat to remove the Thames franchise unless Dallas was returned to the BBC. After further long and acrimonious negotiations with Worldvision, Dallas went back to the Beeb.

* * * *

Before the announcement of the licence settlement, Young had one more piece of house-cleaning to put into effect. Ever since he became chairman he had been bewildered and irritated by having one member of the board of management, David Webster, based in New York. To be an effective director Webster had to attend board meetings, which meant numerous expensive Transatlantic flights – one every three weeks on average, some in the splendour of Concorde.

Webster is a large man in most respects; tall, plump, extravagant, persuasive, doing nothing by halves. In build he resembles Aubrey Singer. Colleagues would lump them together as the Pooh Bahs, Gilbertian aristocrats who gathered authority to themselves by virtue of their physical presence and self-confidence as much as through innate skills. The seventies were a fruitful time for such figures in the BBC. Webster had been a producer of current affairs programmes and then assistant head of current affairs at Lime Grove under John Grist. During a stint as head of the New York office in the early 1970s, he bought for the BBC a lavish apartment in United Nations Plaza, then one of the most exclusive buildings in the city. Back in London, his powers of persuasion were put to good use when he was made controller of information services. In 1977 he joined the board of management as director of public affairs, charged among other things with putting the BBC's case to Members of Parliament. It had been a rapid rise.

In 1980 Webster married Elizabeth Drew, a respected Washington journalist who wrote for the *New Yorker*. She clearly was not going to throw up her thriving career to fulfil the role of a corporation wife in London. Ian Trethowan, then director general, valued Webster's contributions to board meetings and suggested that he go back to New York as a US-based director, taking a particular interest in the then promising field of direct broadcasting by satellite. He would be replacing John Grist, due to return to London after four years. The chairman George Howard (another Pooh Bah) approved the appointment but, aside from him and Trethowan, there were few senior executives who saw any logic in it.

Grist and Webster had never been mutual admirers. At Lime Grove Grist had been the senior of the two but as director of public affairs Webster had controlled international relations, which meant Grist was working under him. Webster arrived in New York while Grist, a difficult and sometimes irritable man, was engaged in tricky negotiations with Trethowan about his future. (They ended in his leaving the corporation and becoming managing director of Services and Sound and Vision Corporation, a film and broadcasting production company linked with the Ministry of Defence.) Grist's mood was not improved when he heard that the first thing Webster had done after arriving in New York, before even introducing himself to the staff, was to ring the office manager, Werner Hebman, to discuss changing the carpet. So when Webster went to call on Grist at the BBC's Fifth Avenue offices, Grist sent word to the receptionist that he was out. Webster instead went in for a chat with Peter Foges, an old colleague. On the way out he put his head round Grist's door, to see him writing at his desk.

'Hullo,' said Webster. Without looking up from his writing, Grist responded steelily:

'Get out of my office, you fat fool, and don't come back until I've gone.'

Webster tottered back to Foges' office and sat down, looking pale. 'Do you know what he called me?' he stammered. 'He called me a fat fool.'

Surviving this setback, Webster began to imprint his personality on the New York office as soon as Grist pulled out. Needing more space to cope with his additional responsibilities for satellites, he rented a suite on the floor above and had a spiral staircase installed to link them. When word of this reached the Fleet Street gossip columns, it was pilloried as an example of BBC extravagance, and so were some of the fairly basic electronic office gadgets he had installed. This did not worry Webster but it did increasingly cause concern at Broadcasting House, because it helped feed the generalised impression of corporate expenditure getting out of control. When Young became chairman he identified it as just the kind of excess that he, as an accountant, had been hired to do something about. Milne, who had never seen the logic of Webster's role, agreed. What was needed in New York was a competent production person, not a high-level board member – especially since by 1984 it was becoming clear that satellite television was not an immediate prospect. It was not as if Webster's presence obviated the need for other senior executives to visit the States. American trips were invariably enjoyable and heads of department could always find a pretext for crossing the Atlantic in person to finalise deals, rather than leaving it to the director on the spot.

In the summer of 1984 Young and his wife visited the United States to attend the Olympic Games at Los Angeles. Webster had cut short a holiday to be in Washington when they arrived. He sent a chauffeur-driven limousine to meet them at Dulles Airport and on their first evening took them for dinner at the Jockey Club, a discreet and extremely expensive room at the back of the Ritz-Carlton Hotel on Massachusetts Avenue. It is the kind of place where regular customers such as Webster know the *maitre d'hotel* by his first name, and where any evening or lunchtime you are likely to meet influential members of the US administration. Later Webster hosted a party for the Youngs, where the guest list provided proof that he and his wife knew a large proportion of

Washington's movers and shakers. Young was impressed but it was not in any sense his milieu and the evening only reinforced his doubts about whether the BBC really needed that level of representation in the United States. Like anything Webster was involved in, it did not come cheap.

Young's impression was strengthened when he went to see the set-up in New York. It was not the staircase and the electronics that bothered him – nor, as was later rumoured, any slights he felt he and his wife had endured from the Websters. He felt the sheer scale of the American operation was unnecessary. He told Webster that, unless he was prepared to return to London, it would be better if he parted company from the Beeb. It took a while to negotiate his comfortable compensation terms, which included a consultancy deal on satellites, but he finally left in February 1985 and was succeeded in New York by Peter Woon, former head of television news, not a member of the board.

* * * *

The Peat, Marwick, Mitchell report on whether the BBC gives value for money was presented to the board of governors on Thursday, 31 January 1985 and to the Home Secretary, Leon Brittan, the following day. It would be a month before the contents were published but Stuart Young gave a broad hint that same weekend that the findings were favourable to the Beeb. On the Channel 4 interview programme, Face the Press, Young said the study had found, as he always believed it would, that the BBC does give value for money, but that some 'fine tuning' might be needed. Later he was to declare, in a phrase he would come to regret, that the report gave the corporation 'a clean bill of health'. This was taken to mean that it supported the financial calculations and inflation forecasts behind the claim for a £65 fee.

On 5 March, Peat, Marwick's main conclusions and recommendations were published, but not the annexes that made detailed points about departmental activities and recommended thirty specific cost-saving measures. At a self-congratulatory press conference, Young repeated his assertion that the report proved the legitimacy of the £65 claim and rashly predicted that

it would be met in full. BBC1's Nine O'Clock News, in an excess
of enthusiasm, went further, stating erroneously that the report
had specifically backed the claim and moreover had found no
over-staffing – mistakes that were the subject of embarrassed
apologies a few days later.

Next morning Young and Milne, who were coming to be
obsessed by *The Times'* coverage of their licence application,
eagerly picked up the paper to see what its reporter had made of
it. They were surprised and relieved to read the headline above
David Hewson's story: BBC PRAISED FOR QUALITY AND
EFFICIENCY IN BUSINESS STUDY. The text beneath was
scarcely less pleasing, making the point that the accountants had
praised the corporation's commitment to quality and efficiency.
Hewson added the proviso that the largely favourable nature of
the report did not necessarily mean that the Beeb would get its
£65 fee, because of the 'breadth of opposition' that had come to
light since the application was made.

Young's and Milne's relief was short-lived. Next day *The
Times* decided it had been gullible in accepting the Peat,
Marwick report at the BBC's own valuation. Hewson's
front-page story, headlined REBUFF FOR BBC ON £65 FEE,
quoted a response from Peat, Marwick's John Fielden to Young's
'clean bill of health' assertion:

> I think he has been reading very selectively. The report is a
> mixed judgment on the BBC. The very fact that the BBC is
> implementing 30 recommendations from it can't mean it is a clean
> bill of health. . . I was disappointed at the emphasis in the BBC
> news of our report. It reported us as saying there is no
> overstaffing and we supported the licence fee. . . We were not
> asked to comment on the level of the licence fee and staffing was
> outside our remit.

Fielden added that in his view the whole report should have been
published, including the secret annexes.

Hewson returned to the attack on the next two days, implying
that the BBC had fixed the terms of reference to prevent the
investigators from considering staffing levels, and suggesting
that the Home Office believed the report to have little bearing on
the level at which the fee should be set. This provoked an
outraged response in the correspondence columns from Geoff

Buck, director of finance, who pointed out that Peat, Marwick's terms of reference had been drawn up in concert with the Home Office.

Young was angered by all these quibbles, which had the inevitable effect of suggesting that the BBC was behaving shiftily and had something to hide, negating the upbeat effect he had intended from his 5th March press conference. He complained to Peat, Marwick and received a letter from P. J. Butler, senior partner in the firm, regretting Fielden's comment that Young had been selective: 'We know this to be untrue.' He confirmed that the published part of the report contained the main findings and the annexe had not been intended for publication. He thanked Young for apologising about the inaccurate news report on the 5th. The letter satisfied the chairman's *amour propre* but did not repair the damage caused by the confusion.

The most specific ill effect was in the mind of Leon Brittan, the Home Secretary, the man who would have the strongest voice in setting the licence fee and who had insisted on the inquiry in the first place, partly to mollify his back-benchers. He knew that those of them most opposed to the BBC would seize on the doubts raised by the *Times* reports and the BBC's maladroit response to them. It had, he believed, been grossly mishandled by Young, and he told him so. It was demonstrably wrong to present the report as a clean bill of health that confirmed the justice of the BBC's application. On the other hand, Brittan recognised that some of the critics had vested interests. Despite the protestations of its editor, when *The Times* ran five editorials on a subject (a fifth had appeared at the end of February) this smacked of something more than a strongly held view that happened to coincide with the interest of its proprietor.

Brittan and a small group of ministers outside the Cabinet formed a committee to decide the level of the fee. On Wednesday, 27 March, Brittan invited Young to his room at the House of Commons. The news was bad but scarcely unexpected. The licence fee would be set for the next three years at £58 – a full £7 below the request. This was close to the level that commentators had forecast. It was a nice figure in a political sense, representing a large enough increase over the present fee to take inflation into account, but far enough below the requested figure to deflect some – but in the event by no means all – criticism that the government had once again been led by the nose by the smoothies of Portland Place.

Naturally, Brittan did not present it to Young in those terms. Although he began the meeting by declaring: 'We don't believe the public should be asked to pay £65,' he explained that the final award was based on the BBC's own detailed application. In arriving at £65, the corporation had included a sum of £5.70 for the enhancement and development of broadcasting services. Brittan said there should be a freeze on such development, at least until the future of broadcasting had been determined by the means he was about to explain. In addition, Peat, Marwick had said that their recommended economies could save £20 million a year.'We want you to do better than that,' Brittan urged Young.'We want you to save £65 million.' That came to £1.30 per licence. Added to the development money, it amounted to a cut of £7 – which miraculously took the figure down to what was politically acceptable.

The second part of Brittan's proposal had again been quite widely anticipated in the press. He was going to appoint a committee to look into the consequences – both to the BBC and to rival media – of accepting advertising as a replacement or supplement to the licence fee, and to consider other ways of raising money for broadcasting. It would not necessarily have to make recommendations but could if it wished confine itself to laying out options. Its chairman would be Professor Alan Peacock of Heriot-Watt University in Scotland. That was another piece of bad news for the Beeb. Peacock, a former chief economic adviser to the Department of Trade and Industry, was one of that breed of free-market economists that had inspired fear in all public institutions since Mrs Thatcher became Prime Minister and clasped them to her bosom. He had also held a post at Buckingham, the private university with a right-wing reputation. On the plus side he was fond of music, so could not be a total barbarian: and he insisted that he would not play the role of a 'hired gun' to kill off the BBC.

The committee was given plenty of time to complete its work. A report was not expected until the summer of 1986 and Brittan told Peacock that he would sooner have a thorough report than a speedy one – the politician's traditional way of hinting that he would not be displeased by an element of delay. By the time the Cabinet had decided what, if any, action to take on the recommendations, the next election might be in the air, and the Conservatives would probably prefer to put any broadcasting reform in their manifesto rather than tackle it right away.

That at least gave the BBC some breathing space but it did not mean any let-up from the attentions of the Murdoch press. After *The Times'* attempts to argue the case against the corporation from the intellectual high ground, its stablemate the *News of the World* adopted the knee-in-the-groin tactics that come more naturally to it. On Sunday, 14 April, it spread over two pages the headline: BRITISH BONKERS CORPORATION. The story beneath it was a conglomeration of allegations about corporate overspending:

> The BBC have an army of 140 staff covering the two tables at the World Snooker Championship. . . At last year's SDP conference in Buxton, Derbyshire, there were said to be 250 BBC staff and only 400 delegates. . . The Beeb's new soap opera, East Enders, costs twice as much to make as Channel 4's Brookside. . . In November a cash storm blew up when BBC executives took their wives on a £30,000 trip to the Far East.

One of eight current affairs journalists whose contract had not been renewed (as an economy measure) told how his letter of dismissal had been sent in a chauffeur-driven car 60 miles to his home in Reading while he was working at Lime Grove. 'We're the scapegoats for an empire of incompetence,' he said. And Richard Somerset-Ward, who resigned as head of music and arts after scandalous allegations in *Private Eye* about his personal behaviour, made further charges of waste, saying: 'At times I could have managed with half or even a third of my staff.'

The article was composed of sketchy anecdotes and generalised abuse rather than any original research. ('There were so many BBC people there I started interviewing them by mistake,' an unnamed producer was quoted as saying.) It could have been that the editor of the *News of the World* had the idea of investigating BBC extravagance independently of Murdoch and of the campaign in *The Times*. But the battered warriors of Portland Place and Television Centre could be forgiven for suspecting that there was more to it than that, and that Murdoch's apparent campaign against them would now be sustained until the Peacock committee produced its report.

Chapter 9

YES, MINISTER

PROFESSOR Peacock's first appearance on a public platform after his appointment to head the inquiry into BBC funding was at the Edinburgh International Television Festival in August 1985. In retrospect the Edinburgh debates of the previous year, with Max Hastings and others thundering away about the collapse of standards in public service broadcasting, seemed frivolous. They amounted to nothing more than the pleasurable sport of pecking away at the Beeb and urging it on to more laudable things – pleasurable because the BBC always suffers its wounds publicly, openly writhing in anguish and pecking back in a predictably churlish manner. In the intervening year the government had finally moved in with what had all the appearance of a tangible threat, an inquiry into the future funding of the BBC that was in reality more than that. As the 200 or so delegates, dressed casually for a summer Sunday, sprawled on the uncomfortable seats in the main hall of the Assembly Rooms on George Street, Janet Morgan, one of Alasdair Milne's two special advisers, explained that the Peacock inquiry would be looking at the very legitimacy of Britain's broadcasting arrangements. It was not just a matter of economics, she argued: it involved public policy and philosophy. Given that the philosophy of the government – and of Professor Peacock – differed sharply from that of the BBC management, the odds seemed stacked against the broadcasters. Because the festival delegates were nearly all broadcasters themselves, the mood in the hall was defensive. The wagons were drawn into a circle, the better to fend off the unwelcome approaches of Peacock and those few of his allies who were present.

The altered role of Brian Wenham, director of programmes and TV Centre's house intellectual, was the most telling example of the difference the year had made. In 1984 he had been reduced to reeling off lists of creditable BBC television programmes to counter suggestions that the corporation had gone to pot. Few were swayed by that argument and he came in for some rough handling, from both his own employees and outsiders. This year he was on the side of the angels – or rather the angels were on his. The hall was full of people doing nicely out of the broadcasting duopoly and not keen to risk any radical alteration. Wenham argued in detail against some of the alternatives that had been proposed to the licence fee and then made the general point that, if it was desirable to have more channels for a wider variety of broadcasting, it made no sense to cripple those that already existed and were performing creditably. Even when satellite and cable TV came on stream, there was no reason why some channels should not remain free of advertising. It was a negative argument, but it was what the audience wanted to hear.

Peacock was scarcely more positive. He seemed anxious to allay the fears of the broadcasters that he was some mad axeman bent on chopping down all the trees in the wood, no matter how many years of vigorous life they still had in them. A Scot with a mild and persuasive accent, his moderate manner belied his awesome reputation and his intellectual rigour. He stressed that he and his committee – whose members included that other redoubtable Scot Alastair Hetherington – had not been appointed simply to do the government's bidding.

'I detect a touch of frenzy in the air,' he said, 'as if my committee had the power of life or death over television. That is as far removed from reality as soap opera. . . Any suggestion that we are going to serve up a dish of pre-cooked political nostrums should be dismissed.' They were independent people and would judge the issues on their merits.

Peacock left everything so open that there was little scope for criticism from the hall. Other panellists were more forthright.

Rodney Harris, the advertising man who had fuelled the debate with his article in *Marketing Week* in September 1984, went over the arguments for commercialising the Beeb. The independent producer David Graham restated his case for funding public service broadcasting by selling leases on the many channels that would come available through cable and satellite, rather as leases for oil exploration are sold in the North Sea.

The man who appeared to relish most the role of bogeyman was Andrew Neil, editor of the *Sunday Times*. He is a popular target for the BBC and its defenders because his paper is owned by Rupert Murdoch, whom Alasdair Milne had accused of advocating the break-up of the corporation so as to get his hands on some of the action. Neil, another Scot, is philosophically opposed to cartels, which he believes invariably operate against the public interest, benefiting only those who are part of them. He likened the cartel in broadcasting (in other words the duopoly) to that among the Fleet Street print unions: by making newspapers inordinately expensive to produce, they render it impossible for anyone but a millionaire to own or launch one. Neil challenged the article of faith among the professionals that British TV is immeasurably better than that in the United States or anywhere else, comparing the down-market BBC comedy series Are You Being Served? with the cultural treats available on cable in New York. This provoked Michael Grade to snarl from the audience: 'A lot of us don't like what masquerades as journalism in the *Sunday Times*'. This rare breach in Grade's suave facade was evidence of the depth of feeling among BBC management over the conduct of the Murdoch papers.

Neil's point about labour practices had been underlined in a debate the previous day when representatives of unions in the broadcasting industry declared their support for the *status quo*. In particular, they opposed any increase in the role of independent producers, in whose houses the unions are not as powerfully represented as in the BBC or the ITV network companies. They deplored the measures the BBC had announced in July as their first response to the licence settlement and the Peat, Marwick report. Milne had unveiled an economy package involving the loss of up to 4,000 jobs, partly through putting such services as cleaning and catering out to private contract. As part of the package, the BBC pledged to devote 150 hours of screen time a year to the work of British independent producers by 1988. These concessions to Thatcherite economics had been urged on management by the governors. The unions saw both the dismissal of manual staff and the increased use of independent production houses as part of the same process of 'casualisation' – a dirty word in the vocabulary of organised labour. Large public corporations, employing full-time staff, are easier for unions to deal with, because the bigger they are the more vulnerable they must be to the threat of industrial action. Broadcasters and union leaders are among the favourite bogey groups of the radical right. With both united against change, how could any self-respecting Thatcherite administration resist inflicting it upon them?

* * * *

As a topic, the future of British broadcasting had to share the limelight at the 1985 television festival with a sensational incident that had occurred two weeks earlier. Like so many of the programme disputes of the last two decades, it concerned Northern Ireland. The BBC was about to screen a documentary in the Real Lives series that included an interview with a man reported as being the chief of staff of the Provisional IRA. Hearing of this the Home Secretary, Leon Brittan, wrote to the chairman of the governors, Stuart Young, asking for the programme to be withdrawn. The governors held an emergency meeting and took the unusual step of viewing the programme in advance. Having done so, they rejected the unanimous advice of the board of management and banned the film, provoking a ferocious dispute and a rash of front-page headlines that lasted for days.

Throughout the spring of 1985, there had been a feeling on the board of management that the governors were working up to some kind of a showdown. It was reinforced by a cluster of incidents in April where the governors made statements critical of decisions by Milne and his staff. They appeared to have abandoned the notion that public solidarity with management was paramount.

The first occasion was at Easter, when the managing director, Bill Cotton, and his senior colleagues at TV Centre decided, with Milne's approval, to end the long-standing practice of televising the Pope's annual message to his flock, on the grounds that it attracted an audience of only 200,000. The decision angered leading Catholics. Cardinal Basil Hume, Archbishop of Westminster, wrote to Young to complain. When the matter was raised with the board Sir William Rees-Mogg, himself a Catholic, was prominent among those who insisted that the message should be reinstated in ensuing years. Young wrote to Cardinal Hume assuring him that this would be done. Milne went along with the decision, despite its representing a rare departure for the governors. Their role *vis a vis* specific programmes was normally to praise or blame in retrospect, although they had on occasion intervened to prevent controversial programmes from being shown, as was their right. This was the first time anyone could remember their taking the opposite course and issuing a direct and public order that a particular programme *must* appear on the screen.

Two weeks later they went on record again to disown a management decision, this time in more sharply critical terms. For some days the newspapers had been exciting themselves with revelations about the family background of Princess Michael of Kent, a minor member of the royal family by marriage. It had been discovered that her father, a German, had once been a member of the Nazi SS. The independent breakfast television company TV-am secured an exclusive interview with the princess, screened on the morning of Wednesday, 17 April. Buckingham Palace had indicated that they would like the BBC to be given access to parts of the interview for their own breakfast programme, but TV-am would not agree. The commercial company was still smarting over events six months earlier, when an IRA bomb exploded at the Grand Hotel, Brighton, during the Conservative Party conference. Independent Television had no live news coverage and the BBC would not share its own. So TV-am saw no reason to do any favours over Princess Michael.

Faced with the refusal of permission to screen extracts from the interview, the BBC simply took the law into its own hands, recorded it from the screen and aired it without any acknowledgement. The decision was taken by David Lloyd, the editor of Breakfast Time, in consultation with Ron Neil. head of news, who informed Alan Protheroe, the assistant director-general. When Protheroe went into Milne's office later that morning and confessed to what had been done, Milne was appalled. 'We have gone absolutely wrong,' he declared. Nevertheless, when TV-am sought an injunction against the BBC later that morning, to prevent any .repeat showing of the interview, Protheroe went to court to contest the claim, and the BBC even appealed – unsuccessfully – when the injunction was granted.

Milne did not discuss the matter with Protheroe again until the next morning, when there was a governors' meeting. He asked who had been responsible for the decision to pirate the interview, and Protheroe offered no specific reply. So when the governors asked Milne the same question, he was obliged to confess that he had no answer. This irritated the board, who pointed out that more than twenty-four hours had passed since the incident, and they thought the director-general should have made it his business to discover what had gone wrong. Led by Young and his deputy Rees-Mogg, they described the incident as unprincipled and deplorable. Milne said he would make it his business to find out exactly what had happened and report back to them, but they were so angry that they refused to wait. After giving Milne an exceptionally rough time they issued a press statement deploring the incident and apologising for it.

Milne felt foolish and aggrieved. When the BBC was under attack from many quarters, he thought he was entitled to expect the governors to stand behind management, at least in public. The governors saw it differently. They believed that when politicians were sniping at the BBC for being out of control, it was incumbent on them to demonstrate forcefully that they were in charge, pursuing their supervisory function with vigour.

Less than a week later they received another unwelcome surprise, when they learned that the corporation was going to have to pay around £1m in costs to extricate itself from a libel case that had been in court for 87 days. Dr Sidney Gee, a Harley Street slimming expert, was suing for damages over an item in

Esther Rantzen's programme, That's Life. Everything had gone wrong for the BBC in the conduct of the case: the judge seemed unsympathetic and had dismissed the jury; counsel had been stricken by illness; two of the BBC's witnesses modified their evidence during the course of the trial. People connected with the programme felt that they had a chance of victory, and Milne instinctively wanted to fight on, but to extend the action until a verdict was reached could have doubled the costs. The governors, horrified at the spiralling expense, persuaded him to settle.

The spring sequence of misfortunes – the dropped balls and missed catches, in the sporting parlance popular at the Beeb – persuaded Young and his colleagues that there was something essentially at fault with the corporation's senior direction. Looking at the composition of the board of managemement, they found it top-heavy with programme people, arts graduates and former producers, lacking the streak of worldly realism that Young, as an accountant, detected and admired amongst the business executives he was used to dealing with.

At their May meetings the governors discussed changes at the highest level. At one point the position of the director-general himself was called into question, although there was never a serious move to replace him. At the beginning of June, press speculation about changes mentioned the possibility of Milne being replaced by Jeremy Isaacs, the head of Channel 4. Isaacs had lunched with the governors some months earlier but he had not been offered the post. (Since Milne had been present also, it was scarcely an appropriate occasion for such an approach.)

When the anticipated reshuffle was announced after the board meeting in Plymouth on 6 June, only one position was involved. Alan Protheroe, the scapegoat for the Princess Michael debacle, remained assistant director-general but ceased to be Milne's *de facto* deputy. He also lost responsibility for the information division. Michael Checkland was made deputy director-general. He had been director of resources for television and was a money man like Young, more familiar with cash flow than camera angles. It was a clear sign that the governors wanted commercial criteria to play a stronger role in management decisions. Somebody must rein in the programme people. The corporation had to operate in a more businesslike fashion.

In a perfect application of Sod's Law, the first time Checkland had to stand in for Milne was in a dispute over programming rather than management. Despite the high regard in which he was held by the board, he was unable to head off a graver public relations disaster than any that had occurred that spring, or for years previously. The governors' long period of muscle-flexing culminated in the delivery of a damaging punch to the Beeb's vital organs.

* * * *

Real Lives was a BBC1 series produced by Will Wyatt's documentary features department at Kensington House. The linking theme was implied in the title. The programmes focused on people, often in stressful situations, and in the case of known figures it sought to penetrate their public image to explore the reality beneath. Its summer season in 1985 was expected to be its last, because Michael Grade was averse to providing too many fixed spots for documentaries in his schedules at prime time.

In 1984 Paul Hamann, a producer with fourteen years experience in the BBC and something of a specialist on Northern Ireland, made a film called A Company, about four disgruntled soldiers who had been in the army when troops were sent there in 1969. One of them had been responsible for the army's first killing. Hamann took them back to the province and they gave their views on the rights and wrongs of the dispute. Some Protestant partisans had objected to the film and Lucy Faulkner, the BBC's governor for Northern Ireland, expressed their and her concern to the board. But Hamann had earlier made a film that angered the Republicans. It was called Fighting for Life and concerned two British soldiers horribly injured by an IRA bomb, and the efforts of neuro-surgeons at Belfast's Royal Victoria Hospital to secure their recovery. When that was screened he received a telephoned threat from the IRA; so he felt justified in regarding himself as an impartial chronicler of the affairs of the province.

Hamann wanted to make another Northern Ireland film for Real Lives in 1985. Sir John Hermon, chief constable of the Royal

Ulster Constabulary, tipped him off that during that summer's marching season, when Protestants stage provocatively trium-phant marches through the towns and cities, more trouble than usual was anticipated. The police planned to stop or divert some marches and there would be confrontations. Hermon initially offered Hamann generous access to film the RUC as they implemented this policy, but in early April he changed his mind and withdrew the offer.

Hamann now had a camera crew at his disposal in Northern Ireland but no film to make, so he discussed alternatives with the producer of the Real Lives series, Eddie Mirzoeff (the man involved with Wyatt in the E. P. Thompson row a few years earlier). They agreed that he should try to get the agreement of two leading and opposing politicians in Derry (Londonderry), Ulster's second city, to make a film about the conflict as seen through their eyes. They decided upon Gregory Campbell, leader on the city council of Ian Paisley's Democratic Unionist Party, and Martin McGuinness of Provisional Sinn Fein, alleged in a *Sunday Times* report to be the chief of staff of the IRA (which he denied). Both are elected members of the Northern Ireland Assembly and both advocate violence, although neither has been convicted of carrying out violent acts. Hamann's first thought was to call the film Elected Representatives. At a later stage that was changed to At the Edge of the Union.

Campbell, who had received comparatively little national media exposure at that point, was keen on the idea from the start, but McGuinness took some persuading. He did not want to be accused by his Sinn Fein colleagues of seeking personal publicity. His wife Bernie was also opposed to the project and remained reluctant to participate even after McGuinness eventually agreed.

After Carrickmore, the BBC had strengthened its rules about interviews with people believed to be involved in terrorism. On page 52 of the News and Current Affairs Index, the following sentence appears in bold type:

> Interviews with individuals who are deemed by ADG (assistant director-general) to be closely associated with a terrorist organisation may not be sought or transmitted – two separate stages – without the prior permission of DG.

242

In addition, the rules demand that the controller in Northern Ireland should be consulted about any programmes concerning the province. Since those rules were framed, however, the position in Northern Ireland had changed. The Republican movement had begun to operate in the political arena, as well as espousing violence. The previous May, Sinn Fein had fifty-nine representatives elected to local councils. Despite the fact that most, including McGuinness, had links with the IRA, they were often interviewed on television in the province. There was no question of referring such interviews to the director-general.

When Wyatt learned that Hamann's revised contribution to the Real Lives series involved interviewing McGuinness, he told Mirzoeff to assure himself that this did not place the programme in the category that had to be referred to Milne. Mirzoeff consulted Cecil Taylor, acting controller for Northern Ireland in the absence of James Hawthorne, who was away sick. Taylor advised him that as an elected politician McGuinness was not in that category. Wyatt also confirmed that Taylor had told Protheroe about the programme. He was convinced he had done enough to comply with the reference procedures, and so it would doubtless have proved were it not for an unfortunate and unforeseeable combination of circumstances.

Hamann had the film in the cutting room when, in June, Arab hijackers took over a TWA aircraft and held it at Beirut airport for several days. The American television networks gave the event extensive publicity, including interviews with the hijackers, who went so far as to organise a press conference. There was much criticism of the extent of the coverage and in July the Prime Minister added her voice at the American Bar Association's convention in London. 'We must try to find ways to starve the terrorists of the oxygen of publicity on which they depend,' she declared, to rousing applause.

Hamann feared the effect this statement might have on the reaction of his superiors to the programme. His distinctive style of film-making involves letting the characters speak for themselves, with no commentary and no challenging questions from an interviewer. So when McGuinness and Campbell spoke of violence and its inevitability, there was nobody to ask a question to weaken the impact of their advocacy. The film also showed them at home with their families, pointing up the contrast between their violent words and their peaceful domestic lives. Hamann foresaw that all this could be construed as offering a platform for terrorism and lending it a human face. He was additionally worried by a scene in which Campbell was shown loading a gun.

He was much relieved, therefore, when neither Wyatt or Hawthorne, when they saw it, suggested major changes. 'Difficult subject, well handled,' was the verdict of Hawthorne, who asked Hamann only to shorten a section where old news film showed the brutality of the RUC against Catholic civil rights marchers. Hamann did so. Wyatt had no changes to suggest. The programme was scheduled for 7 August and a three-page feature, with large colour pictures of the two men and extensive quotations from both, appeared in *Radio Times*.

But if Wyatt and Hawthorne had not recognised the new climate created by Thatcher's comments on publicising terrorists, the sharp journalists at the *Sunday Times* had. The first hint of the paper's interest came on Tuesday, 23 July, when Hamann received an apparently innocent call from Barrie Penrose, a reporter specialising in major investigations. Penrose wanted to confirm that the programme included an interview with McGuinness. Hamann saw nothing sinister in the approach and was glad to help him. Producers naturally welcome advance publicity for their programmes and there was to be a screening for the press on the Friday.

Hamann did not bother to tell anyone else about Penrose's call until two days later, when he heard from Gregory Campbell that the *Sunday Times* had been in touch with him as well. 'I think they're trying to dig up a story,' said the Loyalist leader. The reporter had asked him whether he knew that McGuinness was going to be in the film when he agreed to take part in it. Campbell had responded scathingly that yes, of course he had known. The reporter seemed disappointed.

Hamann thought it sensible at this point to alert the BBC press officers about the newspaper's interest, and they in turn phoned Wyatt, who was not unduly alarmed. He advised them to respond that both McGuinness and Campbell were entitled to a salary from the British government as elected representatives in Ulster and were therefore legitimate interview subjects.

On Friday Penrose began seeking official reaction to the proposed film. He sent hand-delivered letters to Leon Brittan and Bernard Ingham, the Prime Minister's press secretary, inviting their comments. He spoke to Douglas Hurd, Secretary of State for Northern Ireland, who said he was 'alarmed' to hear of the interview. 'Giving space to terrorists has a very powerful effect and it is up to the broadcasting authorities to understand this,' he added.

What Penrose needed to make his story work was a comment from the Prime Minister herself. Not only had she made the 'oxygen of publicity' remarks but she had also been the intended victim of an IRA bomb in Brighton ten months earlier. She was now visiting Washington where Mark Hosenball, one of the paper's correspondents, was instructed to ask a question about the programme. The only chance he had was at a briefing for British reporters on Friday evening. Anxious not to alert rival papers to the story, Hosenball asked a general, hypothetical question without going into the details of the Real Lives documentary. How would the Prime Minister react if she learned that a British TV company was going to interview the IRA chief of staff? She replied that she would 'condemn them utterly', adding: 'The IRA is proscribed in Britain and in the Republic of Ireland. We have lost between 2,000 and 2,500 people in the past 16 years. I feel very strongly about it and so would many other people.' Next morning, the day before the *Sunday Times* appeared, a Downing Street spokesman phoned the paper to stress that Thatcher had been speaking hypothetically, not about any particular intended programme. Penrose did not make that clear in his report.

Alan Protheroe told Penrose that the film was 'responsible and balanced'. But a fatal weakness in the BBC's position was that the person ultimately responsible for it, as for all programmes, was still serenely unaware of its existence. A week earlier Alasdair Milne had set off for Scandinavia with his wife Sheila for a fishing holiday. It had begun in Norway and continued in Finland, where he was being looked after by Finnish Television. On Monday, 29 July, he was due to move on to Sweden.

There were two routes by which he should have heard of the

Real Lives programme before he left London. By a strict interpretation of the News and Current Affairs Index, Wyatt ought to have told him. The second way was through the minutes of the fortnightly target meetings. These were convened by Brian Wenham for the specific purpose of pinpointing possible areas of controversy in forthcoming programmes, especially on Northern Ireland. Milne did not attend the meetings but received the minutes. Since the beginning of the year, though, the meetings had ceased through what Milne later described as administrative inertia. Wenham thought there was a good deal too much unproductive chat in the BBC and this was one meeting he could dispense with. Milne did not seek to dissuade him.

Had he been made aware of Hamann's film through either of these channels, Milne might have asked to view it for himself. At the very least, he would have mentioned it to Stuart Young. It is his habit to alert the chairman to any potentially troublesome programmes and to assure him that he is satisfied they can be defended in the event of criticism – which, in the majority of cases, does not materialise.

With the benefit of an advance warning signal, Young would not have been taken by surprise when, at his North London home in the late afternoon of Saturday, 27 July, he received a call from Lady Faulkner, telling him that she had just been telephoned by the *Sunday Times* seeking her comments on a programme of which she had not hitherto been aware. In her case, too, the usual referral procedures had failed to operate. Hawthorne's normal practice was to warn the Northern Ireland governor of any network programme concerning the province, in much the same way as Milne kept Young informed. But at the end of July Lady Faulkner would end her seven-year stint as governor. By the time the programme was due to be aired she would be replaced by Dr James Kincade, a Belfast headmaster. She had already attended what everyone believed would be her last board meeting, where formal farewells had been bidden. Hawthorne thought it inappropriate to discuss with her a programme that would be shown outside her term of office.

In her phone call, Lady Faulkner warned Young to expect an approach from the *Sunday Times*. It came almost immediately, in the form of a letter pushed under his door by a messenger who did not even wait long enough to ring the bell. The letter outlined the nature of the programme and asked for an interview with Young about it that very day. Young phoned the duty press officer who rang back to confirm that there was such a programme and that the *Sunday Times* was next day running a story saying that the government were critical of it.

Young was surprised that he had not previously heard about the film but believed that the row would be containable. He would assure himself that the correct consultation procedures had been followed. (The *Sunday Times* reported, falsely as it turned out, that Milne had given his permission for it to be broadcast.) Then he and the governors would defend the programme, at least until after it had been shown and they were able to appraise it critically. On Sunday he telephoned Sir William Rees-Mogg, his deputy, and Michael Checkland, doing his first stint as acting director-general since his appointment as Milne's number two. He also contacted David Holmes, the secretary, arranging to talk to him in the office first thing on Monday.

Checkland summoned the board of management to Broadcasting House early on Monday to see the film. Milne was the only one absent. It had not seemed to Checkland that the issue was important enough to warrant trying to reach him in Finland by telephone. The board decided to a man that Real Lives: At the Edge of the Union should be shown as scheduled, though most thought it would benefit from an introductory statement about its aim and a round table discussion on terrorism afterwards, probably on Newsnight. There was talk of a possible change to one of the captions. At 10.30 Checkland and Protheroe went to Young's fourth-floor office to report in those terms to the chairman and David Holmes.

Their meeting had been under way for about half an hour when Holmes was called away to take a phone call from Wilfred Hyde, a senior Home Office official. Hyde said that the Home Secretary had asked him to read over the phone a message that he was releasing to the press about the Real Lives programme. Holmes, a former reporter, took it all down in shorthand and rushed back to the chairman's office to read it aloud. It amounted to a public request to the governors not to show the film because of its security implications. It appeared to be 'giving succour' to terrorist organisations. 'It gave them the opportunity for public advocacy of terrorist methods by a prominent member of the IRA. This gave spurious legitimacy to the use of violence for political ends. It would be contrary to the national interest that a programme of the kind apparently envisaged should be broadcast.' If it was to be shown as scheduled, Brittan would like the chance to view it in advance. The Home Secretary insisted that he respected the BBC's independence and invited Young to telephone him whenever he wished.

Brittan did not see his move as unorthodox or as an attempt to exert improper pressure. As minister responsible for law and order he felt he had a right to express his opinion on the question. The fact that he was also minister responsible for broadcasting was not, in his view, a reason for staying his hand. Among the many criticisms made of him in the wake of the affair, it was pointed out that most of his predecessors would have sought to deal with the matter confidentially, without involving the press. Brittan, a lawyer by training, prefers to operate above board, not by off-the-record winks and nudges. A precise man, he appears, at least in public, to lack warmth and good fellowship. He had been made Home Secretary – an important promotion from his former post as Chief Secretary to the Treasury – because he shares Thatcher's brand of strict conservatism on financial and social issues. But he is not an instinctive politician: he is insufficiently calculating when it comes to assessing the consequences of what he does and the manner in which he does it. He was dismayed by the proposed interview with McGuinness and saw no reason not to make the point publicly.

Young was surprised and angry at what he saw as a blatant attempt by the government to lean so heavily on the BBC as to make nonsense of the independence that Brittan claimed he recognised. He told Holmes to phone the Home Office back and urge them to retract the message. He was certain the BBC was the victim of a *Sunday Times* set-up and that Brittan's intervention would compound it. But Hyde told Holmes it was too late. The text of Brittan's statement had already been released to the press.

Within half an hour the first edition of the *Standard*, London's evening paper, was delivered to Young. The main front-page story was headed BBC TOLD: BAN IRA FILM and it contained long quotations from Brittan's statement. As soon as he saw it Young telephoned Brittan, incensed at having read his comments in the newspaper before they had been conveyed to the BBC in writing.

'Do you really want a letter?' asked Brittan, who, having made his point publicly and forcefully, but informally, would have preferred to avoid committing it to paper. Young insisted. He was, he said, planning to summon an emergency governors' meeting the following day and needed a record of the precise terms of the Home Secretary's request. Without waiting for it to arrive, Holmes rang round the governors and to his surprise, seeing that it was August, he received promises from all but one of them to report to Broadcasting House on the following morning, Tuesday 30 July.

Brittan's long letter was not delivered at Broadcasting House until ten past seven on Monday evening. It began by insisting that the decision whether to broadcast the programme lay with the corporation alone.

> It is no part of my task as the minister with responsibility for broadcasting policy generally to attempt to impose an act of censorship on what should be broadcast in particular program-mes. To do so would be inconsistent with the constitutional independence of the BBC, which is a crucial part of our broadcasting arrangements. I do, on the other hand, also have a ministerial responsibility for the fight against the ever present threat of terrorism. . .

The BBC would be giving an immensely valuable platform to those who have evinced an ability, readiness and intention to murder indiscriminately its own viewers. Quite apart from the deep offence that this would give to the overwhelming majority of the population and the profound distress that it would cause to families of the victims of terrorism, it would also in my considered judgment materially assist the terrorist cause. Recent events elsewhere in the world have confirmed only too clearly what has long been understood in this country: that terrorism thrives on the oxygen of publicity. . . Even if the programme and any surrounding material were, as a whole, to present terrorist

organisations in a wholly unfavourable light, I would still ask you
not to permit it to be broadcast.

The deliberate echoing of Thatcher's phrase about 'the oxygen of
publicity' was a less than subtle hint by Brittan that his initiative
represented the collective position of the Cabinet. In fact he had
not discussed the issue with Thatcher. Several other ministers,
while approving the sentiment behind the letter, later questioned
his confrontatory tactics. But at that stage only one of the
principals, Stuart Young, seemed aware of the gravity of the
position that had been created by Brittan's *demarche*. The other
man most intimately concerned with this government assault on
the corporation, the director-general, had, astonishingly enough,
been informed for the first time about the dispute scarcely an
hour before Brittan's letter arrived.

* * * *

Alasdair Milne had fished in Norway and Finland and was
about to fish in Sweden. His Swedish friends told him that quite
the most delightful way of travelling from Helsinki to Stockholm
was on the boat that left the Finnish capital at 6 p.m. every night,
steamed through the Gulf of Finland and across the Baltic Sea to
arrive in Sweden at 9 a.m. next day. Soon after 5 on 29 July he
and Sheila boarded the boat and were making themselves
comfortable in their cabin when he was summoned to the
purser's office by loudspeaker. It was a message from his hosts,
Finnish Television. There had been a call from London. Would
he telephone Checkland as soon as he could?

By now the ship was less than half an hour from sailing time.
There were three phone booths on board but they needed Finnish
coins and he had changed all his into Swedish. Even had he been
able to borrow some, all the booths were occupied until just
before the boat sailed. Only when it left port was he able to use
the ship-to-shore radio link to contact his deputy in London.

Checkland gave a rundown of the events of the weekend and
told him the governors would meet next morning. It was the first
Milne had heard of the contentious Real Lives programme.
Checkland's main concern was to have his chief's advice on what
to do if the governors insisted on viewing the film in advance of

transmission. Milne equivocated. He told Checkland to argue with conviction that they should not go against precedent; but if they felt they could not answer Brittan's letter sensibly without seeing the programme, that was their right. Then he asked if there was any chance of the meeting being postponed to allow him to attend it. Had he been contacted earlier on the Monday he would have been able to get back by Tuesday morning. Now that the boat had left port it would be Tuesday before he reached dry land again, so there was no chance of getting back to London for the meeting unless it could be postponed. Checkland replied that he thought a postponement out of the question, since the governors had already been summoned.

That casual exchange was to become a critical moment in the drama. Checkland had not raised the possibility of postponement with anyone on the governors' side. It had not occurred to him. He had every confidence in his own ability to act properly in Milne's place, and after the events of recent months the director-general certainly needed his holiday. So did his wife Sheila, who had not been at all well.

Milne had not specified whether he was talking about putting the meeting off until Wednesday, when he could be there if he was willing to break his holiday, or until the following week, when he was due back in the office anyway. While Young would not have delayed the meeting for a week, he maintained later that he would, if asked, have postponed it for a day. But he was not asked. Some suspected that Checkland did not encourage Milne's return because he was keen to flex his muscles as acting DG for the first time. This is an unlikely explanation, for Checkland himself went on holiday shortly after the governors' meeting: had he been motivated by self-aggrandisement he would no doubt have altered his own arrangements. The likeliest reason is that he saw no point in Milne disrupting his private plans for what he thought was only the slimmest chance of altering the situation. It was an unfortunate decision, though, for in the event Milne's absence proved a key factor in persuading the governors first to view the film and then to ban it.

The morning of Tuesday, 30 July, was showery and miserable, an apology for high summer. Nor were the BBC governors in a sunny mood as they ran the gauntlet of photographers and reporters outside Broadcasting House. Some had been dragged up from holiday homes in the country: but they managed to look reasonably businesslike for the cameras as they walked into the newly refurbished art deco lobby and took the lift to the third floor board room.

The governors are an assorted bunch, but nowadays not assorted enough to satisfy those critics who, in the wake of this dispute, charged them with leaning too heavily towards the philosophy of the government – or, more bluntly, of being political placemen. As she showed when declining to appoint Mark Bonham-Carter as chairman, Thatcher has no time for consensus politics or its practitioners. When a vacancy occurred at the end of 1984 for a governor connected with the arts, the management were asked for suggestions. They proposed John Mortimer, the popular playwright and author who, as a lawyer, defended several cases involving human rights and freedom of expression. That made him too libertarian for the government, who instead appointed the Earl of Harewood, 62, a cousin of the Queen and former managing director of the English National Opera. Even under Labour and less ideological Conservative Prime Ministers, the board has tended to settle to the right of centre, simply because that is the natural political alignment of those from whose ranks the governors are mostly drawn.

Apart from Young and Harewood, the members of the board who met that day to discuss *Real Lives: At the Edge of the Union*, were:

Sir William Rees-Mogg, 57, vice-chairman, chairman of the Arts Council and former editor of *The Times*.

Lady Faulkner, 60, Northern Ireland governor, due to retire the following day. (Her successor, **James Kincade,** headmaster of the Methodist College in Belfast, also sat in.)

Watson Peat, 62, Scottish governor, in farming and meat production.

Alwyn Roberts, 51, Welsh governor, director of extramural studies at the University College of North Wales.

Sir John Johnston, 67, former diplomat and also on the point of stepping down.

Daphne Park, 63, another former diplomat and principal of

Somerville College, Oxford.

Lady Parkes, 59, educationist, chairman of the College Advisory Committee.

Jocelyn Barrow, 56, born in Trinidad, former vice-chairman of the Campaign Against Racial Discrimination.

Malcolm McAlpine, 68, an executive of the building and property company that bears his family name.

(Sir John Boyd, 57, former president of the Confederation of Shipbuilding and Engineering Unions, was the only governor who could not attend the meeting on 30 July.)

A worthy bunch, but it is easy to understand the prevailing view at the Beeb that, with one or two exceptions, they are not of outstanding calibre. Most members of the board of management were there, and so was James Hawthorne, invited because of his special interest in the programme. Proceedings began at 10.30 a.m. with Young extending an especially warm welcome to Lady Faulkner, saying how much the other governors appreciated her attendance on her last day in office, after the formal farewells had been endured. Some felt that by paying that tribute Young, probably inadvertently, was placing Faulkner in an unusually strong position, increasing the chance that her view of the proper course of action would prevail.

When Young had explained the position he invited discussion on whether the governors should view the film and asked members of the board of management to speak first. Checkland admitted that there had been what he called a 'technical foul' in the matter of procedures. The programme should have been referred to the director-general, but was not. However, the rest of the management board had seen it and were confident that they could speak for Milne in their decision to show it under the conditions they had agreed the previous day. For this reason he felt the governors should not see it but, echoing the director-general's guidance of the evening before, he conveyed that he would not be fervently opposed if they decided on a viewing.

Bill Cotton, on the other hand, was adamant that the governors should not break with precedent by seeing the film, and he argued his case with passion. The last time the entire board had viewed a programme in advance was in 1967, the subject being bull-fighting. As for Yesterday's Men in 1971, only about half the board were present when Lord Hill decided on a screening. Alan Protheroe warned the governors to be careful about their reaction to something that had begun as a newspaper stunt. 'This mischievous action by the *Sunday Times* has taken the BBC and its procedures by surprise,' he declared – a characteristically neat turn of phrase, though its meaning was far from clear. Brian Wenham then argued for the specific format that had been agreed by management the day before, in which the programme would be followed by a discussion. He pointed out that, whatever happened, the film when shown would receive more than usual attention because of the dispute that had grown up around it.

When the governors began to speak it was clear that they resented having been put in a virtually impossible situation by a combination of the failure of management's reference procedures and the improper pressure being applied by the Home Secretary. It was true that the BBC had to be seen to be independent of government influence. It was also true that as governors they had the obligation to consider representations from all responsible sources. They were not at liberty to refuse to recognise complaints because they did not like the form in which they had been made.

At this point it became apparent that Milne's absence would have a crucial bearing on the outcome. If the director-general, the editor-in-chief they had appointed, had seen the film and passed it, the governors would in all probabilty have accepted his judgement, reasoning that not to do so would be to imply a lack of confidence in Milne personally. But Checkland's endorsement could not be regarded as of equal weight. He was, after all, a man whose experience was in administration rather than programmes. How could he judge the fine line between what was acceptable on the screen and what was provocative? In Milne's absence it was up to the governors to exercise final editorial control. They could not simply tell the Home Secretary that no, they had not seen fit to view the film, and neither had the director-general, but yes, they were all satisfied that the BBC ought to show it.

Nor could the governors fail to take into account previous occasions in recent months when they had been told that the director-general had been unaware of a set of circumstances that developed into a crisis. There had been the Princess Michael interview, the Gee libel, the Pope's Easter message. The BBC was a large organisation and nobody could know everything that was going on inside it, but there did seem to be something wrong with Milne's intelligence system. Michael Swann had been convinced that the position of editor-in-chief was too onerous to be combined with all the administrative duties of a director-general, and he had insisted on the appointment of a director of news and current affairs to perform exactly that function. Richard Francis was the first to hold the position – and the last, for it lapsed when Milne became director-general and made him managing director, radio. The appointment of a DNCA had not prevented the Carrickmore uproar; but were it still in existence it would have provided a safety net for an accident-prone board of management.

The argument in favour of the governors viewing the Real Lives film was put most forcefully by the vice-chairman, Sir William Rees-Mogg. He exerted a powerful influence on the board because, amongst a group just below the first rank in British public life, he stood out as the best known, a man who moved easily in politics and journalism, who had Cabinet ministers to dinner at his house in Westminster. He was known to have favoured Young's appointment as chairman. Moreover, the vice-chairman had firm views on most issues and the ability to express them vividly – a gift developed while writing leaders for *The Times,* and one that Young lacked.

Rees-Mogg's view of the Real Lives programme was coloured by his suspicion of a deliberate bid by Hawthorne – despite the Ulsterman's denials – to keep it from Lady Faulkner. He did not accept that her impending departure from the board was an excuse for not keeping her informed. Earlier, Lucy Faulkner herself had surprisingly opposed viewing the programme, partly because, some years earlier, she had been outvoted by the other governors when she wanted to preview a programme about Ireland that discussed the role of her late husband. She pointed out that Brittan's chief fear seemed to be security and the board had no qualification to pronounce on that. (That was why some governors felt the right action would be not to rule on the programme at all, but to invite the Home Secretary to ban it, using his reserve powers under the BBC licence agreement, if he thought it a security threat. But the majority felt that, in the light of Brittan's letter, to take that course would be to dodge the issue.)

The arguments swung from one view to the opposite. Young, although he preferred as chairman to play a neutral role, thought on balance that they should watch it. He believed it would put them in a stronger position *vis a vis* Brittan when they decided – as he was convinced they would – to broadcast the programme as scheduled. All the same, the decision to view the film in advance was a narrow one.

The governors moved to the adjoining dining room for lunch, a cold buffet with BBC house wine. As the coffee was being served the film began to run on the five screens scattered round the room. It was clear almost from the start that the group, staring in almost total silence, did not like it. A sullen, disapproving mood prevailed, like an impossibly extended catching of the breath. Afterwards Rees-Mogg and about half the governors went into a conclave near one of the screens. The management people thought that ominous. There were suggestions that someone should go and break up the circle. Nobody did.

After the viewing the governors returned to the board room to reconvene in formal session. Rees-Mogg was invited by Young to speak first and did so in immoderate terms, striking a keynote for the other governors. The programme was 'totally unacceptable' and ought not to be shown. It was not a technical foul, as Checkland had argued, but a major failure to apply safeguards that had been devised by the management and approved by the governors. The reference system existed so that programmes such as this could be considered at an early stage at the highest level.

Rees-Mogg is a strong believer in rigid lines of authority. Looking hard at Hawthorne, he said there had been no convincing explanation of why Lady Faulkner had not been consulted at an early stage. While there was no formal obligation on the controller's part to refer such matters to her, he had until now customarily done so and it was proper that he should. Both the usual procedures and standing instructions had been breached. If the rules were wrong or impossible to apply, they should be changed. If they were simply ignored the editing system broke down and decisions like these became purely arbitrary.

Turning to specific criticism of the programme, Rees-Mogg said it had given McGuinness the opportunity to make propaganda on behalf of the IRA, not countered by any effectively stringent questioning. This derived from Hamann's technique of letting the characters speak for themselves, rather than in an argumentative interview that would allow the flaws in extremist arguments to be pointed out instantly. He referred the board to another part of the News and Current Affairs Index. Dealing with the coverage of violence, page 79, paragraph 14 states: 'Great skill is required to tread the thin line between explanation of the role of these elements in the conflict and providing a platform for propaganda. Political rhetoric may be illustrated in a programme, but it should not be allowed to pass unchallenged.' In this case, it had been.

Rees-Mogg accepted Young's caution that if the governors banned the programme they would be attacked for caving in to the government, but they were not entitled to take that into account. Their responsibility was to decide the issue on the merits of the film they had just seen. Brittan had behaved improperly, he was sure of that. But, if the Home Secretary's view of the programme was right, to find against him because it would be embarrassing to find for him would be a betrayal of the board's function as a last court of appeal in BBC matters. *Real Lives: At the Edge of the Union* would offend many people and should not be shown.

Lady Faulkner spoke next, beginning in a combative manner. 'I can see, Jimmy,' she said, turning to Hawthorne, 'why you didn't tell me about this' – a sally Hawthorne found hurtful because he believed from earlier conversations that she had accepted his explanation of why he had not done so. She continued in the same vein, clearly feeling that Rees-Mogg's powerful opening speech gave her a licence to criticise the programme with a level of passion that she was normally chary of deploying. She said she was 'utterly horrified' by the film, which was inflammatory and would almost certainly lead to intercommunal violence in Northern Ireland. She especially disliked the file footage of the police in action against civil rights marchers – the segment that had been shortened at Hawthorne's request – pointing out that it was not balanced by any portrayal of violence by the IRA.

Stuart Young was by now seriously alarmed at the drift of the meeting. His hopes that the viewing would lead to approval of the broadcast – albeit with amendments – were clearly not going to be fulfilled. He pointed out to the governors the gravity of banning a programme at the government's behest. However genuine their reservations about the film, if they did not allow it to be shown they would certainly be accused of bowing cravenly to official pressure. The consequences, he warned, could be 'immeasurable'.

But he was powerless to alter the direction the meeting was taking. Johnston, Peat and Lady Parkes, while they did not match the extreme views of the first two speakers, all articulated worry about the film. McAlpine gave his verdict in two words: 'No show.' Harewood began his contribution by declaring: 'I hate it, I hate it, I hate it,' going on to describe the programme as 'smooth, odious and hateful'. Park was equally opposed to it. She said the scenes showing McGuinness with his family had the effect of domesticating the IRA. Barrow called it sinister, and made one point that had a powerful effect on some of her colleagues. She said that many young, disadvantaged black people believed violence was the only way to improve their condition. They would welcome this film because it lent legitimacy to that view. In a later contribution she objected to the fact that the army patrol in the film had been led by a black soldier, who had been made to look silly.

Kincade, although he had no formal vote, was asked for his view and showed solidarity with Lady Faulkner. He said he would have to consider his position as a governor if the film were broadcast. Young quipped that he could scarcely resign before taking office but in reality the chairman was in anything but a flippant mood. He could see now that the board were almost unanimous for banning the programme. He repeated his earlier warning, with scarcely any hope that it would be heeded. When he went round the table for a second time to confirm the governors' view, Roberts was the only one who voted against a ban.

Now the problem was how to announce the decision in a way that would limit the damage. A small group was set up to draft Young's reply to Brittan's letter. They felt it important to stress that they thought the Home Secretary had behaved badly.

> We would now wish to discuss with you the profound issues raised in your letter to me (it said). We are anxious that those discussions be conducted in a neutral and dispassionate climate. Having seen the programme, the board of governors believes it would be unwise for this programme in the series Real Lives to be transmitted in its present form: the programme's intention would continue to be misread and misinterpreted.

The letter represented a subtle modification of what the governors had actually decided. The majority of them had assumed during their debate that they were talking definitively about whether to show the film or censor it. The phrase 'in its present form', leaving open the possibility of a later transmission after amendments, was inserted only in the drafting stage and formed the basis of the eventual compromise.

With the letter agreed, Young summoned the board of management back into the meeting room. It had, he said, been a tiring day, a momentous day. What he was now asking was that the management should show solidarity with the decision that had been taken by the governors. He knew they would be disappointed by it, but he felt that as loyal corporation men they had a responsibility to rally round at a time when the BBC would certainly come under heavy attack from the outside. He wanted them to defend the decision in front of their subordinates. If Young really believed he could coax support from the professionals, he was quickly disabused of the notion. 'We can't be solid on this one,' Cotton told him. That made Young and the other governors angry. They dispersed on a sour note.

* * * *

The BBC management had believed that the governors would conform with precedent and decide not to view the film; that they would accept the judgement of the professionals that it should be broadcast. It was expected that the meeting would be over by lunch time. Will Wyatt sat in his office at Kensington House awaiting a call from Bill Cotton. When it did not come he phoned the press office, who told him the meeting was still going on and it could last a while yet. Even when he heard that the governors had decided to look at the film, Wyatt was not unduly worried. He thought the decision misguided but did not expect it to affect the eventual outcome.

The first indication that things had gone seriously wrong came at about 5 in the evening, when Wyatt was asked to join Michael Grade in Cotton's office at Television Centre to await the managing director's return from Broadcasting House. As the two men sat there expectantly, Cotton phoned his secretary with the message that the film had been censored. So when he arrived with Brian Wenham, in the middle of the Six O'Clock News, they already knew the worst. The four were joined in Cotton's office by Graeme McDonald, controller of BBC2. Over drinks, they discussed how they could limit the effect of what they all agreed was a profound crisis for the BBC. The staff, they knew, would react badly. The quintet stayed to watch the extensive coverage of the governors' decision on the Nine O'Clock News; then Cotton, Grade and Wyatt went out for a Chinese meal, returning to Cotton's office to watch further criticism of the decision on Newsnight. They went home shortly before midnight, knowing that a grave event had occurred, wondering how serious the consequences would be.

It did not take them long to find out. All next morning's newspapers carried front-page headlines about the governors' decision and comments were sought from relevant bodies and personalities. In general, Conservative MPs and the right-wing press supported the ban, while organisations concerned with civil liberties and press freedom denounced it. On Channel 4 news, Sir Hugh Greene said it was 'one of the most fateful days in the corporation's history'. He went on: 'To put it mildly, I find this decision deeply disturbing because however it may be wrapped up in talk of further consultation with the Home Secretary, it is a case of giving way to government pressure. I cannot imagine BBC boards of the past giving way to such pressure.'

The Times and the *Telegraph* both made the point that the government's position was inconsistent. If Brittan thought the programme a threat to national security he had the power to forbid its broadcast on his own responsibility. 'Both the Prime Minister and the Home Secretary have emphasized the absence of censorship, though Mr. Brittan's quasi-diktat is scarcely distinguishable from it,' *The Times* wrote. Brittan contested that energetically. He was against censorship. He had been surprised first by Young's decision to call a meeting and secondly by the governors' reaction to the programme. He was glad they had banned it but he had not expected them to do so. He had assumed when he made his protest that they would go ahead with the programme regardless of it. In that case he would have made his point without creating such a fuss. He certainly had no intention of using his powers to enforce a ban.

The *Financial Times* commented: 'Independence is what the BBC is all about. It is what its reputation rests on at home and abroad. Where is that reputation now? Ultimately, one must ask: without independence, what is the point of the BBC?' While the *Guardian* said of the governors: 'They copped out; they caved in.'

* * * *

Of all the senior BBC executives, James Hawthorne was the man wounded most by the fracas, and in a profoundly personal way. It was he, after all, who had cleared Hamann's film for transmission, and it was he who had been assailed by the redoubtable Rees-Mogg for failing to disclose its existence to the Northern Ireland governor. By an embarrassing coincidence, on that very Tuesday evening Hawthorne was due to host a cocktail party and dinner for Lady Faulkner at BBC headquarters in Belfast, a tribute to her on her retirement from the board.

As the meeting in London dragged on, it became clear that neither of them would be able to make the cocktail party in time, so that was cancelled, but they rushed together from Broadcasting House to Heathrow airport, on to the shuttle, and arrived only a little late for the dinner. Both were asked excitedly to report on the day's events and they did, though they managed to conceal in public the gravity of the differences between them. Both made friendly and mutually flattering speeches. In particular, Hawthorne gave no hint to Lady Faulkner or anyone else that he had as good as made up his mind to resign.

The decision had been taking shape since the governors agreed the terms of their letter to Brittan. Part of the reason for his disillusion was what he saw as the shabby hypocrisy of indicating in the letter that the programme might be shown in an amended form later, whereas he had been at the meetings where the governors had expressed their total rejection of it: 'No show, no show. . . I hate it.' He felt it important that someone should be seen to behave honourably. He wanted to tell people what had really happened, and he could not so long as he remained with the corporation. It would, he knew, only be a gesture, but maybe at that stage a gesture was needed to prevent the BBC losing all the credibility it had accrued in its sixty-year existence. When he went home from the dinner he discussed his position with his wife and family. Tears flowed and the talk continued next morning at breakfast. By the time he left home to drive to the office, he had decided what to do.

At half past nine he telephoned Johnny Wilkinson, the director of public affairs in London. He told him he was going to quit, and would hold a press conference in Belfast to explain the reasons. Wilkinson urged him to postpone a final decision for twenty-four hours, and when Protheroe came on the line later to reinforce the appeal, Hawthorne agreed. There was another farewell party for Lady Faulkner at lunch time, this time for the Belfast staff. Hawthorne considered whether he ought to attend, and decided he should. In London, Richard Francis (his predecessor as controller in Northern Ireland) jumped on a plane for Belfast and Hawthorne invited him for dinner. Young had promised to issue a statement expressing full confidence in the management in general and the controller in Northern Ireland in particular, but that by itself would not have been enough to change Hawthorne's mind. He was more influenced by Francis's point that if anything was to be salvaged out of the rubble it was essential that the management should avoid dramatic gestures of this kind; although that did not mean they should refrain from expressing their dismay at the governors' decision.

By the time Francis left after dinner, Hawthorne was all but persuaded to withdraw his resignation. Next morning, Thursday, not long before lunch, Young telephoned him. With the BBC under pressure, said the chairman, it more than ever needed people like Hawthorne. 'I beg you, I beg you, I beg you to remain,' he pleaded. Hawthorne had already decided to hold a press conference for 4 p.m., where he was going to announce that he was not quitting after all, but he thought it appropriate to keep the chairman in suspense, promising only to think about it. He told the press conference that he would stay on, saying he had received assurances that the BBC's integrity would be maintained. When, three days later, Hawthorne appeared on ITV's The World This Weekend and made remarks criticising both the governors and the government, the chairman may have wondered whether he should have let him go after all.

Young had managed to keep the management intact, but stood no chance of mollifying the staff at lower levels. As current affairs and features producers wrote letters of protest to the press, members of the National Union of Journalists at the BBC decided to strike for twenty-four hours on Wednesday, 7 August – the day the programme was originally supposed to have been screened. They were supported by other unions as well as by journalists at Independent Television News. Staff of the external services at Bush House had never struck before, but because they perceived the issue as being of such extreme gravity for the corporation they came out with their colleagues on the home side. In doing so, by an odd irony, they helped to restore their service's reputation. It had looked as though the international good name of Bush House might become an incidental victim of the dispute. Although the overseas services are funded by the Foreign Office, they are proud of their comparative freedom from direct political interference. In the wake of the Real Lives affair other overseas broadcasting services, particularly those of Iron Curtain countries, were able to score propaganda points, maintaining that the incident proved all British broadcasting to be subject to government censorship. By striking for a day and forcing the world service to broadcast nothing but music, the staff demonstrated a degree of independence unthinkable for those who worked for the broadcasting services that criticised them.

Both for this reason, and because of their hostility to the governors' decision, senior management had sympathy with the strike, although they were naturally inhibited from saying so too openly. Alasdair Milne was kept in touch with events by Michael Checkland. Now on dry land in Sweden, the director-general could have returned whenever he liked, and he considered doing so early in the week. After the Tuesday meeting was over he asked Young, Checkland and Protheroe whether he should return the following day. They all advised against it, even though Checkland himself was starting his holiday the following day. Milne calculated that he would stand more chance of rescuing something from the ashes of the relationship between the two boards if he kept to his timetable and delayed his return until the weekend, when passions might have cooled a little.

When he arrived home on Saturday, 3 August, a cassette of the programme was waiting for him, and he viewed it that evening. He decided right away that the board of management were right, and that it could be shown with only a couple of minor amendments. On Sunday he telephoned some of his management colleagues to discuss how to proceed. They agreed to come to a decision at the regular weekly board meeting the next day. He telephoned Young and arranged to talk to him on Monday, too. Although his favoured solution would have been for the programme to be shown as scheduled, he recognised that there was no chance of the governors agreeing to lose face to that extent.

What he hoped was that, without meeting again, they would authorise him to announce a firm date for the showing of the film, with the minor changes he thought necessary, no later than the autumn. This, he believed, might be enough to persuade the unions to call off the strike.

When Milne put that plan to him on Monday, Young said he would go along with it if Milne could persuade the other governors. That afternoon the director-general telephoned as many of them as he could find. Five agreed to his plan, but Daphne Park and Sir William Rees-Mogg did not. Young decided he would have to call another meeting the following day. It was nearly 7 p.m. before he made that decision, and he was again surprised next morning that they all turned up – even Sir John Boyd, who had not been there the previous week. Boyd indicated his position at the beginning, when he advised the other governors to stick to their guns and not be swayed by pressure from the press.

The hard-liners were one below strength because Lady Faulkner had now ended her term of office and her successor Kincade, freed from her influence, was more inclined towards compromise than he had been the previous week. Relieved of the cares of office, Lady Faulkner was now not inhibited from expressing her views in public. In a powerful article in the *Listener* that week, she was scathing about the film: 'The shots of McGuinness – who says he would be proud to be the chief of staff of the IRA – were like those foxes produced years ago for the anti-blood sports campaigners, pretty animals, like collie dogs. What one didn't see were the fowl in the hen-run with their heads pulled off.' And she placed the dispute in an interesting broader perspective: 'The BBC must get its act together. This is not the swinging sixties, when the winds of change were heady with promise and in-fighting was permissible.'

At the meeting on 6 August, Rees-Mogg was still proving the chief obstacle to a settlement. He did not want Real Lives shown at any time, however amended. He hoped – although he recognised it was unlikely – that Milne would take against the film and ban it on his own account. In the political context created by the governors' action that would have been virtually impossible for the director-general, even if privately he had disliked the work; which as it happened he had not.

Despite the support Milne had assumed from his Monday telephone calls, the governors would not name a date for the screening at their Tuesday meeting. Instead, they issued a long statement that began: 'The board of governors are the BBC and are therefore responsible for the editorial policy of the corporation. They devolve the day-to-day management to a director-general, whom they appoint, who is the editor-in-chief.' The statement concluded that the main issue was one of censorship by the government, which the board would not accept. They were disturbed at being accused – wrongly, they felt – of yielding to official pressure.

The journalists had charged the governors with censorship and now the governors were appearing to try to off-load the responsibility by accusing the government of the same thing. The journalists were not won over and Wednesday's strike was now inevitable. Milne admitted later that at this point he had considered resignation but decided, along with the other members of the board of management, that he should stay to steer the Beeb back to calmer waters. Alwyn Roberts, the single governor who had opposed the ban, also revealed that he had contemplated resigning.

The one-day strike crippled all the news programmes of the BBC and Independent Television News. The NUJ sponsored a screening of the banned film at the Institute of Contemporary Arts. During the discussion afterwards Gerald Kaufman, the shadow Home Secretary, pledged that a future Labour administration would free the media from controls. Lord Annan, chairman of the commission that produced the 1977 report, came up with the most memorable quotation of the entire affair when he described Brittan as 'a demented poodle who has been knocking over the china in his excitement'.

Young, Milne and Protheroe went to see the demented poodle that afternoon. It was not a cordial meeting. Brittan said he had the same rights as anyone else to comment on BBC programmes, and that he had not forced the BBC to accept his advice. It was a curious position to adopt. If he truly believed it – and there is nothing to suggest that he did not – then it was evidence of a political naivety rare in a senior Cabinet minister. It was left to Milne to point out to him that being secretary of state responsible for broadcasting did place Brittan in a more sensitive position than other citizens.

Although no agreed statement emerged from the meeting, Young left convinced that it would be a long time before any future Home Secretary took an initiative (or a liberty, as he was more inclined to regard it) comparable with what Brittan had done. Milne issued a stirring and defiant message afterwards, criticising Brittan's comments on a programme he had not seen.

> When such comment is further accompanied by a direct request to remove the programme no matter what its actual content and context – in this case by a minister of the crown – it will be assumed that the government is seeking to dictate programme policy. The BBC will firmly resist such pressure.

He added that he had considered resigning. 'I consulted my colleagues but in the end there is a job of work to be done here, so there will be no resignation.' With the rousing declaration: 'I am the editor in chief. I am in charge,' he gave an assurance that, after emendation, Real Lives: At the Edge of the Union, would be transmitted. He said the same in a longer statement the following day, although he was still not able to give a firm date: 'The governors feel they need time to allow the dust to settle.' So he was not *absolutely* in charge after all.

* * * *

The BBC studio in Queen Street is not large enough to accommodate all 600 delegates to the Edinburgh International Television Festival at any one time. It works as a venue only on the assumption that not everyone is interested in all the subjects under discussion and some have better things to do. Occasionally the system breaks down. At the 1984 festival, when Arthur Scargill went to criticise TV coverage of the miners' strike, an overflow meeting was organised in a separate hall and the proceedings were fed to it by closed-circuit television. In 1985 there had not been time to make that arrangement for the screening and debate on the Real Lives film, hastily added to the festival schedule for the afternoon of Saturday, 17 August. It was something nearly everyone in television wanted to talk about. By 4 p.m., half an hour before the start, the studio was full and the pavement outside seething with angry delegates demanding to know why they could not be allowed in.

Nobody was in any doubt about the significance of the occasion. Michael Blakstad, the independent producer chairing the session, introduced it by observing that when Stuart Young nominated Sir William Rees-Mogg to lead the governors' debate after they had seen the film, it amounted to 'one of the most important moments in history'. Nobody accused him of hyperbole. Brian Wenham, the only representative of the BBC's board of management, sat towards the back of the hall with a group of colleagues including Hawthorne, Michael Grade and Patrick Chalmers, controller in Scotland.

Aubrey Singer, still regarded as an honorary member of BBC top management, sat with them. He had distinguished himself the previous week by writing a ferocious attack on the governors in the *Listener:* 'The board has been gradually packed with pro-establishment government supporters. . . the collective decision smacks of pusillanimous sycophancy. . . The programme

267

will have to be shown, and shown quickly.' He had suggested that in future the director-general and heads of the output directorates should sit on the board of governors, and had even managed to get a sly dig in at his old enemy Bill Cotton, asserting that the television hierarchy was too steeped in show-business experience and knew little about current affairs. Speaking in the debate he went further and called for three governors to resign and be replaced by three of a different political colouring, for balance. He won the loudest applause of any speaker: an unlikely hero.

The debate was a show of complete unanimity. Nobody, from Wenham down, disagreed with the proposition that the programme had to be broadcast quickly for there to be any chance of the wound healing. Roger Bolton said that if a date was not fixed soon the whole board of management should resign, together with those responsible for the BBC's journalistic output: 'We can't afford to wait past the end of September.' Hawthorne said the charge that the BBC had not applied its referral procedures properly was a red herring. Vincent Hanna, a leading figure in the strike ten days earlier, castigated the governors' behaviour as 'not the thin end of the wedge – we're half way up it'. Chris Dunkley of the *Financial Times* wondered whether the board of management could not put out the programme on its own authority, regardless of what the governors said. Wenham pointed out that the governors had the power to fire him and the rest of management if they acted unilaterally in that manner.

Melvyn Bragg, the novelist and head of arts at London Weekend Television, proposed that a resolution should go from the meeting to Stuart Young, with copies to Milne and Brittan, insisting that the ban be lifted. It was agreed unanimously. 'We urge you to show it unimpaired and before the end of September,' the letter said. 'We see this as the most serious public test of the BBC and believe that if the BBC does not survive it, then its integrity will be completely undermined.'

It was past 7 p.m. (there had been a short interruption for a false fire alarm) before the meeting ended. Everyone left it feeling that a blow for virtue had been struck. But when they mingled in the bar of the George Hotel afterwards, delegates heard rumours of another BBC sensation that was to break in the

Observer the following morning. It cast still further doubt on the corporation's independence and, for the time being at least, relegated the Real Lives debate to the status of yesterday's news.

The front-page headline read: REVEALED: HOW MI5 VETS BBC STAFF. The report, by David Leigh and Paul Lashmar, was a thoroughly detailed piece of work that began: 'The *Observer* has obtained concrete evidence for the first time of the way the security service, MI5, secretly controls the hiring and firing of BBC staff.' The vetting, hitherto denied by the BBC on MI5 instructions, had affected the careers of numerous people, especially in the areas of news and current affairs. The MI5 writ even extended to the editorship of the *Listener:* Richard Gott, features editor of the *Guardian* had been chosen for the post by an appointments board but vetoed by MI5 because in his twenties he had opposed the Vietnam war and supported left-wing causes in Latin America.

Some people had been blacklisted by mistake. When Alastair Hetherington wanted to hire Isabel Hilton as a television reporter in Scotland, he was told she was a member of a pro-Communist group supporting friendship with China. In fact the body mentioned, the Society for Anglo-Chinese Understanding, is not pro-Communist and Hilton had not been a member of it. As a Chinese linguist, she was once secretary to the equally innocent Scottish-China Association. Hetherington had asked the security people to look at the case again but, frustrated by the delay, Hilton let her application lapse and became a journalist with the *Sunday Times*.

The *Observer* reporters had discovered that the vetting took place inside Broadcasting House in Room 105, the office of Brigadier Ronnie Stonham, whose job title is special assistant to the director of personnel. An officer with a background in intelligence work, he had joined the BBC in 1982. According to the report, he provided a direct link with MI5 records and kept in his office sensitive files about employees with a suspect political past. Such people's regular employment files were marked with a Christmas tree device to denote that a second, more confidential file existed and should be consulted before the person was considered for advancement. The subjects of the files had no idea of what was in them, so they could not challenge their accuracy.

The story represented the low point of a deplorable summer for the BBC and for its director-general. Milne was in Edinburgh that Sunday, sitting in the Assembly Rooms in his stone-coloured suit, listening to the debate in which Professor Peacock was taking part. As he had done the previous year, he sat towards the rear of the hall and said nothing. He was gratified at the tone of the discussion. Contributions from the floor were overwhelmingly supportive of the BBC and its continued existence as half of the broadcasting duopoly. But he must have recognised, too, that the *Observer* revelations, coming so soon after the turmoil over Real Lives, meant that the corporation would not automatically be able to count on such support any longer. As the BBC soaked up a seemingly endless series of body blows, of revelations calling its cherished independence ever more seriously into question, its defenders inside and outside the industry could be forgiven for wondering whether such an organisation deserved their continued support.

For years the BBC has been subject to two conflicting assumptions about its political bias, both of which it denies. The Left believes it to be a tool of the establishment. The most persistent advocates of this view are the Glasgow University Media Group, who regularly produce studies seeking to show bias in BBC (and ITV) news and current affairs output against organised labour and in favour of established authority. For those who share the Glasgow assumptions, the events of the summer confirmed them. The Right, meanwhile, traditionally view the Beeb as a nest of left-wingers and subversives. It is hard to square that with the *Observer's* revelation that such characters have been systematically excluded for years, but the more dedicated right-wing tabloids are never stuck for a rationalisation. Their editorials chastised MI5, not for trying to vet BBC employees but for not doing it effectively.

Most of the corporation's employees had always assumed that some sort of security procedure was applied to appointments. It would be a surprise if it did not happen in an organisation of more than 26,000 people run with a high degree of bureaucracy. Yet to discover the physical details of the operation and its extent still came as a ahock. Staff unions complained and demanded assurances that in future all security checking would be done with the knowledge of its victims, who would be given the right to examine their files. Milne's first instinct was to play the issue down. He pointed out that some BBC personnel had access to top-secret plans for keeping broadcasting going in the event of war: it was vital to know that they were reliable. There was a case for vetting senior people in the external services at Bush House. He added that the scope of vetting had been under review for some time and was likely to be cut back – a promise put into effect ten weeks later.

Like the minor aftershocks of an earthquake, there were more small revelations to come. The *Observer* said that MI5 provided regular background briefing notes to the BBC about alleged subversives in the trade unions. The *Guardian* disclosed that, every day, secret Foreign Office cables were supplied to selected personnel in the overseas services. Moreover, the Special Branch had sometimes been allowed to film demonstrations from the roof of Bush House. The tabloids returned to more familiar ground, with allegations of extravagance among the Beeb top brass. There were stories of helicopter trips, lavish weekend conferences for executives, luxury corporation cars. Any company expenditure can be represented as wasteful by ill-willed critics and the BBC had valid answers to the charges. The effect of the sniping was to irritate rather than wound. It was significant chiefly for the contribution it made to lowering still further the corporation's depressed morale.

Not until September, coinciding with a last-minute improvement in the dreadful summer weather, did things begin to look up. At the first governors' meeting of the month, when Milne asked for permission to show Real Lives: At the Edge of the Union in October, the board agreed. Rees-Mogg was still in favour of suppressing it but most governors, badly shaken by the events of August, took Milne's point that it could not be business as usual at the Beeb until the ban was lifted. It was screened on 16 October and watched by 4.8 million people – respectable enough for a documentary but less than a quarter of the figure for the soap opera East Enders, the BBC's most popular show. It attracted sixty calls from viewers, no more than the average for a programme of that nature. About half the callers complained, while the remainder could not see what the fuss was about.

Brittan by that time was no longer Home Secretary. He had been moved sideways (at the most generous interpretation) to the Department of Trade and Industry, not specifically because of the nonsense he had made of the Real Lives affair but because of the overall lack of political instinct of which his misguided letter had been a symptom. Early in 1986 that lack of instinct was to prove even more damaging when he was forced to resign from the Cabinet in the fallout from the Westland Helicopter affair.

News stories have a short-shelf life and the BBC dropped out of the headlines as the autumn of 1985 approached and the party conference season began. Peacock and his committee were busy preparing their report, which would not be published for a year. Just in case Milne thought everyone was losing interest, though, his adversaries at *The Times* published another MORI poll indicating that people would prefer the BBC to take advertising rather than constantly put up the licence fee. This time it fell to Brian Wenham to give the corporate response, in a speech to the Marketing Society. The poll questions were still being asked in a loaded form, he maintained. To answer them adequately, respondents needed to be informed that people in the broadcasting industry believed a commercial BBC would lead to inferior programmes. It was the familiar argument that would be made many more times before Peacock reported. But it sounded no more convincing or less defensive with repetition.

Small wonder that the governors and management, united on this one point at least, decided that the BBC needed to improve the presentation of its case if it was to win over public opinion. The advertising agency Lowe Howard-Spink Campbell-Ewald was hired to spend £500,000 on sprucing up the BBC's by now limp image. Their first campaign was a series of full-page newspaper advertisements for the BBC2 serialisation of Scott Fitzgerald's Tender is the Night. The slogan the agency devised, 'compelling is the viewing', was derided as unwieldy and the campaign was not too well received. At the beginning of 1986, some commercials featuring John Cleese, stressing the variety and value offered by BBC television, gained a better reception.

The newspaper campaign did not deter *The Times* from writing yet another editorial at the beginning of November. Headlined PAYING FOR WALLPAPER, it was inspired by IBA research revealing that many people use television simply as a background to other activities, rather than giving the programmes the detailed attention their makers believe they deserve. 'For the average viewer,' said *The Times,* 'television is a mild and mindless form of entertainment, wallpaper which moves and emits friendly sounds. . . It is no more an overwhelmingly important source of information than were the penny dreadfuls.' It was a slur calculated to offend those news, current affairs and documentary producers who are serious about their work and are among the stoutest defenders of the BBC's independence. The editorial noted that Douglas Hurd, the Thorn Birds critic who had replaced Brittan at the Home Office, had indicated that he might not be in any hurry to implement the Peacock report once it was published. The paper argued against any delay: 'It could be politically insensitive not to act.'

The autumn brought one piece of better news for the Beeb. Ratings were at last going up.

Chapter 10

ANY ANSWERS?

The debate on the future of British broadcasting is dogged by a lack of agreement on its terms. In this chapter I shall try to clarify the terms, using the device of self-interrogation. Common ground is scarce, because the conflicting sides begin from opposite premises. The BBC prefers to limit the scope of discussion to the claim that it does its job better, cheaper and more comprehensively than any comparable organisation anywhere. That is probably true; but it begs the question whether it should be doing that particular job at all.

After a year as controller of BBC1, Michael Grade had succeeded in reversing the decline in its ratings. By the autumn of 1985 the two BBC channels combined were attracting 47.5 per cent of viewers, where the figure had been less than 40 per cent when he arrived. In exceptional weeks the corporation's share would advance to just over half. This was chiefly due to the success of the new early evening format. The soap opera East Enders was overtaking Granada's Coronation Street as the most watched programme on any channel, with a rating of 16 million; although this was partly the result of a peculiar ratings rule that allows the numbers for the weekend omnibus edition to be added to the figure for the original weekday showing.

Grade could not count this as a wholly personal triumph because the series had been planned during Alan Hart's time as controller. But Grade had been responsible for its scheduling as part of his evening package – in the autumn he shifted it back half an hour to 7.30. He had come to Television Centre with a reputation for getting programmes in the right order and it proved to be justified. The entire BBC1 schedule had a more convincing, thought-out look to it. More programmes appeared at recognisable fixed points, on the hour and half hour rather than at seemingly arbitrary fractions of the hour. And he had displayed a meticulous attention to detail. His first instruction to Robin Day, the veteran interviewer, was that he must stop saying 'sleep well' at the end of his weekly Question Time, because it could be seen as an insulting comment on the next programme.

Yet although Grade had taken a grip, it was now less likely that he would be rewarded with the job of controlling both channels, which Cotton had dangled before him during their 1984 negotiations. The board of management had finally abandoned that idea because they thought it would create as many problems as it would solve. With the future of the corporation uncertain, at least until Peacock reported, it was a bad time to be introducing fresh instability into the chain of command, however feeble the 1985 crises had shown it to be.

Thanks to Grade, then, the ratings decline that had seemed one of the BBC's largest problems in the early 1980s was for the time being halted. The argument was no longer heard that the corporation's claim on the licence fee was illogical because it served only a minority. Yet because of the lack of consensus on what the debate on broadcasting is really about, it has been easy for critics to turn even that success against the Beeb. It is like one of those computer adventure games where the player escapes from one mortal peril only to find he has landed himself in another tough spot, still more threatening.

With the ratings up, the critics assert that it is no great feat for the BBC to gain audience parity with ITV by the simple device of duplicating its programmes. Nobody doubts that it can command the necessary skills in abundance. Observing that Coronation Street was regularly close to the top of the chart, the decision was taken to make a series resembling it in nearly every respect except the location – shifted from Lancashire to London. East Enders was done with flair and imagination and there was no stinting resources. By deploying a franker, tougher approach to contemporary issues it achieved a more modern feel. But while it silenced the 'Why subsidise the elite minority?' argument, it provided fuel for the opposite criticism, characterised by the Thorn Birds fracas. Why should a broadcasting service funded by a tax on the public squander its resources in providing fare that is popular enough to be financed commercially? In what sense are East Enders and Dallas of public benefit?

What are quality programmes?

The BBC uses its 'quality' argument flexibly. Its supporters say Britain has the finest quality television in the world, thanks to both the corporation's own efforts and the uplifting effect these have on the competition. Although no longer universally accepted, this is probably true. But there are two kinds of quality programming. In one sense it means serious drama, coverage of the arts, conscientiously produced documentaries, responsible and impartial reporting of the news – the 'public service' element of broadcasting. Such enterprises are generally expensive and popular with only a minority of viewers. But there is also high-quality entertainment of a less elevating nature – soap operas, star interviews, comedy series, pop shows, giveaway quiz games. They have scant artistic merit, but they are good of their kind. Ask your orthodox Beeb man which of the two sorts of quality he aspires to and he will say both. One BBC, from Wogan to Wagner. So long as the corporation can make the best soap operas and quiz games, measured by the highest professional standards, that is as much part of its job as mounting the plays of Shakespeare. It's not what you do, it's the way that you do it.

Hasn't that always been the BBC's role?

No, it is the very opposite of the philosophy on which Lord Reith founded the Beeb. One of his most often quoted dicta states that it is futile to aim at giving the public what it wants because the public has no very clear idea what that is. 'He who prides himself on giving what he thinks the people want is creating a fictitious demand for lower standards which he will then satisfy,' he wrote.

There was no more truth in that in the 1920s, at the birth of broadcasting, than there is today, but it was a viable and comforting precept for running a monopoly radio service that controlled all the available channels. You could mingle improving programmes with moderately popular ones, provided they did not pander to any public taste Reith did not approve of (and that would rule out half today's BBC output). If significant numbers of people did not switch off between Variety Bandbox and the Brains Trust you might be fulfilling a useful social purpose by exposing them to cultural experiences they would not otherwise have sampled. No doubt such flashes of enlightenment occurred, although it would be difficult to substantiate the thesis that any dramatic general uplift of popular taste occurred as a result of the BBC monopoly in radio and the early years of television. If it did, then its effect was short-lived: consider, for instance, the current state of the tabloid press.

By virtue of its monopoly position, the BBC quickly became a powerful cultural influence in British life, as well as an important patron of music and drama. In wartime, with radio by far the fastest source of news and the best means of delivering uplifting messages to the nation, the BBC came to be counted as part of the war effort, a psychological weapon against the enemy. Even its comedy programmes were regarded not solely as entertainment but as devices for improving national morale. This elevated and distorted the public perception of the BBC's role for many years afterwards. Memories of the war receded but the corporation's self-importance did not. It was only jolted back towards reality by a combination of two factors: the success of the alternative services offered by Radio Luxembourg and later the pop pirate stations, and the coming of commercial television. These proved that the Reithian BBC had attracted large audiences in spite of its high-toned attitude to listeners, not because of it. Offered a choice, people devoured the less demanding alternative. If the Beeb was aiming to occupy the middle ground, it had seriously miscalculated where this was. Sir Hugh Greene recognised that. It was his achievement to convert the creaking institution into a modern entertainment and information service able to compete with independent television on the audience's terms rather than its own.

But the old notion of the BBC dies hard. Many still think of it as a body whose significance transcends the sum of its parts. One veteran recalls being told by Huw Wheldon: 'You must understand that there is something called the BBC which is more important than you are.' Alasdair Milne and his lieutenants would not put it in such blunt terms but part their motivation is the belief in a special BBC ethic that places it above other broadcasting organisations. They would resist any change that did not take this into account.

What is the point of a publicly run BBC today?

One of the first of the quangos, it was the perfect creation for the job that had to be done in 1927. If there was to be only one national broadcasting organisation it made sense in the climate of the time for it to be accountable to a quasi-independent governing body, appointed by the state but answerable to the government in only an informal sense. The potential power of the new medium was unknown and a little frightening. It could not be left entirely to run itself. There had to be safeguards against its falling into corrupting hands. And as far as finance was concerned, it was a neat idea to have it funded only by those who owned radio sets.

But assume that 1927 never happened and a British government were today faced with the need to construct a framework for the nation's broadcasting, given the proliferation of radio and TV outlets and the greater number that will soon be created. Radio and television, though important means of communication, are becoming less influential. The more channels there are and the more we come to regard the screen, in the words of *The Times,* as moving and talking wallpaper, so the scope for sinister mass persuasion diminishes.

For any administration, in 1986, to devise for broadcasting the duopoly arrangement we now have would be as unthinkable as instituting a similar scheme for, say, buskers in the underground. Those who played mainly Bach would be subsidised by the state, while those with a more accessible repertoire made do with contributions from travellers. (For a more exact parallel, the commercial lot would be forced by law to include a bit of Bach, though at off-peak times, and the subsidised buskers would feel obliged to play some pop so as to attract an audience large enough to justify the subsidy.) If TV were being started from scratch today the likely set-up would be a single regulatory body, similar to the IBA, responsible for franchising the available channels to public and private concerns and for exercising a mild censorship to ensure that nothing too blatantly offensive or inflammatory was allowed on the air. But it does not necessarily follow that, because the BBC would never be established today, it should be done away with. It does, however, mean that the corporation has to justify its survival in positive terms, rather than adhering to the negative rhetorical questions: We make good programmes, don't we? And has anyone thought of anything better?

Well, don't they? And has anyone?

The respective answers are 'yes, but . . .' and 'no, but . . .' It is no use making good programmes if you cannot persuade the customers to pay for them. When faced with this argument, corporation executives say people would not complain about the licence fee if they could only be made to understand what splendid value it is. Nor would they advocate the BBC taking advertising (as in repeated opinion polls the majority invariably do) if it were explained to them what a deleterious effect it would have on the programmes. Yet if so powerful a communications organisation cannot convince its viewers and listeners on these two central points, it must be a peculiarly difficult case to make.

The argument against the licence fee is anyway more fundamental than the fact that people do not like paying it. As presently constructed, the licence system means that the Beeb relies ultimately on the goodwill of the government for its funding – a fact that governments, whatever they say in public, seldom allow them to forget. So it gets trapped in the kind of untenable position it occupied during the Real Lives drama in 1985. Officials of both the BBC and the Home Office insisted that there was no connection between the Real Lives row and the discussion over funding – but they can scarcely have expected anyone to believe it. Politicians make their mark primarily by striking attitudes that they hope will appeal to the electorate. Politicians also have ultimate responsibility for voting funds to the BBC. It would be a poor politician who forswore striking popular attitudes about an institution on which most of his constituents have decided views.

Insidious political influence is exercised and it is not confined to programme content. The decision not to appoint John Gau as controller of BBC1, giving the job instead to Alan Hart, was just as much a matter of politics as the decision to ban Real Lives. The governors most concerned about the corporation's coverage of Northern Ireland effectively blackballed Gau because of his role in the Carrickmore affair and his refusal to repent it. The increase in the number of political rows over broadcasting in recent years cannot be put down simply to bad luck. It is evidence that the BBC, for all its glittering past, is an institution in decline, destroying itself through its inability to cope with the contradictions inherent in the way it is administered.

How can it adapt to the 1980s?

What the Peacock Committee and the BBC should be seeking is a method of allowing the production of excellent programmes to continue while ensuring that the ways in which they are financed are freed from the possibility of commercial corruption or political control. In Chapter 8 I described some of the most interesting proposals put forward.

The BBC, although it declares itself ready to look at suggestions, finds reason to quarrel with all of them, especially those that involve breaking it up into smaller units.

Its supporters insist with fervour that its size, more than anything else, makes it the world's best broadcasting service. The phrase 'critical mass' is often deployed. Break it up and you would squander all those years of accumulated experience in quality broadcasting. It is impossible to test this assertion except by actually doing it, but it does not seem overpoweringly logical. If the Beeb as we know it were abolished the talented people would still be there, making programmes for whatever alternative outfits took its place.

Some producers have told me that the size of the BBC and its access to resources is indispensable to the making of fine programmes. Others insist that the weight of the bureaucracy is a deadening influence.

What could take its place? How would it be financed and administered?

These are the Peacock questions – at least the second one is, but it is unrealistic to suppose that they can be discussed separately, since the nature of any new institution will depend to a high degree on how it is proposed to pay for it. If you discount the 'critical mass' argument there can be little doubt that the BBC is too big. That was another lesson of Real Lives. If Alasdair Milne did not have charge of 6,000 television programmes a year, as well as the domestic and external radio output, it is reasonable to suppose that he would have been able to exercise more effective supervision over the troublesome programme.

The most vivid symbol of how the BBC has outgrown its strength is its physical spread from its Broadcasting House headquarters. Almost every street around Langham Place contains one or more Beeb outposts, mainly to do with radio and administration. Similarly, the square mile round Shepherd's Bush Green is peppered with branches of the television service. It is like a fat man whose belly sags uncontrollably over his trouser belt: however hard he tries to diet he still grows larger and larger. By the end of the decade the radio flab should be eased into a copious new complex on the site of White City stadium.

The corporation has a staff of 30,000, with a top-heavy administration that includes the twelve-man board of management and no less than twenty-six people with the title of 'controller'. For a while, in the sixties, the organisational drawbacks of its size, at least as far as television was concerned, were masked by the emergence of such strong and independent department chiefs as Paul Fox, Desmond Wilcox, Aubrey Singer, Humphrey Burton and Brian Cowgill. They were often tyrannical but they had the gift of motivating people. Whether or not they were called controllers, they certainly took control. Their departure, enforced or otherwise, was the result of a growth of centralised bureaucracy that resulted partly from the governors demanding a more powerful voice in matters of detail as well as principle, and partly from their growing concern about costs.

That the governing board should get steamed up about such trivial issues as the astrologer on Breakfast Time and the scheduling of Dallas is a symptom of an organisation where the delegation of responsibility is unclear. Their interference in financial matters is easier to defend, but it has led to a loss of influence for programme people at the hands of professional managers, culminating in the appointment of Michael Checkland, an accountant, as deputy director-general. The governors want real decision-making authority to be in the hands of people they can exert pressure on directly – in other words the director-general and his senior colleagues. But the corporation is too big for that to be an effective form of government.

The initial broad answer to these two questions, then, is that the Beeb could be supplanted by a number of smaller institutions, some financed by advertising or subscription, others by a form of subsidy raised through general taxation or by a levy on commercial broadcasting.

How would that work?

Once the principle of fragmentation is agreed, the Beeb could be split in a number of ways. The most obvious would be into the existing three directorates – television, home radio and overseas radio, plus an extra unit for local radio. Or the production of programmes could be split from the responsibility for their transmission, as I discuss a little later.

A third possibility would be to separate the corporation's public service and entertainment functions. This would pave the way for changes in revenue sources. The network public service elements would continue to be financed by a form of taxation – either direct on the public or on the advertising or subscription revenues of the entertainment channels and local radio. A useful comparison can be made with the theatre: the commercial and subsidised houses exist side by side, and nobody believes that the National Theatre should produce 'No Sex Please We're British' to justify its claim on public revenue.

But is advertising a feasible option?

This is another debate in which the BBC seeks to have things two ways. The Beeb's apologists argue primarily that two organisations competing for the same source of revenue would drive down standards in search of the mass audience. The spectre of three-channel commercial competition in the United

States is often raised to support this view. It implies that quality is incompatible with popularity – the same line peddled by those who opposed the introduction of commercial television in the 1950s. It ignores the facts that the BBC is already competing for the mass audience with programmes such as East Enders, and that with a four-channel system it is economically possible to satisfy the masses and minorities at the same time.

The alternative argument, supported by a weight of statistics and projections and embraced by the independent broadcasting companies, is that there is not enough advertising to go round. This means that if the BBC were to enter the market, some of the existing commercial radio and television stations would be forced out of business. The scenario is hypothetical since the volume of advertising could well expand if the introduction of a new competitor were to coincide with a healthy economy. And even if it did not, it is an unadventurous business philosophy that would forbid entry into a field because it already seems well supplied. Tesco does not refrain from opening a supermarket in a town because Sainsbury's and a number of smaller grocers are already there. They compete as vigorously as they can and are prepared to accept that the weakest may fail. To place artificial restraints on such competition can sap the vigour of broadcasters and grocers equally.

Can't the BBC boost its revenue by developing sales of its programmes and the books, records and videos based on them?
Yes, but not sufficiently to make more than a marginal impact on its overall budget. In 1984-5, profits from BBC Publications and BBC Enterprises (which sells programmes overseas) amounted to £9.1m, whereas expenditure on the domestic radio and television services was £774.8m. Publications made a profit of only £4.3m on a turnover of £63.7m – but at least that was better than the loss of £700,000 in 1982-3. Enterprises did better, making £4.8m profit on a turnover of £35.3m. In 1985 it was announced that the two would be joined in a single trading organisation, which is likely to improve their performance. Among rival publishers, BBC Publications has a poor reputation in terms of initiative and imagination, given that its books start with the enviable

advantage of built-in television or radio promotion, and that their weekly magazine *Radio Times* has a monopoly on detailed programme listings. Selling programmes overseas can never be a major source of revenue. The largest English-speaking market, the United States, has a distinct preference for the products of its own huge film and TV industry. British programmes, though held in high esteem, are seldom sold to the major American networks, being confined instead to the Public Broadcasting Service which caters to a minority audience. PBS is chronically under-funded and can afford to pay very little.

If you shrank the Beeb, wouldn't you be letting out the baby with the bath water?
Not necessarily. There is, for instance, no logic in having the external services, financed by the Foreign Office, within the same organisation as the domestic programmes, funded by the licence. As for local radio, it seems against its essential nature for it to be controlled by a large central corporation. It is a small-scale operation best left to small-scale institutions. The theory is that the staff enjoy the freedom to transfer easily from Radio Northampton to Bush House to Broadcasting House and even to Television Centre. But as Paul Bonner's study group found when it was looking into the establishment of independent production units in 1977, in practice the structure of the corporation does not allow unrestricted cross-fertilisation even between different departments of the same service. In any case, in most branches of the media people switch jobs between competitors as readily as within one organisation. The argument is no more logical than suggesting that the national newspapers should be merged, to give the staff opportunities for more varied employment. Staying in a single institution throughout a working life is not nowadays regarded as necessarily a good thing: even Milne made a brief escape in mid-career from the stifling comforts of the corporate bosom.

The decision to go into local radio may have been one of the most significant mistakes the BBC has made. Some governors – including the poet Roy Fuller – were against it at the time. They warned that it would reinforce the impression of an overweening corporation bent on reaching into every corner of broadcasting. It must learn to say no thanks, I'm full already. The BBC argues that the existence of its local stations means that the national network newsrooms have reporters to call upon when an important story breaks in their locality. That is true, but it is only marginally less convenient to use 'stringers' (freelance correspondents) as newspapers do and as the the BBC did in the days before it had any local radio stations. The fact that many BBC local stations are a success – although some are not – is no more valid as an argument than the observation that the BBC must stay as it is because it makes a lot of good programmes. It is not a question of what is done but of who does it. To deploy the newspaper analogy again: it is harmful that Rupert Murdoch controls so much of our national daily and Sunday press; and it would be worse if he controlled a chain of local papers as well.

Diversity in media control is good for its own sake. The BBC's corporate ethic may be stainless and unchallengeably beneficial for us, but how are we to ensure that it remains so unless there are plenty of vigorous alternatives to test it against?

If the BBC were fragmented and part of it privatised, how would you prevent the Murdochs and Maxwells from adding the juiciest bits to their empires?
The BBC believes that you could not, and that this is the reason for the enthusiasm of the Murdoch papers for the break-up of the Beeb. The rules for ownership of commercial TV stations effectively rule out any one person gaining absolute control, as Murdoch discovered when he flirted with London Weekend Television in the 1970s. If the government were of a mind to frame similar restrictions on any new broadcasting franchises, they could certainly do so. There must be a question, however, whether the *laissez-faire* Thatcher administration would want to.

Couldn't you achieve the desired effect less painfully by keeping the BBC whole and giving greater autonomy to its departments?
Perhaps you could, were it not for the sustained resistance of senior management to any such thing. Look what happened to Alastair Hetherington and Phil Sidey when they advocated more power for the regions. Remember the unbending opposition of

Bill Cotton and Aubrey Singer to the recommendations of Paul Bonner's study group about establishing small production units outside the departmental framework. (See Chapter 4.) As in many large institutions, lip service is paid to decentralisation, but when it comes to the point the people who hold the power at the centre cannot bring themselves to surrender it.

What would happen to BBC news if the corporation were fragmented?

BBC news has established a reputation for reliability and impartiality that nobody would want to destroy. Nearly all the plans for breaking up the Beeb involve keeping an element of public service broadcasting: news and current affairs would presumably form part of that. Today the BBC provides a professional and responsible news service based on contemporary values – but it is not the only such service. Independent Television News, although funded by the commercial stations, is not influenced by any improper external pressure in its selection or treatment of items in its bulletins. In the United States, the three national commercial networks all run their own news services and defend vigorously their independence from the government or from advertisers. Their standards of impartiality are in some instances higher than those of the BBC. For example, they allowed on the air more critical comments on the Vietnam war than did the BBC about the Falklands, and accepted no restrictions on covering the fighting.

The BBC's news and current affairs departments ought to be preserved because the professional judgement and competence they have amassed over the years are a national asset that should not be squandered. But it is not easy to see why it is essential that they should be preserved inside the present BBC framework.

Why does the BBC think it has to keep control over both the production and the transmission of its programmes?

It's the 'one BBC' concept again. The production of programmes and their dissemination are separate functions and there is no over-riding reason why they should be carried out by the same institution, except that it is the way the BBC has always done it.

The commercial companies do not run their transmitters, which are owned by the IBA. In the case of Channel 4, the process of making and transmitting is successfully split into three. The channel buys programmes produced by outsiders and uses the IBA transmitters. Its own role is merely that of the middle man, the impresario.

To suggest any such split is a sure way of provoking a Beeb person to fury. Forced to choose between making programmes and being responsible for their transmission, the BBC would certainly plump for the former. In an interview in *Ariel* in November 1985, Bill Cotton said: 'We have a commitment to try to help independent producers, but it is against the background that the BBC is a major producing organisation and must remain so. We are the cornerstone of a very successful industry in this country and if we don't maintain that it would be a major tragedy for the country, not just for the BBC.' Like many such apocalyptic assertions from BBC executives, it came without any supporting argument.

To sustain the programme output, sacrifices have already had to be made on the technical side. In the package of cuts made in 1985 in the wake of the licence settlement, engineering was the area hardest hit. And in the autumn of that year the governors decided not to take a share in Superchannel, a modest new satellite venture initiated by the ITV companies to beam old ITV and BBC programmes to cable systems in Europe. The BBC agreed to provide programmes but not to involve itself in the channel's financing and operation. It was learning to say no at last. Ideally, the BBC would like to be a satellite entrepreneur, to maintain its engineering division at full strength and to remain the world's largest production house – all three. But it is clearly prepared to hive off the engineering to private enterprise if that is the price of maintaining programme production.

But hasn't the 'one BBC' philosophy established the BBC at the centre of our cultural life? Wouldn't we be the poorer without it?
Yes and maybe. Apart from the brief 'Greene spring' of the 1960s, the BBC's cultural influence has on balance been conservative, with a few honourable and inventive exceptions.

When the Beeb brought Mort Sahl to London in 1961, it neutered him by having Muir and Norden introduce him as though inviting viewers to partake in some mildly naughty indiscretion, like smoking in the dorm after lights out. Politically, as I have indicated in earlier chapters, the corporation has usually been over-careful to avoid offence to the establishment, especially concerning Northern Ireland. It has been outside the scope of this book to describe in detail the many rows over censorship of drama that persuaded some frustrated writers to take their talents elsewhere. Alasdair Milne was responsible for banning both a Denis Potter play, 'Brimstone and Treacle', and 'Scum', which included a homosexual rape and was later shown on Channel 4. This is not to say that any successor organisations would necessarily allow greater latitude for broadcasters. But it is hard to deploy its patchy record on artistic freedom as a convincing argument for the BBC's preservation.

So far you've cunningly dodged the question implicit in the book's title and it's time to nail you down: Are these the last days of the Beeb?
I think that something called the BBC will survive Peacock, but truncated in a fashion displeasing to those who now run it, with some of its functions dispersed along the lines I have suggested in this chapter. The Real Lives dispute, taken with a number of comparable if less sensational incidents, illustrates that the BBC is an unsuitable and unwieldy instrument for broadcasting in the 1980s, too bureaucratic and too big. That has been increasingly evident since the departure of Donald Baverstock in 1965 – the first of the major upheavals that I described in detail in the narrative. A few years ago the critic Peter Black wrote a lively book about the corporation which he called *The Biggest Aspidistra in the World*. The aspidistra is a tough plant, tolerant of much abuse, and some authorities maintain that it needs no serious attention until it splits its pot. The Beeb has done that. Now, to stay healthy, it needs to be divided and put in fresh compost: then new plants can be propagated from the old.

BIBLIOGRAPHY

A selection of books about the BBC and broadcasting:

Allighan, Garry, *Sir John Reith*. Stanley Paul, 1938.
Annan Committee, *Report on the Future of Broadcasting*. Her Majesty's Stationery Office, 1977.
Bakewell, Joan and Garnham, Nicholas, *The New Priesthood*. Allen Lane, 1970.
Beadle, Gerald, *Television: A Critical Review*. George Allen & Unwin, 1963.
Black, Peter, *The Biggest Aspidistra in the World*. BBC Publications, 1972.
Briggs, Asa, *Governing the BBC*. BBC Publications, 1979.
Briggs, Asa, *History of Broadcasting*, vols 1 – 1V. Oxford University Press, 1961–79
Briggs, Asa, *The BBC: The First Fifty Years*. Oxford University Press, 1985.
Burns, Tom, *The BBC: Public Institution and Private World*. Macmillan, 1977.
Curran, Charles, *A Seamless Robe: Broadcasting Philosophy and Practice*. Collins, 1979.
Curran, J., Gurevitch, M., and Wollacott, J. *Mass Communications and Society*. Arnold, 1977. (This contains Michael Tracey's account of the Yesterday's Men dispute.)
Davies, Hunter, *The Grades*. Weidenfeld & Nicolson, 1981.

Bibliography

Day, Robin, *Day by Day.* William Kimber, 1975.

Dunkley, Christopher, *Television Today and Tomorrow.* Penguin, 1985.

Glasgow University Media Group, *War and Peace News.* Open University Press, 1985.

Goldie, Grace Wyndham, *Facing the Nation.* Bodley Head, 1977.

Greene, Hugh, *The Third Floor Front.* Bodley Head, 1969,

Hall, Barrie, *The Proms and the Men who Made Them.* George Allen & Unwin, 1981.

Hetherington, Alastair, *News, Newspapers and Television.* Macmillan, 1985.

Hill, Lord, *Behind the Screen.* Sidgwick & Jackson, 1974,

Hood, Stuart, *A Survey of Television.* Heinemann, 1967.

Mansell, Gerald, *Let Truth be Told.* Weidenfeld & Nicolson, 1982.

Paulu, Burton, *British Broadcasting in Transition.* Macmillan, 1961.

Sampson, Anthony, *The Changing Anatomy of Britain.* Hodder & Stoughton, 1982.

Sherrin, Ned, *A Small Thing – Like an Earthquake.* Weidenfeld & Nicolson, 1983.

Shulman, Milton, *The Least Worst Television in the World.* Barrie & Jenkins, 1973.

Stuart, Charles (ed.), *The Reith Diaries.* Collins, 1975.

Tinker, Jack, *The Television Barons.* Quartet, 1980.

Tracey, Michael, *A Variety of Lives* (biography of Sir Hugh Greene). Bodley Head, 1983.

Trethowan, Ian, *Split Screen.* Hamish Hamilton, 1984.

Whitehouse, Mary, *A Most Dangerous Woman.* Lion Publishing, 1982.

Wilcox, Desmond, and Rantzen, Esther, *Kill the Chocolate Biscuit or Behind the Screen.* Pan, 1981 (paperback); Severn House, 1982 (hardback).

INDEX

Index

Index

Index

Index

Index